MW00851204

Chuck Jones
CONVERSATIONS

CTR. MORICHES PUB. LIBRARY

Conversations with Comic Artists
M. Thomas Inge, General Editor

Chuck Jones
CONVERSATIONS

Edited by
Maureen Furniss,
with the assistance of Stormy Gunter

University Press of Mississippi
Jackson

www.upress.state.ms.us

The University Press of Mississippi is a member of the
Association of American University Presses.

Copyright © 2005 by University Press of Mississippi
All rights reserved
Manufactured in the United States of America

12 11 10 09 08 07 06 05   4 3 2 1

Library of Congress Cataloging-in-Publication Data

Jones, Chuck, 1912–
    Chuck Jones : conversations / edited by Maureen Furniss,
with the assistance of Stormy Gunter.
        p. cm. — (Conversations with comic artists)
    Includes index.
        ISBN 1-57806-728-6 (cloth : alk. paper) — ISBN 1-57806-729-4
(pbk. : alk. paper)
        1. Jones, Chuck, 1912– 2. Animators—United States—
Interviews. I. Furniss, Maureen. II. Title. III. Series.
NC1766.U52J66   2004
741.5'8'092—dc22   2004057172

British Library Cataloging-in-Publication Data available

Contents

Introduction

Aside from Walt Disney, Chuck Jones is probably the most famous practitioner of the art of animation in America. This legendary figure is remembered in many, sometimes contradictory, ways: as an intellectual, a free spirit, a businessman, a teacher, a liberal thinker, a dedicated artist, a gentleman, a philanthropist, and a regular, if sometimes strongly opinionated, guy. The complexity of Jones's public image has made him especially attractive as an interview subject and a favorite icon among animation fans.

Although Jones worked for the Disney, Iwerks, and Metro-Goldwyn-Mayer (MGM) studios, most of his career was spent at Warner Bros. The general public knows him as a director of Bugs Bunny and Road Runner/Wile E. Coyote Looney Tunes and Merrie Melodies shorts that showcase his unique spirit, sense of humor, and timing. However, students of Jones's work know he cultivated a more serious side when it came to considerations of animation as an art form and means of expression.

As a young man during the Depression, Chuck Jones dropped out of high school and enrolled in the Chouinard Art Institute (now known as California Institute of the Arts), then entered the working world. In 1933 he began to work for Leon Schlesinger in the studio that produced animation for Warner Bros. He began directing there in 1938 with *The Night Watchman*. He briefly worked for Iwerks in the 1930s and Disney in the 1950s. During World War II, working after hours, he directed *Hell*

Bent for Election (1944), which advocates the reelection of President Franklin Delano Roosevelt. This film was one of the first productions of what would become the influential United Productions of America (UPA) studio. *Hell Bent for Election* was funded by the United Auto Workers (UAW) union. Jones himself was involved with union activities, having participated in strikes at the Warner Bros., Disney, and other studios during the late 1930s and early 1940s.

In the United States, Jones won three Oscars and a special Academy Award for lifetime achievement, and his films have been placed on the National Film Registry by the Library of Congress. He also has been the subject of numerous tributes and documentary films in the United States and abroad. Although Jones dropped out of high school, he received numerous scholarly accolades, including honorary doctorates and emeritus status as a university lecturer. He and his work have been discussed in newspapers, mass media, and scholarly journals, and he wrote two autobiographical books, *Chuck Amuck* (1989) and *Chuck Reducks* (1996), which further established his public persona. He took advantage of the growing market in animation art, developing the Chuck Jones Studio Galleries and also selling his work at hundreds of other galleries worldwide. Jones maintained a busy schedule of events and lectures until the last few years of his life. He loved to connect with young artists, sharing his philosophies on art and his knowledge of animation techniques and recounting anecdotes about the golden years of the studio system.

In short, Chuck Jones was a multifaceted artist who not only helped to elevate the status of animation worldwide but also assured his own place in history through his talent, energy, and business sense. His many interviews provide glimpses into his personality as it developed through the years. Of course, it should be remembered that published interviews are edited at many steps along the way, so their content generally is not an objective reflection of the "whole truth." The interviewer asks specific questions based on his or her agenda, personal knowledge, and perception of worth. Jones's responses in part reflect his feeling about what is best to say under the circumstances. In preparing a manuscript for publication, an interviewer sometimes compiles the responses from various meetings into one master interview or cuts out portions that could be regarded as irrelevant or weak. After corrections and clarifications are made by the interviewer (and perhaps Jones himself), additional changes may be made by the editor of the publication, depending on space requirements and personal or institutional agendas. In any case, the reader of this anthology should bear in mind that the work published here represents only a portion of the interviews and interview-based materials related to Jones. Additional perspectives can be found in Jones's books and other writing.

The interviews in this volume cover a thirty-year period from 1968, when Chuck Jones was just being discovered by the critical establishment, to 1999, after his popularity had led to his comeback as an animation director. Despite the range of years, one finds in them a number of consistent themes as well as repeated examples. Analysis of these recurring points can help us understand what Chuck Jones saw as key elements to his success as an artist and his vision of the art of animation.

The primary interest of most interviewers has been the body of work that Jones produced while he was an animation director at Warner Bros. from 1938 through 1962. When Jones discussed this period, he inevitably characterized the management, particularly Leon Schlesinger, as an inept, if not idiotic, unwitting target of jokes and a money-grubbing businessman with absolutely no understanding of art. He regarded his later producer, Eddie Selzer, with contempt. Though Jones constantly asserted his love of his job, he regularly mentioned that he and his colleagues were underpaid and denied rights to the valuable properties they created. The upside was that the artists enjoyed a great deal of personal freedom, which Jones saw as enabling them to invest a great deal of themselves in their work. The result of this investment was the development of characters with complex personalities and films that are immensely creative.

Jones admired Walt Disney and defended him as a visionary, rather than a businessman, as he felt Richard Schickel described him in the 1968 book *The Disney Version*. While Jones was careful to acknowledge that Disney had his faults, he recognized him as the person who laid the foundation for the growth of animation in America. Jones spent four months at Disney, an experience that ended when he realized that only one person at the studio could make any decisions. According to a favorite anecdote, Jones told Disney, "There's only one job at this studio worth having: yours." Disney replied, "That job's taken." So, while Jones regarded his own producers as uninformed and ineffective, he saw Disney as a well-informed and controlling figure—who also sometimes stifled individual creativity. He felt Disney produced better films, but he realized he could not have worked in that environment. Jones recognized the freedom Warner Bros. offered, but he often belittled his own productions or dismissed them as incomplete. Thus, his comparisons of the environments and final products created at Warner Bros. and Disney can at times seem contradictory, reflecting the complexity of being a creative artist working in a commercial setting.

Throughout his career, Jones developed many theories about animation that he wrote about and discussed in interviews. For example, he felt that an essential aspect of the animator's art was to move beyond drawing a character's exterior to get inside the character itself. He stressed the importance of students learning the bone structure of animals, which his art instructors had taught him, to understand how a character can move (as opposed to how it wants to move). He described this "internal" approach as both intellectual and emotional. In many interviews (for example, with Mark and Brian for KLOS radio) he quipped that he dreamt of being Bugs, but woke up to discover he was Daffy.

He used this example to stress that animators should relate to their characters as manifestations of their own personalities. Similarly, viewers should be able to recognize animated characters as real entities, not drawings. In interviews he often discussed his thorough understanding of such characters as Bugs Bunny, Daffy Duck, Wile E. Coyote, and the Road Runner. However, Jones insisted he never understood the black African boy Inki and the Minah Bird who appeared in five of his cartoons. It is possible that Jones distanced himself from these characters because they were controversial in terms of racial stereotyping.

Another constant throughout Jones's interviews are frequent references to fine art, literature, and music. He regularly acknowledged his family as being directly responsible for his artistic abilities by encouraging him to draw and read. Virtually every interview contains reference to the work of Paul Klee, Mark Twain, and other artistic and literary figures. In his interview with Mary Harrington Hall, he is paired with author Ray Bradbury for a discussion about creating fantasy (their proposed collaboration on *The Halloween Tree* never materialized; many years later, Bradbury worked on it with Hanna-Barbera). Jones commonly mentioned respect for the work of great actors (such as Lawrence Olivier), filmmakers (such as Jean Cocteau), and operatic composers (such as Richard Wagner). He compared animation to jazz, describing both as significant American art forms.

In his interview with Michael Barrier and Bill Spicer, Jones argued that American animation had an international reputation unmatched by any other country. He noted, however, that Americans were slow to recognize this art form. Tex Avery was acclaimed in France before Americans celebrated him. Jones complained that America didn't begin to appreciate animation until the 1970s; that was about the time when Jones began to be recognized through interviews and awards.

Jones balanced his intellectualism and pride with self-deprecation. In his 1993 interview with the Academy of Achievement he said, "I'm still astonished that somebody would offer me a job and pay me to do what I wanted to do . . . that anybody would be so stupid as to be willing to do that." When Ron Barbagallo asked which project made him the proudest, his reply was that he was not proud of any of them. He later suggested that some of his films were "insufficient" and even "really bad." He rated the works of some other studios even lower. Notably, he disliked the work of UPA, although he and his wife co-wrote the script for the UPA feature *Gay Purr-ee* (1962). Jones left Warner Bros. in 1962, possibly after studio management objected to his "moonlighting" work for UPA. The animation unit at Warner Bros. closed the following year.

Jones seemed to have two objections to UPA work. He contended that the works were too reliant on their soundtracks and that they were not visual enough (he also leveled this complaint specifically at John Hubley, one of the studio's directors). Jones's second complaint was aimed at public statements attributed to the studio, criticizing the animation industry for creating "fuzzy animal" pictures—a position he felt was divisive.

For Jones, the visual element of animation was supreme. In various interviews, he discussed the sound components of his work, including the contributions of Treg Brown, Carl Stalling, Mel Blanc, and June Foray. However, Jones consistently stressed that Warner Bros. tested its animated visuals without sound or color to assure its "readability" on the screen. He placed the ultimate control over these visuals with one person: the director. He supported this view with stories about Schlesinger, the "missing producer" who Jones said was more likely to be at the races than supervising his workers. In this scenario, Jones, as director, made all the decisions. He proudly explained he was bold enough to do exactly the opposite of what his producer bosses instructed. Jones further asserted his control over films by repeatedly telling interviewers that he and his colleagues made the films for themselves. A dominant narrative heard in his interviews is that, lacking sufficient pay or even a boss that recognized his value as an artist, self-fulfillment and his love of drawing kept him at work. This scenario is a familiar story of the "American way" that only strengthens our admiration for Jones as a cultural icon.

Jones was adamantly opposed to the notion that any of his work was created "for children" and he hated the term "kid vid," which was used to describe Saturday morning cartoons. Jones felt that self-consciously writing for children necessarily entailed "dumbing down" the work. He consistently asserted that adults and children should be able to enjoy his films equally. The real test, he said, was if something made him laugh; if so, he thought others would find it funny as well. His assertion that he didn't create films specifically for children also built a defense against critics who said Warner Bros. cartoons were too violent for young viewers. Actually, Jones reacted slightly differently to that accusation in various interviews. In his interview with Joe Adamson, he suggested that if people thought they were so violent, perhaps children shouldn't watch them. More often he maintained that children were smarter than people thought and they could handle cartoon violence.

Jones also argued that the violence in his work tended to be "motivated" and any results were neutralized, as opposed to the random and hurtful actions he saw elsewhere. He contrasted his approach with Bill Hanna and Joe Barbera's Tom and Jerry series at MGM, which he found much more painful and realistic. He cited their bashing in of teeth as too authentically hurtful. To some extent, Jones justified the constant violent struggle of the Coyote in his Road Runner films as a natural predator and prey relationship. He also saw that violence as being removed from reality, as it tended to happen at a distance and in a manner that did not suggest actual pain. Another repeated argument one finds is Jones's description of Bugs Bunny as a counterrevolutionary (as opposed to a revolutionary), because he "reacts" to provocation rather than becoming violent on his own. These points about violence further illustrate Jones's personal aesthetic and his considered opinion about what constitutes acceptable violence and humorous content.

Although Jones praised the work of many individuals he worked with, he targeted a few people for producing substandard work. He criticized Hanna and Barbera not just for the violence in their Tom and Jerry cartoons, but also for their later made-for-television work. Jones felt they squandered their talent on low quality, dialog-driven animation aimed at children. Richard Williams was another target of Jones's criticism. Although he praised Williams as a talented artist, Jones also described him as unfocused because he attempted to do too many jobs, from directing to animating to cleanup.

Jones increased his criticism of Williams's work in discussions of Who Framed Roger Rabbit, a project Jones was involved with in its early stages.

In an interview with Tom Shales, he called the film "a successful *Tron*," suggesting that it was fine technically but it had no substance. He complained that the viewer cares about the human performer Bob Hoskins more than the animated Roger Rabbit. Speaking to Jo Jürgens, Jones said the character (or perhaps the film) is "very well done," but he nonetheless described Roger Rabbit as an example of the problems found in animation made after 1963: the character doesn't slow down enough for people to get to know him. Jones's comments about Roger Rabbit echo a favorite concept in Jones's perception of animation practice: "discipline," using restraints to strengthen the work overall. In his interview with Michael Barrier and Bill Spicer, Jones elaborated on discipline in the context of the Road Runner films. He detailed the limitations he placed on the series and how they enhanced the final product. When artists lack discipline, he contended, the result is uncontrolled and weak.

Clearly, Jones did not like the animation in *Who Framed Roger Rabbit*, so it is not surprising that he was disparaging about Williams, who directed the film's animation. He went so far as to describe Williams as director Robert Zemeckis's "pencil," suggesting that he had no vision of his own. It is interesting to contrast this perspective with Jones's comments about his own bosses at Warner Bros. and Disney, with whom he struggled creatively. Whereas Jones saw himself as triumphant against his higher-ups, he characterized Williams as having acquiesced, ultimately producing a mediocre product.

Particularly in early interviews, we can see that Jones was very sensitive to working conditions and issues related to labor and management. He pointed out that he received no residual earnings from his early creative work. He also discussed the Disney strike of 1941, though it is unlikely that Jones was actually a "leader" in the action, as he sometimes suggested (he later went to work for Disney). In the end, it appears that Jones came out all right. At the age of eighty-five, he signed a fifty-year contract with Warner Bros. to produce new films. That contract certainly validated Jones's value to Warner Bros. management. However, to Jones this opportunity was equally or perhaps more important because it allowed him to train new talent. Although the interviews in this anthology do not touch on Jones's work as a teacher, and little is said about his honorary doctorates, he greatly valued his role as a teacher and a role model.

In the 1990s, as his popularity grew, Jones increasingly was invited to attend screenings, make speeches, and accept awards. These events generated press coverage in many newspapers. Such articles generally have included only fragments of Jones's longer thoughts, boiled down to a series of one-liners inserted into light, entertaining articles or promotional pieces, sometimes focusing on the honors bestowed upon him later in life. Jones tended to be dismissive of such accolades, such as honorary doctorates, saying that "the road is better than the inn." But while he wanted to stay active, rather than rest on his accomplishments, Jones was well aware of how these honors and the news coverage they generated benefited his position as an artist and historical figure. By giving speeches, opening galleries that showcased his artwork, distributing his films, publishing books, teaching young artists, and giving interviews, he guaranteed his place in media history and assured that "Chuck Jones" would remain a household name in America.

Jones was a businessman, although probably he would object to that title, just as he objected to it being applied to Disney. He also was an artist who spread his love for animation throughout the world. A cultural icon in his own right, Jones was as much an emissary for the art of animation as Disney. Chuck Jones left a legacy not only in his films but also in his words. In those words we see a mandate for future generations, which he hoped would continue on his path, developing animation as an art for all people to enjoy.

Before I conclude this introduction, I would like to thank all the authors whose interviews appear in this volume. It is through their generosity that this anthology has been completed. Thanks also to M. Thomas Inge, who invited me to edit this book. I appreciate the assistance of Michael Barrier and Jo Jürgens, who helped me early in my process of collecting essays; Joe Adamson, who spent a great deal of time readying his interview for publication; and Charles Solomon, who helped me at numerous points along the way. I greatly appreciate the work of my assistant editor, Stormy Gunter, who coordinated the permissions and did other organizational work to keep me going. I think all of us have contributed to this work hoping it will add to an understanding of Chuck Jones as an important representative of American culture and the art of animation.

Chuck Jones was devoted to the art of animation, committted to excellence in his work, scholarly in thought, and generous in helping others. I would like to dedicate this book to another person who fits this description, Linda Simensky, who has quietly done so much for the world of animation.

Chronology

1912   Born Charles Martin Jones on September 21, in Spokane, Washington.

1920s   Appears as an extra in Mack Sennett comedies.

1927   Drops out of high school and enrolls in the Chouinard Art Institute (later known as the California Institute of the Arts) in Los Angeles, from which he would later graduate.

1932   Holds a series of short term jobs; begins his first animation-related work as a cel washer at the studio of Ub Iwerks; also works there as a cel painter, cel inker and in-betweener; briefly works at the Charles Mintz Screen Gems studio and for Walter Lantz at Universal; makes money drawing pencil portraits for a dollar apiece on Olvera Street in Los Angeles.

1933   Joins the Leon Schlesinger Studio, the Warner Bros. animation unit, where he would remain until 1962.

1934   Marries Dorothy Webster, an employee of the Iwerks studio.

1936   Promoted to "animator" at the Warners studio, joining the Tex Avery unit. Jones and fellow Warner Bros. animator Bob Clampett are loaned out to the Iwerks studio.

1937   Daughter Linda born.

1938   Begins directing at Warner Bros. on *The Night Watchman*; would eventually direct over 250 animated films there.

1939   Jones's first significant original character, a mouse named Sniffles, debuts in *Naughty but Mice*; Sniffles would appear in other cartoons through 1947. Also debuting is another of Jones's original characters, a stereotypical African boy named Inki, who would appear in five films. Directs the second appearance of Bugs Bunny in *Prest-o Change-o*; the character's persona is still in development, but Jones would become one of the most notable directors of Bugs Bunny cartoons.

1941   Participates in the infamous Disney studio strike.

1942   Jones's short, *The Dover Boys*, released; it is a film in what would become known as the "UPA style."

1944   During World War II, directs Army training films at the First Motion Picture Unit in Culver City, California. Working at night and without compensation, directs *Hell Bent for Election*, a film supporting the reelection of President Franklin D. Roosevelt; this film is supported by the United Auto Workers and created by the studio that would become United Productions of America.

1946   Publishes a critical article on animation and music in *Hollywood Quarterly*.

1950   Jones's film, *For Scent-imental Reason*, receives Oscar for Best Cartoon; his documentary *So Much for So Little* wins Oscar for Best Documentary Short Subject.

1953   Directs *Duck Amuck*, which would become a much-analyzed example of reflexivity in cinema, as it acknowledges the animation process.

1955   Directs *One Froggy Evening*, starring a character later known as Michigan J. Frog; the character would become the symbol of the WB Network in the mid-90s. The Warner Bros. animation studio closes for a brief period, so Jones goes to

Disney for four months, working on *Sleeping Beauty* and early television programming.

1957   Directs *What's Opera, Doc?* at Warner Bros.; one of his best-known films, it would be inducted into the American National Film Registry in 1992.

1962   Jones and his wife co-write the screenplay for the UPA animated feature *Gay Purr-ee*. He leaves Warner Bros. after a management dispute over his authorship of *Gay Purr-ee*; the animation unit closes the following year. Founds Chuck Jones Enterprises; he would be the company's CEO until his death.

1963   Becomes head of MGM's animation department, where he stays until 1971.

1965   Wins Oscar for *The Dot and the Line*, which he directed.

1966   At MGM, creates episodes of the Tom and Jerry cartoon series after modifying the characters. Through Chuck Jones Enterprises, directs the holiday classic *How the Grinch Stole Christmas*, which wins a Peabody Award.

1971   Directs Dr. Seuss's *Horton Hears a Who*, which wins a Peabody Award. Produces, co-writes, and co-directs (with Abe Levitow) *The Phantom Tollbooth*.

1972   Becomes Vice-President of Children's Programming at the American Broadcasting Company (ABC); he remains there for one year. Creates fine art drawings and limited edition images.

1974   A Road Runner and Wile E. Coyote cartoon directed by Jones appears in Steven Spielberg's debut feature, *The Sugarland Express*.

1977   A portion of Jones's *Duck Dodgers in the 24½ Century*, created in 1953, appears in Steven Speilberg's *Close Encounters of the Third Kind*.

1978   Jones's wife Dorothy dies. With his daughter, Linda Jones, he creates limited-edition animation art depicting characters and scenes from his films. This work is exhibited and sold in Chuck Jones Studio Galleries and hundreds of other galleries worldwide.

1979   Serves as an uncredited creative assistant on Spielberg's film *1941*. Releases a feature compilation of past work, Chuck Jones's *Bugs Bunny/Road Runner Movie*.

1983   Marries Marian Dern.

1984   Makes a cameo appearance in Steven Spielberg's film, *Gremlins*. The film *Chuck Jones: A Life of Animation* is produced by David Weinkauf of Edinboro, Pennsylvania.

1985   His works are exhibited at the Museum of Modern Art in New York. Named Lecturer Emeritus at the University of California, San Diego.

1987   Makes a cameo appearance in Steven Spielberg's film, *Innerspace* (1987).

1989   Publishes *Chuck Amuck: The Life and Times of an Animated Cartoonist*, with a foreword by Steven Spielberg. *Chuck Amuck: The Movie* is produced by John Needham of London, England.

1990   Makes a cameo appearance in Steven Spielberg's film, *Gremlins II: The New Batch*; also directs titles for the film.

1991   Wins a Career Achievement Award from the Los Angeles Critics. Awarded a honorary doctorate by Edinboro University, in Edinboro, Pennsylvania; this would be the first of several honorary degrees.

1992   His film, *What's Opera, Doc?* is the first animated film to be inducted into the National Film Registry. Directs an animation sequence for the feature film *Stay Tuned*. Is featured in an episode of the series *The Creative Spirit*, produced by Paul Kaufman. The feature film *The Magical World of Chuck Jones* is produced by George Daugherty.

1993   Signs a deal with Warner Bros. to produce and direct new animated shorts; forms a new studio called Chuck Jones Film Productions in the same part of the lot where he had worked as an animator and director in his earlier years. Directs an animation sequence for the feature film *Mrs. Doubtfire*. His work is the subject of the first major exhibit at the Capital Children's Museum National Center for Animation in Washington, DC; it runs until 1995.

1994   At the age of eighty-two, produces and directs the Road Runner and Wile E. Coyote short *Chariots of Fur*; released with the feature *Richie Rich*, it is the first film created by Chuck Jones Film Productions. The book *Chuck Jones: A Flurry of Drawings*, by Hugh Kenner, is published in Portraits of American Genius series. In *The 50 Greatest Cartoons*, edited by Jerry Beck, works directed by Jones occupy four of the top five slots, including number one; this book was compiled based upon surveys of many top figures within the animation industry.

1995   Receives a star on the Hollywood Walk of Fame.

1996   At the age of eighty-four, is awarded an honorary Oscar for Lifetime Achievement in the Field of Animation. Wins the Smithsonian Institution 150th Anniversary Medal of Achievement. Receives an Honorary Life Membership Award from the Directors Guild of America. Publishes *Chuck Reducks: Drawing from the Fun Side of Life*.

1997   Chuck Jones Film Productions closes it doors. Jones receives an honorary doctorate from the American Film Institute, and his film, *Duck Amuck*, is inducted into the National Film Registry. Has one-man film retrospective at the Museum of Modern Art in New York City. Designs and creates artwork corresponding to four operas for Opera Pacific brochures in Orange County, California.

1998   Wins the Chevalier des Arts et Lettres Award from French Minister of Culture, in Lyon, France.

2000   Television documentary *Chuck Jones: Extremes & In-betweens, A Life in Animation* is produced by Margaret Selby.

2001   Inducted into the Animation Hall of Fame. Develops characters for a new Warner Bros. cartoon, *Timberwolf*, that appears on-line. Establishes the Chuck Jones Foundation to recognize, reward, support, and inspire continued excellence in art and the art of classic animation.

2002   At the age of eighty-nine, Chuck Jones passes away in Corona Del Mar, in Orange County, California, with his wife Marian at his side.

2003   *One Froggy Evening* inducted into the U.S. National Film Registry.

Chuck Jones
CONVERSATIONS

The Fantasy Makers: A Conversation with Ray Bradbury and Chuck Jones

MARY HARRINGTON HALL / 1968

From *Psychology Today*, April 1968, pp. 28–37, 70. Copyright © 1968 Sussex Publishers, Inc. Reprinted with permission from *Psychology Today* magazine.

Ray Bradbury is forty-seven, and he has the presence and the appearance of a moderately unsuccessful Shakespearean actor. His voice is resonant and sure, and he doesn't just speak; he makes pronouncements. He has two rather special qualities: even in casual conversation, he uses the English language like a weaver of rare tapestry; and he has an endearing, terribly male sweetness that warms everyone who meets him. There is no one else like him. He is the best. *Fahrenheit 451, The Martian Chronicles, The Illustrated Man*—what is your favorite Bradbury tale? The American Academy of Arts and Sciences has honored him for "his major contributions to American literature." His new play, *The Anthem Sprinters*, has just opened, and now he is finishing a movie based on Picasso's paintings. He and Chuck Jones met shortly after Hallowe'en and together they are planning an animated film, *The Pumpkin Tree.*

Charles Martin Jones is fifty-four. He looks like a cross between Carl Sandburg and Jackie Cooper as "Skippy," and except for Walt Disney, no one has come along with more consistently creative film animation. He is literate, sophisticated, a pugnacious Pollyana, and probably saved from cynicism by a sense of humor that is a mixture of Puck and Goodman Ace. He invented the Road Runner and Pepé le Pew, and was a father to Bugs Bunny. The only animator-member of Delta Kappa Alpha, the national honorary cinema fraternity, Jones is president of the Alumni Association of the California Institute of Arts, which includes his alma mater, Chouinard. Jones has won three Oscars, and now, with his brave band, he is risking what the experts call the first major full-length fantasy attempt since the great Disney days of *Fantasia.* He is making *The Phantom Tollbooth,* based on Norton Juster's wonderful book.

Enter the world of fantasy. You are sitting with two men of genius. You are there now. MHH is you.

MHH: "The starts they turn, the candles burn, and the mouse leaves scurry on the cold wind bourne. . . ." Those are lovely lines of yours, Ray. And once, Chuck Jones, when I was prey to the hard sell of reality-is-all in our button-down culture, you warned me: "People who look through keyholes are apt to get the idea that most things are keyhole shaped."

Bradbury: The ability to "fantasize" is the ability to survive. It's wonderful to speak about this subject because there have been so many wrong-headed people dealing with it. We're going through a terrible period in art, in literature and living, in psychiatry and psychology. The so-called realists are trying to drive us insane, and I refuse to be driven insane. I go with Nietzche who said: "We have art that we do not perish in the truth." That's what art is for. In our daily lives, we are making do. Things get rougher as we go along, but we make do. We lose love; we lose people; we lose jobs. And the remarkable thing about the human race is the ability to survive. We survive by fantasizing. Take that away from us, and the whole damned race goes down the drain. End of statement.

MHH: Bravo.
Jones: And that, children, is how I met your grandmother.

MHH: Go along with you, Jones. This whole fantasy section was sparked by listening to you and Dr. Seuss spinning off one night on fantasy in literature.

Jones: Have you ever felt drowned in your own minutia? Most people feel so, unless fantasy is one of life's delights. I was supposed to be writing a speech while flying back from Europe—work, work, work. And then we were over northern Iceland and Greenland. Flight is conducive to fantasy. I saw those great, white, unblemished fields. Huge snow fields ten miles wide and ten miles high. And the animator came out in me and got greedy. I thought, if I could only take a giant pencil, a burnt tree or something, and draw on that great cold piece of paper . . . how wonderful, how wonderful.

MHH: That's more like you, Chuck. Now, then, we are gathered here together because you two men are among the few, the precious few, who can create fantasy. What is successful fantasy in the arts?

Jones: You must build an entire world that is believable. Everything about this world must ring true, and the facts of the imagination must become as acceptable as the facts of reality.

Bradbury: What you must do is take one simple, fantastic idea and implement it on every sensual level.

MHH: Remember your man in the attic, the man in "A Scent of Sarsaparilla"?

Bradbury: That's what I mean by implementation. Everything is wrong in his life, and his wife is shouting at him. He gets up in his attic and looks out the window and the year 1905 is out there, firecrackers and sunshine and all. And he looks down the stairs and his hatchet-faced wife is waiting. The only thing good is the past—outside his window. But how can I make people believe this?

I worked and worked on that story. I wanted to go back in time. The attic was my time machine. But I had to prove it. So I opened all the trunks for the reader. There were the mothballs and the old clocks and the smell of machinery, and the prisms of old chandeliers that have caught all the sunlight of other days. I made a list of the things that had been put away so you could smell the attic, taste the attic, feel the old plush, and look at the time and dust put away in that old attic. If I could attack you through every one of your senses so that you believed you were there, really believed in my time machine, then you'd believe my story. Once I wrote that page of description for the senses, I proved my fantasy.

MHH: Then the man pulled up the ladder that led from downstairs up to the attic. I remember. He climbed out that window and was gone, and I believed you. His wife came up and looked out the window at the end. She saw this strange sunlight of another day, and she knew. And she knew she'd never have enough feeling about that 1905 world to follow.

Jones: I know that story. It proves something I believe: there are only two things that matter in life—work and love. And only the love should show.

Fantasy and poetry are horribly under-estimated by people who don't realize that the toughest, the hardest thing in the world to write is poetry. And the second toughest is fantasy. People think there is one set of rules for every form of literature and another set for fantasy, and that's where most mistakes in analyzation are made. The rules are exactly the same. You make sure that both intuitive and sensual logic are involved, not just intellectual logic. We believe only that which is proved artistically.

MHH: And you prove your fantasy with almost-alive people and animals in animated films.

Jones: Not *almost*. The animator is lucky. He is the only artist who actually creates life.

MHH: Tell me about proving fantasy in animation.

Jones: You must give the absolute illusion of reality to something no one has ever seen before. You are dealing with the utterly impossible. That means you can't cut any corners. When my daughter was little, she told me that Terrytoons were "the ones where the water disappears." I checked to find what she meant. When water was spilled or a wave washed into the shore in those cartoons, the water *would* disappear. It didn't remain, because it was cheaper to film by having it disintegrate. That shattered the reality of believable fantasy. All my daughter remembered about those cartoons was that the water disappeared.

You must have a wedding—or at least a liaison—between the logic of your reality and the logic of your fantasy. Ray's story about the sea monster that loved a lighthouse is a good example. It's so simple. Once you know that the monster is there and that the fog horn of the lighthouse and the cry of the monster coming up out of the deep sound exactly the same, there's nothing so incredible about the love.

Bradbury: I wrote a love story recently with just a little twist on reality.

MHH: Imagine you writing just a little twist on reality.

Bradbury: This was about a man who always wanted to be a writer. He wrote millions of words, but he never sold anything. When he was fifty, he took all those unsold words on a train across America.

All though Idaho he dumped these manuscripts on the wind, and they flew like pigeons in the air. He put a million words into the air over North Dakota and South Dakota. Finally, he got off at a little train stop somewhere and he looked in the gum-machine mirror. His hair was wild and his beard had grown.

"Charlie Dickens, is that you?" he said. The mirror image answered: "Yes, yes." Now, all his life he could remember every word ever written by any author he had ever read—Plato, Aristotle, Balzac, but especially Charles Dickens. From that day on, he started to write the novels of Charles Dickens from memory. He found a little boy in Greentown, Illinois, and dictated A *Tale of Two Cities* to him.

Then one day, he heard someone scratch, scratch, scratching away with a pen way at the back of the small-town library. He recognized by the sounds of the pen that poetry was being written, and just what it was. And when a woman came out of the darkness, he said to her: "Miss Emily, is that you?"

MHH: And was she Emily Dickinson?

Bradbury: Certainly. And they got married and lived happily ever after. At the very end of my story, the little Greentown boy says to his grandfather on the porch one October night, "You know, I don't think they're crazy."

Jones: That story illustrates just what the amateur doesn't realize. When fantasy is submitted by amateurs to MGM here it usually has something to do with outer space. And always these amateurs figure if one story element is good, four or five is better. They bury simplicity. And they confuse fantasy and distortion, which is like supposing that those distortion mirrors at the fun house are the same thing as caricature. Well, they're not. They make people look different from what they are. They don't emphasize the thing that makes a person beautiful or ugly. All art is caricature, and all art is editorial—even bad art. Bad art only proves that the artist doesn't know what he is doing.

MHH: What makes a great fantasy character? I puzzle over that. Take your Road Runner. You created him years ago, and he still lives.

Jones: The Road Runner is probably a transference of adult humor to a child's society. What surprises me is the fact that even young children buy it. That proves that children have a helluva a lot more cognizance of the world about them than people give them than people give them credit for.

MHH: But how did you create, how did you invent the Road Runner?
Jones: The Road Runner was intended as a parody of all the chase cartoons. You know, the baseboard pictures, where the camera is so low that all you see is the baseboard of the room and cats chasing mice and dogs chasing cats. But nobody accepted it as a parody, which was a disappointment to me.

I thought I might become the Jonathan Swift of animated cartoons, but people took the Road Runner as a straight character.

MHH: Isn't it lucky Dean Jonathan Swift wasn't taken seriously when he suggested solving the potato famine by eating Irish babies? Fortunately, nobody ate the babies.
Jones: The interesting thing to me about the Road Runner was that it had so many disciplines. I learned a lot about film-making on those cartoons. The more disciplines I applied, the funnier the picture became. I left the dialogue out completely. A discipline. Then I decided the Road Runner had to stay on the road, that's a discipline. The Road Runner never harmed the Coyote. The Coyote only harmed himself by his history of human error. A discipline.
Bradbury: The Road Runner and Bugs Bunny are my favorite TV shows, now that they are regular weekly reruns. Every weekend when Bugs Bunny or the Road Runner is on, the kids yell at me and nothing will keep me away from television. There isn't anything on TV to compare with them.

MHH: Bugs Bunny is real character creation. You say his name, and I can see him now.
Jones: Bugs had many fathers. I did the original drawings, but a lot of us worked to make him what he is. In developing a character like Bugs, first you have to think out who he is, what his motivation is, how he stands, what his weight is, what his personality is. You build out of whole cloth—or whole paper—a character who is understandable by the way he moves.

At first, Bugs Bunny was a sort of Woody Woodpecker. When he stood still, his legs were bent to indicate that he could move suddenly. Then we achieved controlled fantasy, and he never bent his legs again.

He stood with all his weight on one leg and the other leg loose—the classic posture of a man about town. Bugs knows where he's going; he can *go* anyplace. After we evolved that posture, we evolved his way of looking, his way of biting into a carrot. The slow deliberateness.

MHH: My God, suddenly you look like him. It's incredible.
Jones: Oh, an animator does that. How are you going to show all the men who work with you, who draw and bring things off, how a character moves and feels and looks if you don't become the character?

MHH: Tell me about the movie you two are doing together.
Bradbury: I've admired Chuck for twenty years, but we just met six months ago. He decided we should do an animated film. We met just after Hallowe'en.
Jones: I told Ray what had happened at our house. After all the candy was gone, a little boy with a rabbit hood came to the door and held up his little paper bag and said, "trickortreat," all one word. There wasn't a thing left in the house for a treat, no apples or pennies. And the child obviously didn't drink scotch.

"Everything's gone, it will have to be a trick," I said. The little boy's lower lip was quivering, and tears came to his eyes. "All right," he said. And he went out on the lawn and stood on his head.

MHH: Oh, Chuck! That blessed child.
Bradbury: The kid was a walking artifact. He didn't know what he was doing, or why. And then I told Chuck how disappointed I was when Charlie Schulz didn't produce the Great Pumpkin on his Hallowe'en special. It was like promising me Santa Claus and not delivering. It was a tragedy beyond compare.

We got to talking about the evolution of Hallowe'en from the dawn of history. And all of a sudden we decided to do a show and call it either *The Pumpkin Tree* or *The Hallowe'en Tree*.

MHH: I wonder what would have happened if you had met on April Fool's Day. Tell me about your story. Please.
Bradbury: Now I'm not an artist. Chuck is. His paintings and drawings are lovely, and he still studies all the time, but some years ago I did a painting of the Hallowe'en Tree with all the pumpkins on it.

In our story a group of children who are trick-or-treating come to this house where my Pumpkin Tree is, a tree covered with thousands of pumpkins.

Jones: Don't forget that it's the definitive Hallowe'en house, a great Gothic structure high on the hill, black against the gibbous moon.

Bradbury: Mr. Moundshroud lives in the house. He says, "No treat, only trick," and slams the door in their faces. Then he hides beneath the ghost-shaped pile of leaves around the Pumpkin Tree under the pumpkin shine and frightens them, with a skeleton's hand and horror face rising from the leaves. He leaps up. "That," he says, "is a trick!" He offers to show them what Hallowe'en really is all about out in the undiscovered country beyond the town. They run together to an old barn plastered with circus posters, pieces and bits from every circus that ever went through town. They make a huge autumn kite out of the bits of old posters, and Mr. Moundshroud shouts, "Boys, we need a tail for it."

Jones: One of the boys leaps up and grabs the bottom of the kite, and the next boy grabs his leg and soon we have a tail of boys hanging on the kite. Then Mr. Moundshroud opens his bumber-shoot—which is a bat—and they all go flying off into the past.

MHH: Mary Poppins's father!

Bradbury: They land in ancient Egypt and we look at the hieroglyphics and discover the ancient traditions of Hallowe'en. It has to do with our fear of the dark and our fear of death, our fear the spring may never come. All through history, in every culture, we've had to make up mythology to explain death to ourselves and to explain life to ourselves. They find out, as they work their way through history, that the Druids celebrated their Day of the Dead on October 31. The boys see the Catholics move north, with their Day of the Dead on May 31, like our Memorial Day. And someone smart must have said, "Hey, let's go along with the natives and move our Memorial Day to the Druid Day," because the Catholics did just that.

MHH: But when did Hallowe'en become fun?

Bradbury: The Irish did it, with their frolicsome ways, and their carved turnip heads. The boys see witches. Witches were real, you know. They were the doctors of their time. But on another level, the word witch meant *wit*. The witches had no supernatural powers, but they were *proud* of being witches. It was a profession; they were wise people.

Jones: Broom at the Top! And the children and Moundshroud begin climbing on the stone blocks that once were the witches and ogres and monsters of power but which have been turned to stone by the power of the new religion.

Bradbury: As they climb, the stairs build under them and become Notre Dame. When they reach the belfry, the bells go off and Mr. Moundshroud whistles twice. All the old witches and ogres that have been struck to stone come to life and begin to crawl up the side of the cathedral. They become the projections, the gargoyles facing in all directions. You watch that building go up, and you can see without one word how one religion replaces another. The kids look out when they reach the top, and the shadow of Catholicism lies all across Europe. Then they fly away to Mexico and watch what happens there.

MHH: How much easier to "animate" a cathedral to life than to build it from stone. But I don't see how you can put all this in and have entertainment, not solely an amazing educational film.
Jones: Most of the background material Ray has dug up about the historical origins of Hallowe'en will be implied in passing. It's amazing how much you can work in.

MHH: We've talked about what fantasy is. Well, Hallowe'en is an example of the need for fantasy that exists in all of us.
Bradbury: This kind of fantasy, and the kind that comes out in horror stories and horror films is our way of dealing with death. Death comes to all of us, and violence and tears. But death is inexplicable. All kinds of religions have tried to explain death to us for centuries, and we still don't know a damn thing. Science can't tell us anything.

So we have to have explanations for death. When you see *Dracula*, you've watched the essence of death terrifying you for ninety minutes. Then Dr. Von Helsing hands you a cedar stake, and you say, "Dracula, take that." And you go "Voom, Voom, Voom" and you kill death. That's the important thing.

You're free of the hairball. You throw up; you get rid of the sickness.

MHH: Films like *Frankenstein* don't terrify me the way *Wait Until Dark* did.
Bradbury: *Wait Until Dark* is a sick picture. It terrifies you for one hundred and twenty minutes and leaves you with the hairball. That monster can come into your house tonight and kill you.

MHH: Don't, please. I'm still suffering from that movie. I saw it three days ago, and I'm still hoarse. I screamed in terror. So did everyone else.
Bradbury: There, you see, you're never free after you see that film. The people who made that picture don't know the first thing about what we

need to survive as human beings. The purpose of art is to release every tension we have. If we need to cry; let us cry. If we need to laugh; let us laugh. If we need to throw up; by all means let us throw up. Being sick is a means of getting well. That's what sickness is for. You just can't stay sick; you've got to get well or kill yourself. So these new reality films say, "Die, die, die." They don't know that we must lie to ourselves with proper fantasies like *Dracula* and *Frankenstein* that say, "Here's the cedar stake. Drive it into his heart and kill death. For a little while, peace."

MHH: You are not a fan of Dr. Fredric Wertham or new reality reportage.
Bradbury: I read two or three of Wertham's books. His whole attitude is ridiculous. Comics and horror stories ruining children, indeed! Wrong-headed! Books like Truman Capote's *In Cold Blood* are wrong-headed, too. What you call the new reality reportage bothers me.

MHH: Are you sure the new reality isn't a new kind of fantasy? The anti-hero? In Capote's book, the *real* people were the killers, and one pitied them for their inevitable life of crime. The victims were unreal, as two-dimensional as a *McCall's* heroine.
Jones: Wertham came after my childhood, but my mother wouldn't let me go to see Keystone Cops movies and the like. She thought the mayhem and broad humor was hideous fare for my budding libido, that I would try to blow up a policeman when I grew up, that sort of thing. And that's exactly what I did—with a paper and pencil.

Maybe the new reality is partly responsible for the great rise in the popularity of fantasy. Did you know that *How the Grinch Stole Christmas* (Jones-produced) and two Charles Schulz shows—all three of them reruns—were among the five top TV specials last year?

And you know in fantasy films you can't forget *Fantasia*. It was staggeringly wonderful. Deems Taylor and Stokowski were in control. First the music was done as they wanted it, and then the animators took over. It was controlled fantasy.

MHH: Will you ever forget "Night on Bald Mountain?"
Jones: That is a classic, a masterpiece of powerful graphics. Bill Tytla did it. He was to animation what Rico le Brun was to graphics. And think of the cutting, brilliant interpretation of "The Sorcerer's Apprentice."

All right, so the apprentice was Mickey Mouse. It would have taken Marcel Marceau to do it live. The "Tocatta and Fugue" was the first attempt at pure abstraction in films. And "Dance of the Hours"—we can see it freshly now in our minds. Powerful, satirical drawing, and an amusing interpretation.

People tend to judge *Fantasia* on what it is today. Remember, it was made thirty years ago. It cost $3 million then; it could cost $30 million now, but there are no longer enough good animators around to make it. There were terrible mistakes in it. With its interpretation of Beethoven's Fifth, *Fantasia* made miniscule one of the greatest things that ever was. But that was the way Disney saw it.

MHH: The creator has his own right to attempt anything he wants, to tamper with anything, doesn't he? Think of the ballet *Romeo and Juliet*. Where is Shakespeare there?

Jones: Someone is triumphant to the extent that he makes his creation better than the original. If he fails, people say he is trifling with myth. Disney was daring enough to go out and try something no one was doing at the time. Jean Cocteau did the same thing with *Beauty and the Beast*. The important thing to me is that *Fantasia* remains an astonishing effort in film graphics.

MHH: Nobody else still has done anything like it.

Jones: And when it came out, the entire world sat up and cheered. When Disney was making *Snow White, Dumbo, Bambi,* and *Fantasia,* there was never anyone who came near him in genius. Not even Chaplin.

MHH: You and Ray will start making *The Pumpkin Tree* when you finish *The Phantom Tollbooth*. You know, if it comes off, and it looks as though it will, you may have in *The Phantom Tollbooth* a *Fantasia* with a story line. When is it scheduled for release?

Jones: In spring, a year from now. You know, we've always wanted to do a real, full-length children's fantasy. We picked Norton Juster's wonderful *Phantom Tollbooth* because it is becoming a modern children's classic, so MGM and the bankers would believe us. Juster wrote *The Dot and the Line: A Romance in Lower Mathematics*, from which we made a film, and I love to work with him.

Bradbury: You should have won an Oscar for *The Dot and the Line*, where the straight line falls in love with a squiggle.

Jones: We did. *Tollbooth* is an adventure that starts when a little boy named Milo is very bored one afternoon, and the only friend who calls him is a boy named Ralph.

MHH: Ralph wasn't in the book.
Jones: My privilege. It had to be a boy with a name like Ralph. Anybody called Steve or Mike would have called with something to do. Ralph sounds like a wet tennis shoe. And there is Milo in his room. I know what he looks like, so do you. He was so bored when he was walking home that a fire engine went by, and he didn't even notice. And there is a big package in his room addressed to him. He opens it. It is the tollbooth, and a little car, and directions to drive through the tollbooth. He does.

At that point, the real boy we have filmed becomes part of my animated world and himself turns into an animated character, until he returns through the tollbooth at the end of his travels. His adventure shows that anything can be really interesting. Everyone in Milo's travels in the film is obsessed with some *thing*, some *idea*. In Dictionopolis, one city he visits, the people are obsessed with words; you can't use numbers. But its twin city is ruled by mathematicians.

There is a character, Dr. Dischord, who has a fix on noise. It's no big thing, he just likes sound for its own sake. He asks Milo, "Have you ever heard an elephant tap dance on a tin roof at night?"

MHH: I know you conduct your own music for all your films. I know you write and draw and produce and direct. You have the music and the story, but you still don't know what all the characters look like in the *Tollbooth*. How come?
Jones: It requires a great deal of work to find out who a character is. Take the Whetherman in *Tollbooth*. He says it is much more important to know *whether* there will be a change in the *weather* than to know what the weather will be. That sounds like a quick moving fellow, and I remembered a minor actor in the movie *David Copperfield* and his spritely way of moving, like a squirrel. So then you know how the Whetherman moves. I edited him into a longer part. Later in the story, Milo meets Macabre, who is a wicked *which*. Not a witch, but the one who tells people *which* words to use. I made her the Whetherman's sister because I liked his characteristics so much. After all, *which* is obviously the female equivalent of *whether*. And that relieves me of one character. She can move the same way he does.

The successful fantasy in *Tollbooth* means developing characters as believable as Milo. We do hundreds and hundreds of exploratory drawings of every character.

You have to keep drawing and drawing until you get something that works for you in dimensional form. Any living thing has dimension, but there is no such thing as realistic animation. To say that Bugs Bunny is realistic is absurd. A rabbit is a horizontal character—Bugs looks more like a man in a rabbit costume. He is an abstraction; all animated characters are. The thing I am trying to avoid is to have characters appear as drawings. People don't believe in drawings as characters. You have to get reality and feeling and movement, and voice. And you should create a voice, not steal one.

The animator is the actor. He must be prepared to perform on a bare stage without setting or costumes, not like a performer in a Cecil B. DeMille epic, an actor whose art form is buried. The animator must be able to perform with these simple tools: a pencil and a series of blank pieces of paper—twenty-four to the second, to be exact. You hold these drawings up before you, and by flicking them, you achieve life. So animation exists. It's like walking past a picket fence and hitting it with a stick.

MHH: You love this art form, don't you?

Jones: I say I am trying to make fantasy for the audience, but I can really only make it for myself. I am making films for myself that children endorse, or you endorse. I know this is true of Ray's writing, and when Ted Geisel has made a Dr. Seuss book, it is on the basis of what he enjoys. It has to be so. You must do what you do with no thought of audience.

MHH: *Phantom Tollbooth* is a modern *Alice in Wonderland*.

Jones: How I would like to make *Alice* and animate all the original Tenniel illustrations. Isn't that a frightening thought? One thing I have noticed about fantasists—if there is such a thing—is extreme concern about their ability to continue to produce, fear of the open canvas, the fear of keyboard, fear of that empty page in the typewriter.

But coupled with that is an extreme incisiveness and courage when you actually start work. It is like a dive into cold water, and at that point the artists are one with the universe (or with God, depending on what your persuasions are). They have absolute certainty and confidence in what they are doing. Then they stop, and the fear is there again.

Bradbury: Amen. Always there. And to stop is death.

MHH: So you keep rising again and risking. Ray, I'm confused in our definitions. What is the difference between fantasy and science fiction? Science fiction *is* fantasy, but what else?

Bradbury: It is a confusing and fine line. Most people call *The Martian Chronicles* science fiction, but only portions are. In large part, it is really a fairytale of the future. But when you deal with the possible results of a machine's influence on a community, then you set up a civilization of the future and work it out—and *that's* science fiction.

For instance, I've just finished writing a story about the last man in England, and why not? Ireland is almost deserted today. The potato famine, plus travel around the world, plus all the young men leaving have reduced the population drastically. Everyone's getting out of the islands. They've even had to restrict passage. Well, I said to myself, wouldn't it be interesting to write a story called "A Lasting Sceptre, A Final Crown" in which the last man in England says good-bye to his friends who are going off in the last helicopter. They're all going to the summer islands, to Africa, to Australia, to Santa Barbara, to Los Angeles. The warmth, the sun calls. Norway is deserted; Sweden no longer exists. Why? Because of the airplane and the credit cards and the job openings in all parts of the world. Now, this story is science fiction because it takes off on the idea of the influence of the airplane on the family, on society.

And so England is deserted and the last man says, "I will wander about and I will represent the ghosts. I will wander the Roman roads; I will defend our coast from the invasions of the Normans and the Saxons. I will meet Caesar on the shore. I will be in Big Ben on New Year's night. I will sit me on the stone of Scone and crown myself Harry the Ninth, the last King of England."

MHH: The importance of the machine fascinates you.

Bradbury: Sure! Who set the Negroes free? The automobile, not the liberals. The automobile came along and said to the Negro, "Do you want to get out? Do you want to get away? Put a gallon of gas in that 1928 Nash and fly!" And they flew. And they're in Watts now because of the automobile. They set themselves free, ten cents at a time.

MHH: Oh, come on, Ray. *The original* Lincoln was *not* a car.

Jones: I know a southern plantation owner who tried to drive a cedar stake through a carburetor.

Bradbury: Of course. He has to make that death because they're pulling out and leaving his fields. Anyhow, the difference between fantasy and science fiction is that science fiction could happen. England *could* be empty some day.

MHH: On the other hand, in *The Martian Chronicles* you have a meeting between a Martian from one time period and an Earthman from another. They see through each other and neither knows which is the ghost from another time.
Bradbury: That's pure fantasy.

MHH: If each of you had to make a list of the best fantasy, the works that will last—what would you include?
Jones: I think I might begin with James Stephens's *The Crock of Gold* and go on with Thurber's *The Thirteen Clocks*; Tolkien's *Hobbit*; Milne's *Once on a Time*; one of the Dr. Seuss books, *Horton Hears a Who*; T. H. White's *Sword in the Stone*, the book not the Disney version; Disney's *Dumbo*, and Mark Twain's *Mysterious Stranger*.

MHH: How about you, Ray? Do you want to add other titles to the list?
Bradbury: Indeed I do. *Alice in Wonderland* would be one, and all the Oz books would have to be included. You know, most of the librarians of the world don't think anything of the *Oz* books. Won't have them in the place.

MHH: The library didn't carry them when I was a child. That's how I discovered the second-hand book store. Who else will last?
Bradbury: Jules Verne will be around for a while, for as long as you need time. And H. G. Wells. I have a sneaking suspicion that one of my books might make it: *Something Wicked This Way Comes*.

MHH: What a great title! That's the one about the two boys and the carnival and the merry-go-round that makes you older or younger, depending upon the way it revolves, isn't it?
Bradbury: That's the one. It fell off the cliff when it was first published, but now it has climbed back safely. I wrote it for the kids. I wanted to make a book for boys that would scare the hell out of me and out of boys. It's in the tradition of Mark Twain. I have a great love for Twain. I've always wanted to be in that company—Twain, Wells, Verne and the Stevenson of *Treasure Island* and *Kidnapped*.

MHH: You want the young readers always, don't you?
Bradbury: If I can be read by young people—from ten to seventeen—I'm happy. I'm closer to that age group; I like that kind of mind. Chuck Jones

and Stan Freeberg are the only two people who make me behave like a boy, though. Then I say everything I really think. We become utterly honest, real, villainous children.

MHH: What do you remember about when you were a child?
Bradbury: I remember all kinds of things about my early months. I remember being suckled. A while back I asked my Victorian mother how long she suckled me, and she said, up to the third day. "I remember it," I said, "What day was I circumcised?" "On the second day," she said. And well I remember being circumcised, too. The doctor, and the knife, and I remember the atmosphere of the hospital. I remember the pain.
Jones: And on the seventh day he rested.
Bradbury: What's so unusual about remembering? An infant is a living creature; most of its senses are pretty well developed. Lots of the stories I've written over the years are tied in with the memories of the first weeks after I was born, including the first day. I wrote a short story about a baby who resents being born and plans to kill off his parents because of it. The baby is born fully aware and therefore dangerous. He goes around the house and shakes up the parents and kills people. My oldest daughter had nightmares when she was a month old.

MHH: How do you know they were nightmares?
Bradbury: You can tell the difference between a hunger or wet cry and terror. So I said to myself, Hey, wait a minute, what's happened to her life? Nothing! So what's she dreaming about? She's dreaming about being born. That's all. Logically there's nothing else to dream about . . . there's been no fire around, no wolves, no accident. There's been nothing; a completely uneventful life, with only one big event—being extruded forth into the cold world, suddenly, after being comfy all those months. So that sent me back to my own memories of my nightmares in my crib when I was a month old. I remember the angle of the crib and everything, and lying there and my mother coming and picking me up.
Jones: And what is fantasy? Mark Twain says he told his first lie when he was three days old, crying that a pin was sticking him when it wasn't. I don't remember my childhood nightmares or lies—just a family with lots of children. What bleating lambs are to Bengal tigers and Old Grandad to alcoholics, having babies was to my mother. She's a marvelous woman.

All of us grew up to be artists, sculptors, weavers, cartoonists. Father kept trying to start new businesses, buying new letterhead stationery, and everytime the business failed, we children inherited a new legacy—ample drawing material. While every other child on the block was lucky to get one shabby sketch pad a month, we children were rolling in lovely white bond paper and the finest Ticonderoga pencils. And we were free from criticism.

The thoughtless criticism of child's art by an unqualified adult can do great harm—not only to the child's future as an artist but to his future as a man.

MHH: Ray, why are children so often villains in your stories?
Bradbury: It's the truth about children, and it's the truth about all of us. The old Grimm fairytales showed an understanding of the need for horror fantasy. Violence in various forms lets children destroy their hostility by acting it out. You know, every child has wanted to kill some teacher along the way. The instinct to kill is in us all.
Jones: And the instinct to reach out and save someone else. Do you know how to make friends with any child when first you meet? You just say, "Hello, have you ever been stung by a bee?"

An Interview with Chuck Jones

MICHAEL BARRIER AND BILL SPICER / 1969

From *Funnyworld* 13, 1971, pp. 4–19.
Copyright © 1971 Michael Barrier.
Reprinted with permission.

Charles Martin Jones is probably the most famous living cartoon director and arguably the greatest. For nearly a quarter of a century, he was a director for the Warner Bros. cartoon department, bringing to the screen such characters as the Road Runner, the Coyote and Pepé le Pew, and refining and developing established "stars" like Bugs Bunny and Daffy Duck. His best cartoons are models of subtlety, precision and carefully expended energy, with none of the "mindlessness" and "sadism" that ignorant critics sometimes impute to the Warner cartoons.

Bill Spicer and I interviewed Chuck Jones in two one-hour sessions on June 4 and 5, 1969, in his office at what was then the MGM cartoon department. Before the start of the first session, we joined Jones in viewing an unfinished National Film Board of Canada film on computer animation. When the interview began, our conversation turned first to that subject.

—MIKE BARRIER

SPICER: With computerized animation, would it eventually be possible to, say, program two extremes—of someone walking, for example—and have the computer do all the fill-in work?

JONES: It would, I think, in a rigid sense. But great animation depends as much on the character and placement of the in-betweens as on the primary drawings. For example, take a draggy, slow walk by a tired man. If you have one extreme of the legs crossing, and being pulled along the ground, and the other extreme with the foot way back, and the following extreme with the foot forward, the in-between position is not in-between. Because the foot is heavy, it tends to stay on the ground. So you'll have several drawings with the foot very close to the back extreme, and then, in release, the foot will drag through quite quickly, to the center position, and so on.

SPICER: But could this be programmed with a few in-between drawings?

JONES: It could, but what you'd have to do then is make a programmer out of your animator. I'm not saying it can't be done, and I'm not saying it wouldn't be desirable to do it under certain conditions, but I am saying that the true animator makes different decisions on practically every movement. I think it would take him longer to do the programming than it would to do the actual drawings.

Unquestionably, computer animation is going to be a very valuable thing. I was startled to see that they could take what seemed to me to be two-dimensional information and turn it into three-dimensional perspective drawings of an airplane. That's pretty sophisticated.

SPICER: It would require an awfully sophisticated computer to actually do all those hundreds of in-between drawings, using reference points along the way. . .

JONES: I can envisage several areas where I'm sure it would be useful, just as Xerox is. For example in *One Hundred and One Dalmatians* (1961), they had a hundred and one dogs, and in a couple of shots there were acres and acres of puppies. There the Xerox helped them tremendously, because they animated eight or nine cycles of action, of dogs running in different ways, then made them larger or smaller, using Xerox, knowing that if there are a hundred and one dogs, and if there are eight or nine distinct cycles, and they're placed at random in this rabble of dogs, no one will know that they all haven't been animated individually. You might say that this could be carried further. Say we're animating the classic walk of Bugs Bunny. We could simply refer back to that, if we wanted to use that walk another time, and call on the computer to print that same cycle of drawings, smaller or larger.

SPICER: Do you ever see the day when a computer might replace everyone connected with animation besides the animator, the director, and the background artist?
JONES: That may be the ultimate goal, but it would take a pretty far-reaching version of the computer. Right now, computer animation costs more than the traditional method.

BARRIER: How much has Xerox helped in bringing down costs?
JONES: I would say it helped Disney tremendously. They were able to bring in *One Hundred and One Dalmatians* for about half of what it would have cost if they'd had to animate all those dogs and all those spots.

   Of course, only the Disney studio would think of doing a hundred and one spotted dogs. We have trouble doing one spotted dog.

BARRIER: I've noticed that there seem to be a lot more characters in the average Disney cartoon than in the average Warner cartoon.
JONES: Right. As you know, we used a very austere kind of cutting. Our pictures, by and large, involved two characters in some kind of conflict, and there was a great deal of inter-cutting, so that on the screen at any given time, there was seldom more than one. Mark Twain, in *Huckleberry Finn*, was talking about this sleepy little country town on the Mississippi River, and there were posts along the covered sidewalk, and he said, "There was as many as one loafer leaning against each post." So I think we used as many as one character in most of our scenes. In *The Phantom Tollbooth*, however, we have some pretty elegant crowd scenes, and I'd say that was a two-or-more-character picture.

BARRIER: Computer animation has been advocated for doing things in cartoons like rolling boulders, which I've heard is pretty difficult to do.

JONES: We don't roll many boulders except in Road Runner cartoons, but we use a great deal of perspective, and we employ what we call the "telephone pole theory," both in graphic work and in animation. That is, say you have two telephone poles, one in the distance and one in the foreground, and if you draw a line from the top of one to the bottom of the other, and vice versa, a line drawn perpendicular at the intersection is at the halfway point. This is a very striking and startling thing, and I don't think many animators know this, because that intersection is so much closer to the pole in the background than it is to the pole in the foreground. The tendency is to put the line exactly in between, and that's one of the problems I think you would run into with the computer. But I suppose it would be very simple for the computer to understand these matters and be so programmed. However, to me it was always fun to do them a little differently, a little more in comic dramatization. Since I'm in business to enjoy myself, I wouldn't call on a computer to animate my boulder.

BARRIER: I'd like to go back to your beginnings. You started with Ub Iwerks, didn't you? How long were you there, a couple of years?
JONES: The first time I was there was probably for not more than a year. I really don't remember. I started out as a painter, as everybody else did. Then I graduated to cel washing, and inking, and then, eventually, to in-betweening. Then I went to Walter Lantz for a short time; these periods were all very brief, the whole time period that embraced my tenure at Ub's and then Universal and Oswald with Bill Nolan and Walter Lantz was less than two years. Then I worked for Charlie Mintz [Screen Gems] for a short time. I really wasn't sure I wanted to be an animator. I didn't see much future in it. So I went down to Olvera Street and had what you might call my hippie period— although then it was called a "Bohemian period." I worked on Olvera Street, this little Mexican street in downtown Los Angeles, doing sketches of people for a dollar apiece. Eventually I came to Warner's. I suppose that whole period covered a year and a half or two years. In 1933, I went to Warner's as an assistant and spent the next twenty-eight years there.

BARRIER: What kind of man was Leon Schlesinger? Did he exercise any artistic control at all over the cartoons?
JONES: No. We had two kinds of producers. I won't go into who the other one was, you can figure it out for yourself, but he was a sort of

prototype of Mister Magoo.[1] But Schlesinger was absolutely out for money, and he didn't care how he got it. He was very lazy in the sense that he never bothered us. He didn't want to have to make artistic decisions; he wanted the pictures to go out and play and make money. That was fine with me; I was very happy to have it that way. The only time he'd look at a picture was when it was finished, and if he didn't like it, he might get around to saying, "Four more pictures like that, boy, and you're out." One time he bought a yacht from Richard Arlen and named it the *Merry Melody*. We asked when he was going to take us for a ride on his boat, and he said, "I don't want any poor people on my boat." Of course, he was the reason we were poor. We were grossly underpaid, but we still did what we wanted to do. Daffy's voice and Sylvester's voice, which are the same voice, really, except that Daffy's is speeded up a little, are really very similar to Leon Schlesinger's voice, because Leon too lisped when he talked.

He was a darling; he was so pure. He had other interests; he owned Pacific Art and Title, which today is the biggest art and title company in the industry. He didn't do the titles himself, but the same thing happened there: he put the necessary money into it. He helped underwrite *The Jazz Singer.* He was related remotely to the Warner brothers—a cousin or something—and he had some money, and at the time of *The Jazz Singer* the Warners were so hard up they needed anything they could get. Of course, when *The Jazz Singer* hit, they became very close. He was the man who underwrote Harman and Ising; that's where Looney Tunes and Merrie Melodies really all started.

Anyway, he exerted no artistic control at all. He had a man working for him named Ray Katz, who was the production manager and who gumshoed around trying to run the place, but who knew practically nothing about the business. He really didn't know what was going on there. He was a very nice man, as it turned out, but he tried to preserve this air of being mean. The building where we worked was very long, like a string of stables; it was where the first Vitaphone sound pictures had been made, and it hadn't been changed when we moved in.

---

[1] Jones's reference is to Edward Selzer (1893–1970). Selzer was director of publicity for the Warner studio from 1933 to 1937, and head of the trailer and title department from 1937 until 1944, when Leon Schlesinger (1884–1949) sold out to Warner's. Selzer became president of Warner Bros. Cartoons, Inc., until that subsidiary was dissolved in July 1955 and merged with the parent company.

Ray was always catching people asleep or reading the newspaper. One animator had the worst kind of insomnia—he couldn't sleep at work. He had an office with an open door—all the doors were open, and he could see Ray walking down the hall. One of the other animators was an electronic wizard, so he rigged up a whole electric light system throughout the building, and every animator, back under his desk, had a little red light. When Ray would start down the hall, this fellow would press a button, and all the lights would go on, and everybody would snap to attention. Everybody, that is, except writers and directors, who all worked in adjoining rooms. What they did when the lights went on was to *stop* working. For a year and a half, Ray never caught a director or a writer working. He'd walk into a room, and one would be polishing his shoes, another would be reading a newspaper, another would be sleeping, and there wouldn't be anything on the storyboards. Ray was embarrassed and didn't know what to do about these people, because they were kind of outside his little area. So, he'd walk back down the hall, and the writers would go back to work, and the animators would go back to sleep. He'd come back, and the directors and storymen were doing exactly what they had been doing before; the fellow who had been shining his shoes an hour earlier would still be shining his shoes. This was very puzzling. Sometimes when he'd leave, the men would pull out all the work that had been done, and completely cover the story-boards with material they had hidden in their desks. So he'd come back, and they were doing what they'd been doing before, but now the whole damned place would be covered with story sketches. As I've said, he was too embarrassed to ask anybody what had happened.

The other (anonymous) producer's attitude toward animation was that laughter didn't play any part in it. He once came in on a bunch of us when we were just sitting around talking and laughing. When we looked up, there he was, standing in the doorway smoldering, and he said, "What the hell has all this laughter got to do with making animated cartoons?" That was one of his classic lines. The first time I met him, we were sitting in the theater looking at a cartoon, and he said, "There's something new take it out." One sentence, no comma. Also, he aggravated me in quite a different manner. He said Pepé le Pew wasn't funny, no one would go for that bastardized French, or whatever he called it. Nevertheless, when *For Scentimental Reasons* (1949) won the Academy Award, he went up and took the Oscar as producer. Our unit won two that year—the other was for a documentary, *So Much for So Little*—and he took them both.

BARRIER: Was there every any thought while you were at Warner's of making feature cartoons?

JONES: No. When Schlesinger first saw *Snow White and the Seven Dwarfs* (1937), he said—this was another of his favorite expressions—"I need a feature like I need two belly buttons," or words to that effect.

BARRIER: Even after all the money it made, he still felt that way?

JONES: Oh, yes, because by that time *Fantasia* (1940) had come out and fallen flat on its financial face. He said, "See, I was right all the time, fellas. We'll stick to shorts. Hit 'em on the run, I always say. Put a lot of jokes in it."

BARRIER: I've heard that the Schlesinger studio back in the thirties had pretty primitive facilities; for example, when the cameraman had instructions for a "camera shake," he'd hit the camera.

JONES: That's a new one on me; I'd never heard that. I would doubt that. Johnny Burton, a great talent who was in charge of production, never would have permitted such a thing, even if it would work, which it wouldn't. But it was primitive, there's no question about that. We had a wonderful cameraman by the name of Hank Garner, who shot the tests. He was a real primitive, from the swamps of Arkansas—we called him the "Swamp Rabbit." "Smokey" was also his nickname. He had what John Steinbeck called the "mechanic's thumb," and he could fix anything. The camera we used for tests was actually a 1904 camera, a wooden, box-like thing. But Smokey had this way, he could do more with a rubber band and a beer-can opener than most men can do with all the hardware in the world; a wonderful cameraman.

BARRIER: Back in the thirties, the Disney studio was dominant. How did people at other studios look at the Disney studio?

JONES: With absolute awe. We didn't really believe we were doing the same thing. From the time of *The Three Little Pigs* (1933), most of us felt that, there was Disney, and here were the rest of us, just hacking away at the edges. We didn't consider ourselves in the same league. And today, when you look at the animation of a cartoon like *The Tortoise and the Hare* (1934)—I saw that just the other day—I really don't know how you could improve it. It's still a smashing picture. I think you'll find that everyone was affected by the marvelous speed that was achieved in *The Tortoise and the Hare*. That was really the break-through in speed. Up to that time, no character had moved the way Max Hare did. You see, the point about our films and the point about Disney's films was that our experimenting was never overt. We didn't sit down and say, "Look at us, we're experimenting." But think of the *Toccata and Fugue* in *Fantasia*; that was the first abstract film since Len Lye did his thing in the thirties. It was the first of the abstractions to appear commercially. The "Baby Weems" sequence in *The Reluctant Dragon* (1941) was the first of the restricted-animation pictures, and it's probably the best ever made. You look at it today, and you wonder why somebody didn't learn from it: when you use limited animation, use good drawing.

Walt represented something to this business that few of our people will acknowledge. There's a great deal of pontificating about what is happening in the European "schools," and I think they're all very interesting, but the Europeans have been at it longer than we have, and they're never yet developed a school of animation of any kind. People talk about the "Zagreb School," but I just came back from Yugoslavia, and I know they're going off in all directions. The Disney studio did develop an identification, and as a result each studio, all of us, began to develop characteristics. Disney was to me what Harold Ross was to *The New Yorker*; he created an atmosphere where animators could flourish. In so doing, he pointed the way for everybody else to animate creatively. He still is the most important man in animation and not necessarily for the reasons that most people think. What's startling is that so many animators overlook the fact that Disney not only created a great ground for them to work, but he also was probably the first motion-picture maker to break the international boundaries. *The Three Little Pigs* was accepted all over the world, and no motion picture previous to that time had been able to do that. In international cinematic communication, Disney was the first one to break through. *Snow White and the Seven Dwarfs* was certainly the first feature to be internationally accepted. Walt was probably a dreadful man in many ways, but he was the only man who had the daring to even think of doing *Fantasia*. When you consider the condition of the motion-picture industry at that time and of animation in particular . . . I admire these young people who are doing experimenting today, but it's about like Stanley Kubrick or John Boorman saying D. W. Griffith didn't have any meaning. Practically every tool these men use was invented by D. W. Griffith, and practically every tool we use today was originated at the Disney studio—not necessarily by Walt, but his men couldn't have originated them unless he had encouraged them to exist. I have a real quarrel with Richard Schickel over *The Disney Version*. Calling Walt

Disney basically a businessman is a complete distortion. That is as wrong as you can get, I'll say that for Schickel. *Roy* was a good businessman. Till the day he died, when Walt went out to Disneyland and wanted something new put in, he'd tear out anything else to do it, because he wanted it in, no matter how much money the other thing was making. He was one of the few men in the world who was lucky enough to be a child, a millionaire child, who could do anything he wanted. A business-man was exactly what he wasn't. If the war hadn't come along, he prob-ably would have gone bankrupt.

BARRIER: I've heard the reverse, that the war hurt him, by cutting the market for his features in half.

JONES: You're overlooking the fact that there were only three of his entertainment features in existence at that time. I think the films he did for the government during the war were actually what put him back in financial shape. Nobody can say for sure. But I don't think it makes any kind of sense to talk about him as a businessman. I don't adore the man, but I know what he meant to all of us, and it's poor history to ignore that. If it hadn't been Walt, maybe somebody else would have done it, but you can mention any UPA picture ever made to most of the people in the United States, and most of them will have been forgotten . . . you can talk about John Hubley, and among the aficionadoes Hubley is very important. I think John is that important to many animators, but Disney was overwhelmingly important to the world. I repeat, he's the reason we're in existence, and we don't even have to like him to acknowledge that.

SPICER: What else didn't you like about *The Disney Version*?

JONES: Schickel starts out with a nonscientific approach. I'm doing a book now on the diversity of living things with a professor at the Uni-versity of Calfornia at Davis and another at Stanford, just because it inter-ests me, and I've discovered that the scientific method is that you start out with a premise and then you try to disprove it. Schickel starts out with a premise—and a prejudice—and then spends the whole book trying to prove it correct. You can reach into that book and take pieces from it, out of context, and make at least a full chapter of nice things he says about Disney, but the overall effect is bad.

To me, the average book on animation today, Halas or Schickel or Stephenson, goes on the supposition that animation is only the modern European thing plus what you might call the palette animators in

America, the fellows who do the little specialized films. I think they're doing very good cartoons, but from the public's viewpoint and even from an animator's viewpoint, most of these people simply do not have much influence. Does it take me to tell you that?

BARRIER: How did you become a director? How was the choice made?
JONES: Well, a man named Henry Binder was Schlesinger's assistant, and for some reason he thought I'd make a director. I don't know why.

It's my supposition that nearly all of us fall into the line of work we do more by chance than by choice. It'd be nice if it happened the other way, through destiny, but when I think about it, nearly all the animators of my generation, at least, were born or raised or went to school in New York or Kansas City or Hollywood. So, if I'd been born in Butte, Montana, the chances are pretty good that I'd have ended up a cowhand. If an Eskimo wants to be a surfer, the chances are against him.

BARRIER: Your first cartoon as a director was *The Night Watchman*, which was released in 1938. Do you recall how you went about making that cartoon?
JONES: Well, I was pretty scared. The writers had come up with a rough idea for *The Night Watchman*, of a little cat who has to take his father's place as night watchman of the house. At that time, the Merrie Melodies were supposed to have a Warner Bros. song in each cartoon; that was their avowed purpose, to plug songs. Things changed later, but at that time they always had to include one complete chorus. We used this swinging version—which still sounds pretty good—of "In the Shade of the Old Apple Tree."

BARRIER: Something that intrigued me was that the little kitten in *The Night Watchman* is a ringer for your Sniffles, who I guess came along about a year later, in *Little Brother Rat* (1939).
JONES: Yes, that's true. Charlie Thorson, who was working for me—he was the one who made the first model sheet of Bugs Bunny—had actually designed Hiawatha for Disney, so he was instrumental to a certain extent in forming the Disney style. He infected our style somewhat. I didn't draw terribly well at that time. Bob Givens had come over, and he drew beautifully; he was about nineteen years old, and he was fantastic. My style, whatever it is, developed over a period of many, many years. Don Graham of Chouinard Art Institute was very important to me; I spent maybe fifteen years going to night classes with him. I was kind of

a late bloomer as an artist, as a "serious" artist. By that, I don't mean that the work was serious, but that I was serious about it. I never made a dollar from drawings and paintings until I was past forty-five. So the whole thing was like discovering girls when you're forty. Most of the men had long since run through the whole idea of doing watercolors, but for me it was fun, and it was new. I'd been to art school, but I didn't really have that much youthful talent. However, I found that whatever talent you have, if you keep at it long enough, then you acquire facility, and I think I have some graphic facility now.

But anyway, at that time, I needed help, and so Givens and Thorson were helpful, and I suppose there was a subconscious development of a style of my own. Charlie did the drawings of both the Minah Bird and Inki, who was very similar to Hiawatha, although a non-stereotyped Negro. But I designed all my later characters, and I had some effect on the earlier ones.

BARRIER: Something I've often wondered is how the characters were parceled out at Warner's—that is, who decided who was to make so many Bugs Bunny cartoons, and Daffy Duck cartoons, and so on, and as a corollary to that, whether the directors tried to co-ordinate their versions of the same characters.

JONES: The characters tended to be different in different directors' cartoons, a little bit, but we also tended to learn from one another. Actually, there was a troika situation with the three directors—Friz Freleng, Bob McKimson and me—running parallel. We were called directors, but we were really producer-directors, because we had absolute control over our material. We had to do a certain number of cartoons with basic characters like Bugs Bunny, but we also had specialized characters that nobody else used. For example, Friz used Yosemite Sam and Sylvester; I occasionally used Sylvester with Porky Pig, but he wasn't really the same cat. He was a well-drawn cat, and I enjoyed working with him. I did all the Road Runners and Pepé le Pews until I left Warner's. So far as allocation was concerned, the distributing organization in New York would simply tell us how many Bugs Bunnys they wanted in a given year, usually six or eight, which would mean that each director would end up with two or three Bugs Bunnys a year. You had to keep an eye out for good Bugs Bunny ideas.

There were certain characters who evolved slowly, like Bugs Bunny and Porky Pig. Tex Avery, I think, must be given the basic credit for the character of Bugs Bunny, although there were a few Bugs Bunnys made before Tex's first Bugs Bunny. But Tex was the first to have him say, "What's up, doc?" and give him what you might call controlled insanity, as opposed to wild insanity. Originally, Bugs was very much like Daffy.

BARRIER: I've heard that you consider the rabbit in your *Prest-O Change-O* (1939) the ancestor of Bugs.
JONES: That was one of them. It was made before *A Wild Hare* (1940), Tex's first Bugs Bunny, but *A Wild Hare* really set Bugs's personality.

BARRIER: You had a cartoon called *Elmer's Pet Rabbit* (1940), which was released several months after *A Wild Hare*. It seems to be the first cartoon in which Bugs is identified by name. The Bugs in that cartoon is like the rabbit in your *Elmer's Candid Camera*, which was released early in 1940, and Hardaway and Dalton's *Hare-um Scare-um*, which was released in 1939. Both came before *A Wild Hare*.
JONES: I'm not sure of the chronology, but the Bugs Bunny personality has to be started with *A Wild Hare*. That and two or three Tex Avery cartoons after that really made Bugs what he was.

BARRIER: I've read in Bill's *Graphic Story Magazine* that you used stylized animation in one of your cartoons, *The Dover Boys*. Rudy Larriva said that it was done before the UPA cartoons but along those lines.
JONES: Yes, it was made in 1941 and released in 1942.

SPICER: How was it accepted?
JONES: Not very well. New York was shocked. I don't think they would have released it at all except that they had to have a picture. Today it would go very nicely, and does, but it was considered then by many people to be a kind of breakthrough. I know John Hubley always considered it so. But the storyline itself went back to when I was a kid, when I used to read the Rover Boys book. So yes, that was an experiment, but probably my only overt experiment. I did a hell of a lot of experimenting. The Road Runner and Coyote cartoons are now used in many art schools to show objects working in space. Pure space. One of the goals in drawing is to achieve an object working in pure space.

BARRIER: I want to get back to the Road Runner in a little while, but still on stylized animation, I've heard that your *The Aristo-Cat* (1943) with Hubie and Bertie the mice drew protests from theater owners who felt that they were being short-changed with an unfinished picture because of its highly stylized backgrounds.

JONES: Really? I hadn't heard that. But the background were stylized, and we were trying for pretty dramatic stuff. John McGrew did the layouts on both *The Aristo-Cat* and *The Dover Boys,* and he had very interesting ideas that I was willing to try. (But if it failed it was my neck, not his.) *Fox Pop* also had stylized backgrounds. But there was a consistency in *The Dover Boys.* The basic thing we did in *The Dover Boys* that was quite different was the restricted animation, which I felt was called for. I evolved a kind of movement, or pattern, from one extreme to the other. So I would say it was stylized but not necessarily modern.

BARRIER: You left Warner's for a while during World War II, didn't you? Were you in the service?

JONES: No, but I made films for the service. That's where I met Ted Geisel [Doctor Seuss]. He was over here at "Fort Western," as they called it. If you were an animator and you got drafted, instead of working for Warner's you were sent over to Western Avenue and Sunset Boulevard, dressed in a private's uniform. Some of the more prominent Disney people became officers, and so did Rudy Ising, who was about the least likely officer who ever lived. He became a major overnight. He was the head of "Fort Roach." All the animators worked at either "Fort Western" or "Fort Roach," or out at Long Island, where the Army motion picture unit still is. I made most of the Private Snafu pictures during the war; Ted Geisel and some of the other Army people did the storyboards, and I produced them at Warner's.

BARRIER: How many were there in the series?

JONES: There were about twenty of them; I did ten or more.

BARRIER: I've heard that you were somehow involved in the early days of UPA with *Hell Bent for Election* in 1944.

JONES: Yes, I directed that on my own time.

BARRIER: You never actually left Warner's then?

JONES: Only once. When 3-D came in, we made a 3-D cartoon with Bugs Bunny, called *Lumber Jack-Rabbit,* which Johnny Burton worked out. Johnny was a very creative technical man, who could do a hell of a lot with a camera, way ahead of his time, actually. He's now with Pacific Art and Title. John figured out what you had to do to make three-dimensional cartoons. Technically, you can't make a 3-D cartoon in the usual sense. You can get characters working on different levels, but they'll remain flat. That was when Jack Warner made *The Wax Museum,* and he decided, I guess, that the entire world was going to wind up wearing Polaroid glasses. This was the whole future. He was a pretty brilliant man in many ways, omniscient, I guess. He decided that the animated-cartoon business was through, since it was too expensive to make three-dimensional animated cartoons, so he laid off everybody. He couldn't lay off a few of us, because we were under contract, but I didn't want to work there if none of my people were there. I called up Walt Disney and asked him if I could come over there for a while. He said, "Sure, come on over." I was there for four months.[2] I worked on *Sleeping Beauty* and the beginning of the television show. But I couldn't adjust to waiting for Walt . . . the Disney people were raised that way and used to it. You'd finish a sequence, and then you'd wait, maybe for weeks. Five or six men, just sitting around waiting for Walt to come around. When he did come around, he'd already been there the night before when the plant was dark and looked at the boards, and everybody knew he'd seen the sequence, but they still had to show it to him as though he hadn't. Eventually, I felt I just couldn't take it any more, so I went in and talked with Walt. He said, "Well, what do you want to do? We can work out something for you." I said, "Well, you have one job here that I want, and that's yours," because he was the only one there who could make a decision. He said, "I'm sorry, but I'm afraid it's filled." So we shook hands, and I left. By that time, Warner's had decided to start up again, because 3-D hadn't completely revolutionized the world. That was the only time I left Warner's until they closed it down again in 1962.

BARRIER: How much warning did you have that the Warner cartoon department would be closed down in 1962?

JONES: You could kind of smell it coming. Theaters were closing, and television was coming up, and Hanna-Barbera was doing all Saturday-morning programs. Friz and I had put together the Bugs Bunny television show for Warner's. We had produced, written and directed the thing together, the only time we really worked together. This method didn't work out too well either, even though the product was good. It wasn't my fault or his fault; it's just that we were too independent and had

---

[2] From July 13, 1953, to November 13, 1953.

always been independent. It was obvious, with rising costs, that Warner's wasn't going to spend more than they'd been spending on shorts, and they wanted to spend less. They finally decided not to do any. They apparently weren't going to spend the money to go into new cartoons for television; in any event, they hadn't shown any evidence of wanting us to do that. So they said to hell with it and closed the place down. I guess you could feel it coming for maybe a year.

BARRIER: In your interview in *Psychology Today* [April 1968 issue], you mentioned the disciplines you imposed on yourself, the very sparse lee-way you allowed yourself on what the Road Runner and Coyote could do. Would you describe those disciplines?

JONES: The basic one, right away, was that the Road Runner was a road runner and therefore stayed on the road. You make up your own rules as you go along . . . but having made them up, you must adhere to them. I think the same thing was true of Chaplin's movies, in that his costume did not vary. Marcel Marceau allows himself nothing on the stage except a couple of blocks. So, allowing it's a road runner, the first rule is that he only leaves the road when he's lured off, by the simple device of draw-ing a white line, or a detour, or something of this kind.

Second, the Coyote must never be injured by the Road Runner; he always injures himself. The Coyote is what all of us would like to be, a perfectionist in whatever we'd like to accomplish, and yet in the Coyote's case there's always a slight error; that's what usually happens. The Road Runner never enters into it, except perhaps coming up behind him and saying, "Beep, beep," which seems not too violent.

Third, the cartoons were set in the American Southwest desert, and although we used a lot of different styles in the pictures, in the back-grounds and such, it always had to be in that context. As we went along, the Coyote's primary enemy became not even explosions, but gravity. Since we were in an area where there are plateaus or mesas, we could give him all kinds of gravitational problems. Speed and gravity soon became basic factors in our series.

Fourth, the sympathy always had to be with the Coyote. The Coyote was never hurt or in pain; he was insulted, as most of us are when we suffer misfortune. I had my house broken into yesterday, and a couple of things were taken. I thought about it afterwards, and they didn't steal any of my drawings. Kind of a reverse insult. If they had stolen the drawings, I might have felt better . . . although I had an artist friend

once and his burglar carefully cut all the paintings out and stole the
frames, which is even worse.

Of course, timing is very important, and I discovered that eleven gags
seemed about right for a seven-minute Road Runner cartoon, except for
what you might call a "cumulative" gag. I hoped when I left Warner's
that I'd eventually be able to do a cartoon where you'd start at the beginning with just one gag and simply keep going, all the way.[3]

BARRIER: A girl I know who's not too interested in animation referred to
the Road Runner cartoons just recently as the "most sadistic" cartoons,
and I've heard other criticism of the violence in cartoons. I wonder how
you'd reply to such criticism?

JONES: There's no completely convincing way of replying. I think one
question you might ask her is what she thinks of the James Thurber cartoon of the duelist lopping off another man's head and calling,
"Touché!" Or what she thinks of the original story of the Three Little
Pigs, in which the wolf, after eating the other two little pigs, actually,
goes down the chimney and is boiled to death and eaten by the third little pig, which made the third pig a sort of second-degree cannibal. All
the Hans Christian Andersen stories, the Laurel and Hardy comedies,
early Chaplin, the very things that I think she probably would adore. I'm
curious what she would think about such "violence." When I lecture at
universities, I find that people usually talk about this when they're doing
a term paper on motion pictures and pick out certain things that they
feel are indicative of black-and-white values. Or else they're graduate
students in teaching. From my viewpoint, I did what I thought was
funny. Sometimes it was violent; sometimes it was not. But I can't think
of any piece of human drama that isn't one of three things: it's violent,
it's sexual, or it's fantasy. It's pretty hard to think of anything else that's
really interesting. The important point is the difference between mean-
ingless violence and comic violence.

What I did, I always tried to do for my own sake—I never thought
much about the audience, I never made pictures for audiences—but for
my own sake, I always tried to put a certain kind of logic to it. It's a natural situation for a member of the dog family to chase a member of the
bird family. It's no less natural for that situation to exist than it is for this

---

[3] In the *Psychology Today* interview, Jones mentions another discipline: the absence of
dialogue.

lady you refer to to eat a porterhouse steak. If she objects to violence, perhaps she'd better go to a slaughterhouse and see exactly how that steak came into being. One of the funny things on radio here is a commercial by an outfit called Farmer John's, which packages sausages and bacon. "Farmer John," they say, fattens his "porkers" (avoiding the term "pig") in the Middle West and then brings them out to the Coast alive, and then they're "processed" here. Now, "processed" means killing. Avoiding the use of the term "kill" doesn't really change the matter at all. We are carnivores; we exist on that kind of violence.

But I put down on film what seems to me to be funny, and I guess that's just about the size of it. There's simply no way to justify it. I believe that children—and many psychologists agree with this—find this a kind of release, providing it's funny. I don't much care for the Superman things. I know kids have tried to imitate Superman, but I don't think anyone's going to try to imitate the Coyote. And they can't imitate the Road Runner.

BARRIER: Do you see any line between the kind of violence you used in your cartoons and the kind of violence Hanna and Barbera used in their Tom and Jerry cartoons?
JONES: The distinction for me was that they would use a kind of personal damage. For example, Jerry might drive a golf ball right through Tom's teeth and all of Tom's teeth would break and fall out. To me, that's pretty painful. Now, the Coyote falling eight thousand feet and landing and getting up immediately, that seems to me to be a broad humor. Abraham Lincoln once told a story about an old dog who was sleeping in a stump while they were dynamiting stumps to clear a field. They didn't know the dog was in there, so they blew up the stump. Lincoln said, "Poor Rover, his usefulness as a dog was about over." Translated into other terms, you could describe the bloody bits. My point is, I don't describe the bloody bits. I don't allow people to be hurt personally. But all this sounds like an apology. I don't apologize for it. I apologize when I'm not funny. Because I'm a particular kind of man, I try to do my stuff tastefully, if broadly. To me, a character like Woody Woodpecker sometimes is wrong because Woody Woodpecker is not always provoked to do mischief. Bugs Bunny is always provoked. The Road Runner is a natural road runner being chased by a natural enemy. With Tom and Jerry, it was natural for a cat to be chasing a mouse. Bugs Bunny is minding his own business, he's in a situation that's natural to a rabbit,

then somebody comes along who tries to deprive him of his foot or send him off in a rocket, or take his hide away, or kill him, or do something like that, and then, "Of course, you realize this means war." I do believe in some kind of a logical, moral situation. Actually, Bugs was a counter-revolutionary, not a revolutionary at all. He didn't go out to bug people; people bugged him, and then he fought back. And I think that counter-revolutionaries are a damned sight more intriguing than revolutionaries.

BARRIER: The style of your cartoons that you've been describing developed rather slowly in the late thirties and early forties. Did you make a conscious effort to develop a broader sort of humor than you had in your early cartoons, or did this just evolve naturally?

JONES: I'm not exactly sure. Certain cartoons are successful, and the results come back to you. I suppose that sub-consciously you begin to apply those principles which seem to have been successful. The styles gradually evolve as you learn from one another. So I don't really know; I don't think that's really answerable. How does any artistic style evolve? I think that can better be determined by someone from the outside than by the person himself. I don't think that a Van Gogh or a Gauguin or a Thurber or anyone else could ever have identified his own style. Frankly, in my graphic works, in my drawings and paintings, people tell me I have an identifiable style, but I have no idea what it is. I think that my drawings vary tremendously, but people can identify the most diverse. After I began teaching, I began to think a good deal about style, and I believe that a person who has a style really is not aware of it. If he's aware of it, then he's imitating himself. The worst pictures at Disney's were made when they were trying to do them in the established Disney style instead of how they felt at the time. I would say that you stop having a style when you prefer doing what's safe or what you're told to do. We quite frankly were out to make pictures that would make people laugh. My entire life has been involved with that particular idea. I never once in my life tried to make an art picture. I never tried desperately to make a picture that in itself was an advance of any kind. What I tried to do was make pictures that were funny within the certain limits of the field in which I was working. If you are making automobiles and you come up with a great idea for making a better bicycle, I don't think that you ought to stay in the automobile business. It's marvelous to make a bicycle, but I don't think you should make a bicycle and pretend you're making an automobile, and that's what's been happening out here.

On the art side of the thing, the people who make these avant-garde films are not doing what is expected of them. The Saturday morning cartoons are not living up to the potential or needs of the audience.

There were two things that were essentially wrong with Saturday morning television when all that super junk was on. One of them was this super syndrome, a far worse thing for children than the violence. After all, what was Hitler? That's the super idea. This person who goes out on his never-ending fight against evil, is he some kind of god? Where does he get the right, outside the law, to protect other people? It implies that he knows what is right and wrong, and God knows, that's the worst thing a child could suppose: that right and wrong are implicit.

The other element is the eternal flatness and repetition, the same thing, the same actions, the same kind of stories. It's like the Chinese water torture. You can't torture a man by putting one drop of water on his forehead, you can't do it by putting ten, with a fairly normal person you can't do it with a thousand. But a million? No man can withstand it for a day, that continual drop-drop-drop. It's the sameness that kills you and hurts children.

The thing is, it's not only that the studios are doing the same kind of work, it's the *same* people who are doing it. The same animator may show up at Filmation, then at Hanna-Barbera, then at DePatie-Freleng. The same man. They're going on a supposition that I believe to be completely erroneous: if you have a different drawing, you have a different character. This is ridiculous; it can't be true. Even in comic strips, it isn't true. A comic-strip artist eventually evolves certain physical characteristics for his characters, which indicate what a character is, not only by the way he's drawn but by what he does. In *Peanuts*, there's the peculiar way Schulz draws that little curly mouth . . . his drawings look simple, but they're disarmingly simple. They're really very, very complicated, even his staging, within that little, simple area. He's kind of like Mondrian, who limited himself to parallel lines. Within that narrow area, he put a lifetime of experience. Schulz never shows a three-dimensional view of Snoopy's doghouse, for instance; you never see the front of it, you don't know what shape the door is. This was true starting with Mutt and Jeff. Mutt and Jeff always did certain things: they held up two fingers when they walked, they hit a particular pose. You can say, "A Mutt and Jeff pose," and every cartoonist knows what that is. The expressions and physical characteristics of characters like Maggie and Jiggs and the Katzenjammer Kids were what made them characters and continue to do

so. That's why many Saturday-morning cartoon characters don't trans-
late well into comic strips, because they've never developed any physical
characteristics. The Flintstones move exactly the same way Yogi Bear
moves, and Yogi Bear moves exactly the same way something at
Filmation moves, and so on. They have evolved a kind of shorthand, and
that shorthand unfortunately can be read by anybody and can be
learned by anybody in a short time.

SPICER: Isn't it the same thing with the Europeans? They have no real
characters that I can see, and they all tend to look alike. They're not
interested in personality.
JONES: No, usually they are not, and personality, after all, is just acting.
Acting in animation is exactly the same as acting in live action, there's no
difference at all. You know a Jack Benny by the way he folds his arms
and looks around and says, "Well . . ." I don't have to look like Jack
Benny in order to get that point across. I *am* Jack Benny by the very
nature of my physical posture. The mimicry immediately identifies a
comedian. In my opinion, a very simple rule about recognition of any
character is that he can be imitated. But these characters on television,
you can't imitate them. Why? Because they're all alike in action. You
might be able to draw them, but you sure as hell can't imitate them. But
you can imitate a Bugs Bunny, or Tom and Jerry, or Coyote, or Pepé le
Pew, or Goofy, or Mickey Mouse, or Donald Duck, any of these characters, because they were identified by their body movements.

BARRIER: Do you think cartoons as a medium are best suited to comedy? In recent years, they've moved away from stories and entertainment, to stating ideas. . . . Is that really suitable to the medium?
JONES: Sure, it's suitable. Anything is suitable for animation. I've done
some science films and some Bell Telephone sequences. I've worked in
a lot of other areas of animation besides humor. Freleng and I won an
Academy Award for a documentary; Friz and I wrote it, and I directed it.
I did many training films during the war. I've had a good bit of experience in non-humorous areas. Unfortunately, the humor tended to leak
into what was intended to be serious.

But it comes back to the same business, the erroneous supposition
that you must destroy something in order to create something. It started
with UPA; up to that time, everybody was willing to let everybody else
live. You might think you made better pictures than anybody else—I
never did, but other people did—but you sure as hell didn't deny the

person the right to do their thing. When UPA started making pictures, their P.R. men surprisingly said, "This contradicts everything that has gone before. This does away with fuzzy little animals," as if Disney had only done fuzzy little animals. He never did fuzzy little animals, because there's no way you can make animals fuzzy in animation. His animals are cute, sure—some of them are sticky. But that isn't what made Disney what he was.

SPICER: Walter Lantz has stated the theory that it's possible to have "movie stars" in animation of the realistically drawn type, accepted just like real movie stars. Do you believe that?

JONES: No, I believe animation is an extension of motion pictures not an imitation. It should go where live action can't go. If I could train a real coyote to do what my Coyote used to do, I'd just as soon use a live coyote. But I have to go in areas where live action can't go. You have to make compromises in some cases. For instance, in *The Phantom Tollbooth*, we had to have a boy who looks like a boy, so we animated a boy in a kind of live-action style . . . but that's because the predominant characters could not be live.

I think realistic animation can be done, but I think it should be done the way they did it in *One Hundred and One Dalmatians*. The important thing about *One Hundred and One Dalmatians* from an animator's standpoint, and this is generally unrecognized, was the development of living characters who were not rotoscoped. Roger was an impressive character, but he wasn't drawn like a real man, because his elbows were in the wrong place, and his hands and his nose were too big, and he was out of proportion. He looked more human than humans do. That's why the term "realistic" wouldn't apply to Roger, but "human" would. He was like a Peter Arno drawing of a man or a girl. He was stylized. If you'd take a Roger Price drawing or a Ralph Barton drawing or a Peter Arno drawing and animate them, I think they'd be bigger than life. Did you ever look carefully at a miniature of Michelangelo's *David*? It's an enormous statue. Big as it is, in miniature the head seems still far too big for the body; it seems all out of proportion. But when you see the real statue, it's on a pedestal, which is just about at eye level, and then you look up at the statue. From that perspective, the head diminishes to the proper proportion. Otherwise, the statue would look like a pinhead. Michelangelo was one of the most profound artists of all time, and he knew what he was doing, just as El Greco did. El Greco probably painted elongated people because his paintings were to be hung high on church walls. One of his most intricate paintings was for a niche where you could look at it only on the diagonal, on a bias, and he painted it so that at that angle of view, it seems to be in proper proportion.

I think there's absolutely no limit to what the animated cartoon should and can do. Again, because you can do one thing, that doesn't mean that you're not supposed to do another. I think that anything that anyone can conceive of for the animation medium is proper and possible. It's just as broad as that. But in any line of endeavor, when you start throwing in negatives—I'm doing this, therefore something else is wrong—you're wasting your time; you're sweating over something you shouldn't even bother with. What do you care what the other man is doing? I am interested, but I don't care. I'm perfectly willing for these people to do this Saturday-morning thing. However, I wouldn't want any children of mine to spend much time looking at it. As an animator, I don't think any animator should ever condemn another animator's way of making a living. But I can criticize it as an art form, and I can criticize what it does to my medium, without criticizing the man. I don't say he's wrong, and I'm right; I'm saying that if I weren't an animator, in my opinion, he'd still be wrong.

SPICER: What do you think is the most neglected aspect of animation today?

JONES: The most neglected aspect, and the saddest thing now, is that there are only two studios, this one and Disney's, that are utilizing the talents of full animators, journeyman animators, in the proudest sense of the term. There are some people, like Bill Littlejohn, who are doing some marvelous stuff in commercials, but unfortunately, the best commercial you ever do, you don't get credit for it. The best commercial that's ever done is dead within a year of the time it's done. So it can't really become a part of the library, or the folklore, of great animation performances. It gets lost, and that's a pity.

The most dynamically tragic thing that can be said about animation today is that if you want to hire a journeyman animator today, you'll hire the same animator that you hired thirty years ago—not the same kind of animator, *the same animator*. The fine journeyman animators today, 95 percent of them are over forty, and 90 percent of them are over fifty. Ben Washam, next door, is fifty-two years old. Abe Levitow, my director, who was considered an *enfant terrible* at one time, is forty-seven or forty-eight years old. The guys at Disney's are all close to sixty. When those people go, there's not going to be anybody to replace them.

SPICER: What about the young guys who are coming along?
JONES: There are not many who are animators; they're practically everything else. Let me put it this way. If there's an acting craft, in films or on stage, there are people evolving who supply actors with the sort of material they must have in order to perform. The Albees and so on grew out of a renaissance of acting. It sort of became popular to have fine acting once again. There was a time when we were all concerned that the great actors were going to die off the way the animators are dying off. There was a corollary situation in the 1930s when everyone got preoccupied with stagecraft, and the actor was pushed into the background. It reached a kind of dramatic head when Norman Bel Geddes, I think it was, built a stage set so enormous that the people in the balcony couldn't see the players, because they had run the stage out over the first thirty rows or so in this theater. There was a sudden revulsion against this sort of thing, with Orson Welles and the Mercury Theater, and they stripped the stages bare and ran actors out in their street clothes to play Shakespeare. Acting came back into focus; that is, to evolve a mood simply by what the actor does and says. Well, obviously, he can't do that unless he has a vehicle to perform. So, getting laboriously back to the point whether there are young animators now, one reason there aren't young animators now is that all the animators are animating on this very thin Saturday-morning stuff. Very few of them know their own craft, just as I think that many television writers don't know their own craft. Anybody who has to turn out a half-hour script every week to survive—or to survive the way he likes to survive—can't write a play of any quality in that time. Maybe you can write just one. That's what usually happens, these men will write a very good pilot, and on the basis of that pilot a series is sold, and then what happens? You have to bring in at least ten writers to finish the series, and you immediately lose control, and immediately you get off into shoddy, unimaginative performances. So, the sadness is not that my animators or the animators at Disney's are not doing what they're capable of doing—they are. The sadness is that many of the old-time animators are working only on these Saturday-morning shows. It's like a violinist playing a triangle and getting paid three times what he used to make. It's a pity. I'm talking now not as an animation director but as a person; I feel a personal loss in this.

When Hanna and Barbera were doing Tom and Jerrys, they were supposed to do ten cartoons a year, ten six- or seven-minute cartoons. They
never did quite that, but let's say they did an hour in toto in a year. The
two of them and a crew of seven or eight men did ten six-minute cartoons; that's what we did at Warner's. Right now, as I understand it,
they have three hours of television that they have to produce every
week. I don't even know how to multiply that in terms of percentages,
but let's say they work forty weeks—that is one hundred and twenty
hours a year, as compared to one hour before.

SPICER: But you can meet this rigorous schedule and still turn out something worthwhile, as Jay Ward did with *Crusader Rabbit* and *Bullwinkle*.
JONES: Those at least had witty dialogue. But you're not talking about
animation, you're talking about illustrated radio. I agree that Jay proved
that dialogue could be better, but you're talking about cartoons being
better in terms of the way they sound. They also could be better visually
with the same amount of money.

BARRIER: You've been doing longer cartoons than you used to do. Has
this created new problems for you, of pacing and the like?
JONES: Yes, you do pace them a little more mildly. There's a tendency
not to crowd as much material in. But even so, some people thought *The
Grinch* was a little over-produced, although it was extremely successful.
I think that was because, basically, television programs spread their
material so thin. A half-hour show usually contains material enough for
maybe ten minutes. It's like spreading your butter too thin, you get to
the point where you almost can't taste it. I still feel that every frame has
meaning. That doesn't mean you can't hold a frame for twelve expo-
sures or more, but you must do it thoughtfully.

On *The Phantom Tollbooth*, fortunately, the nature of the story
helped us a great deal in keeping the pace. It also saved us an enormous
amount of concern in terms of the characters walking. Masterful artists,
like the Disney animators in *Winnie the Pooh*, still have an enormous
amount of trouble with walking human characters. It would seem that
that would be something an animator would learn how to draw rapidly,
but body mechanics are so intricate that the foreshortening of hands and
arms and so on, and the techniques of getting some weight into the
ground, are very difficult. It's practically impossible to do consistently
well. Fortunately for us, during the entire story of *The Phantom
Tollbooth*, the main characters ride in a small electric car. I didn't realize

until we got into it how fortunate we were. Milo doesn't have to walk very much, and when he does, he's usually running or falling or stumbling. But, as I say, because of the nature of the story itself, moving from place to place in an automobile, the stuff sort of naturally paces itself between sequences, growing and evolving, one into the other. The pacing isn't the same throughout; when we go into the broad comedy sequences, it becomes paced very much like an old cartoon.

Of course, I paced things like Pepé le Pew a great deal differently than I paced the Road Runner cartoons, not only because the material was different, but because the characters were different. Pepé, for instance, would never walk at an eight-beat (three steps to the second), he would walk at a twelve-beat (two to the second). He'd walk much more casually, and he'd stop and look at something and contemplate it, instead of going right to it. And, of course, he bounced along to one of Carl Stalling's little themes, a sort of "Sorcerer's Apprentice" theme. He never increased that tempo at all, no matter what the cat was doing. Pepé would always be slower than the cat at the beginning and faster at the end; it was a tortoise-and-the-hare type of thing.

BARRIER: Another of my favorite walks is the Minah Bird's, in the Inki cartoons, to the "Fingal's Cave" overture.

JONES: Those cartoons really baffled Walt Disney. They baffled me, for that matter; I just made them, because I thought they were funny. I wasn't even sure I thought they were funny; they were kind of mysterious. The little Negro was probably the first one who was just a little kid; he was a Negro only because he was living in Africa, not for any other reason. He never acted like a stereotyped Negro.

But people would laugh at that damned bird, and I could never figure out why. Warner's hated it, but it went over very big in the theaters. Walt would run them for his staff, and say, "What the hell . . . why can't you guys do something like that? What is it? What's so goddamn funny about it?" If he'd brought me over, I couldn't have told him. I made five or six of them[4] . . . they were really fourth-dimensional pictures, and I don't understand the fourth dimension.

BARRIER: A great many of your cartoons, including the Inki cartoons, are in pantomime, and there seems to be less use of voices in your

---

[4]There were five: *The Little Lion Hunter* (1939), *Inki and the Lion* (1941), *Inki and the Minah Bird* (1943), *Inki at the Circus* (1946) and *Caveman Inki* (1949).

cartoons than in Freleng's or McKimson's. Did this give you a special kind of freedom? Was there any special reason you decided to do so many cartoons this way?

JONES: I think that I realized I was working in a graphic field, with drawing the basic tool. To me, drawing *is* animation, in a new sense, a consecutive sense. The individual drawing is not very important; it's the flurry of drawings that counts. It requires a whole new drawing style. That's why the best directors, the ones that have been most successful, have come out of animation, and the best layout men, and there are very few of them. I would say Hawley Pratt is one of the very best layout men; he was not an animator, but he's always worked with Friz, who was a good one. Because he was never an animator, some animators fight Hawley's fine drawings a lot more than they fight mine. Friz roughs his layouts, and then Hawley works them over. Friz, as a former animator, tends to body positions that will work in animation. Joe Barbera was a fine animator, and he's a fine layout man and director, too. But for me, it is a little more than that, it is also the feeling that I am just lucky enough to be working in something that gives me the kind of expression that is not available to everybody else. I like to throw in a lot of drawings myself. I guess it is just like a person who paints because he enjoys painting, I feel that the best way to express myself in animation is to accomplish as much as I can without dialogue. Otherwise, I may tend to lean on dialogue.

BARRIER: Do you feel a special kinship with the silent comedians, who worked in pantomime?

JONES: I owe an enormous debt to all of the great ones and even to some who are not great. As a matter of fact, I've seen some old Buster Keaton films recently that I hadn't seen before, and I've seen things which were—I think I've used this term before—retroactive plagiarism. I stole from them without really knowing it. I obviously had seen the films when I was a kid and used things I'd seen—guys running away into the distance, then explosions in the distance; funny little hops. Some of them have been conscious; I used those hopping corner turns, those jumps up into the air, which the Keystone Kops used, and which to me are funny and well worth utilizing.

I was raised around those men. I lived in Ocean Park during the time when most of the Mack Sennett stuff was being shot, when I was a little boy, and I played in some of those pictures almost inadvertantly, because that's how they got crowd scenes, taking whoever was around. They didn't pay you; they'd just say, "You wanta be in the picture, kid? Don't look at the camera." So you'd walk into the mob and be part of it.

I know that those comedians did not think of themselves as profound. Another thing that hits me about your lady friend is that she probably adores these early comedians and goes on the supposition that these filmmakers and actors were philosophers. They weren't; they were artists. The difference is so profound that you can hardly talk about them the same way. A philosopher postulates and hopes that somebody will act according to his postulation, but the artist performs, and then somebody comes along and postulates *about* that. To me, the artist who postulates stops being an artist while he's postulating. He'd do better spending his time drawing. I get very tired of people who can draw and don't, who prefer to talk about it. Many of them are brilliant—they understand everything that's happening in the business. The only trouble is, they're not doing it.

BARRIER: You don't use dialogue much, but you seem to place a lot of importance on music, especially in cartoons like *Rabbit of Seville* (1951) and *What's Opera, Doc?* (1957), in which you use classical music.
JONES: *What's Opera, Doc?* is one many Europeans adore. They call that my "masterpiece," which it may or may not be; I didn't think about it at the time. It was very difficult to do; one hundred and four cuts in six minutes. But there again, every frame counted.

BARRIER: Since you've built cartoons around music, is there any particular approach you've employed in doing this?
JONES: No, I don't think so. I usually would go over the thing more or less for pace, with the musicians, before the picture started. In the Road Runner cartoons, I developed almost a concerto style. I don't know why; I'm not that much of a musician. It had a definite form to it, but I couldn't tell you exactly what that form was, except that it tended to have variables and it tended to grow . . . now I'm doing very much what I said the other people were doing, talking too much about it. I feel that no element of a cartoon—or a stage play or motion picture, for that matter—should stand out as an individual element. If anybody says, "That's great cutting," it's bad cutting. You should never be aware of cutting; you should be aware of the effect of it. If someone's in a stairwell looking up, it's perfectly natural for the camera to look up, too. It's even natural for the camera to have an opinion, in the sense of

emphasizing a story point. If you're waiting for a telephone to ring, and it rings, you immediately cut to the telephone.

SPICER: You satirized the angle shots, the *High Noon* sort of cutting in a western with Porky and Daffy [*Drip-along Daffy* (1951)].
JONES: That was on purpose, absolutely. I had a lot of fun with that. I wanted the audience to think I was kidding the Western, and I wanted every shot that could possibly be put in there. Actually, I would think it would be very tricky to shoot a great Western. The trick would be, you'd have to put the stock stuff in, but you mustn't do it in a way that will offend anybody by using exactly the same shots that they're so familiar with. That's why *Stagecoach* was so great. One of the things that made *Stagecoach* so interesting, and kept you from worrying about so many of the shots, was that John Wayne carried a rifle, he didn't carry a six-gun. You don't know what the hell is going to happen, because it's so contrary to everything you've seen before. In *High Noon*, an emotional situation had been set up so that the angle shots and other things didn't bother you. Cooper's reactions were natural; it's the way I would have felt. And yet all the townspeople's reasons for not helping him were also natural. It was a hell of a fine picture.

BARRIER: Color seems to be less important in the Warner cartoons than in the early Disneys and the MGMs . . . did you pay much attention to color, or was this secondary to you?
JONES: Well, *What's Opera, Doc?* was really a tour de force in color . . . a "tour de farce," if you prefer.

BARRIER: Yes, color's important there, but it seems less important in a lot of earlier cartoons.
JONES: Some of that is a little disarming. We used it quite extensively but in a very, very narrow palette on the Road Runners. Because there we were working with space, and you couldn't have clutter. In my opinion, the old Hanna-Barbera cartoons were cluttered in background treatment, and kind of old hat, even then. It seemed to work all right with their pictures, but it sure as hell didn't add anything. I think every one of our pictures—my pictures, especially, because I had Maurice Noble—was experimental. But I wouldn't say there was anything distinctive about the backgrounds of my early pictures. We had a background department at that time, rather than a background man working with each unit. They painted everybody's backgrounds, and so all the pictures'

backgrounds tended to look alike. They were all pretty bad; their basic color was something we used to call "diaper-brindle."

But Maurice always experimented. In an outer space thing [*Hareway to the Stars* (1958)] we just built a kind of little transparent city suspended in space rather than a planet. That was Maurice's idea, to use those hunks of what looked like transparent plastic. We always tried something new, but it always had to work relative to the business. I didn't want the audience to be conscious that we were doing any fancy experimenting.

Witty Birds and Well-Drawn Cats: An Interview with Chuck Jones

JOE ADAMSON / 1971

Combined interviews from March and December 1971, published in part in Gerald Peary and Danny Peary, *The American Animated Cartoon* (New York: E. P. Dutton, 1980), 128–41. Copyright © 2004 Joe Adamson. Published with permission.

Joe Adamson: I find that when you handle a character and another director handles that same character, there's a distinct difference in the personality.

Chuck Jones: Well, my Bugs Bunny was different from Friz's Bugs Bunny. Friz's were maybe funnier, but I'd say that Friz's were usually a little more physical; when you think about *Sahara Hare* and the others, it seemed to me that there were things that happened quickly. Bugs would cleverly do something at the last moment. My Bugs, I think, tended to think out his problems and solve them intellectually a little bit, and also, I insisted upon perhaps a stronger provocation. Usually I'd get Bugs in a situation in which he was innocent, he's minding his own business, then somebody comes along and tries to do him in, or remove his foot, or send him off in a space ship, or do something with him. And two or three things would happen before he got mad enough. No, he wasn't mad enough, just the *logic* would move in, and he'd say, "All right. So much has happened to me—of course, you realize this means war!" Which is not a pugnacious statement, it's a logical statement. [Karl] Von Clausewitz said, "War is politics carried a step further." At that point, you say, "Okay, hostilities start here."

Bugs simply says that war has begun, and you couldn't get rid of him then. He is willing to engage danger, but only because he's put upon. He's a counter-revolutionary, you know, he's not a revolutionary. He's not a Woody Woodpecker.

Adamson: What about your Tom and Jerrys in comparison with Hanna and Barbera's? Yesterday in the projection room you said you never understood Tom and Jerry.

Jones: Well, I didn't understand them the way Bill and Joe did. I tried to make them like Bill and Joe, tried to think the way they thought, but it didn't work out well, so I just kind of changed the characters to fit my own way of thinking. They used a kind of violence I seldom used, and if I did use it, it was a mistake and I regretted it. One example would be in their golfing film where the ball hits Tom in the teeth and leaves a hole there, and then the teeth fall out.[1] They would have an axe come down and take all the fur off the back, including his tail. That kind of thing, to me, is much more hurtful than somebody falling off a cliff. Or if the Coyote lights a bomb and the whole thing explodes, he's left there all black, and then you cut immediately and he's whole again—death and resurrection. So mine were, I'd say, much gentler than theirs, but probably not as funny. I was never able to get quite as much character in Jerry. I thought they did a smashing job on Jerry; I thought his personality was always delightful. I probably got a more human personality out of Tom than they did, but not the same character. Tom was pretty vicious in their stuff, and was a clear-cut villain.

As I developed (if I developed), it was on the idea that nothing's clear-cut—and it shouldn't be in comedy. You should be able to

---

[1] *Tee for Two*, 1945.

understand either side. You should be with the hero, hopefully, the idea that "Gee, I wish I could be that way"—but with the villain you should also recognize, "There but for the grace of God go I." So you get involved. In all of my things, I get involved. In *The Dot and the Line*, I associate completely with the Line; I knew what he was. But I also understood the Squiggle; I knew what his problems were. That's why *Bully for Bugs* was a particularly good Bugs Bunny, because the losses were equally shared. Bugs had almost as many problems as the bull did.

Adamson: How did the Three Bears originate?
Jones: I was working with a layout man by the name of Art Higham at the time, and Mike Maltese and I got the idea that it would be funny just to reverse the shapes, to have the baby the biggest and wearing a diaper, and the father a little bitty, bombastic character. You see elements in him of Yosemite Sam and Colonel Shuffle, in the bombast: "AAAaaaaa, I hate rabbits." These are the elements of comedy—somebody hates rabbits just because he hates rabbits. I always liked that.

I don't think you can make comedy unless you're involved with the characters. It never occurred to me that these were not living things. I love the Father Bear; he represents part of my character. I think any caricature worth getting involved in represents the bombastic side, or the innocent side, or the evil side, or the ineffectual side of your own character—or what you would like to be romantically, which is what Pepé le Pew is, everything I always wanted to be. I wanted to be irresistible, and in a situation in which I couldn't believe anybody would reject me. Not only was he completely sure of himself, but it never occurred to him that anything was wrong with him. Ever! I was always aware of my broken shoelaces or my body odor, or whatever. I always knew that there must be great areas of me that were completely repugnant to girls. And Pepé was quite the opposite of that.

And Bugs, of course, is based on many things, but one of them is the idea of how wonderful it would be to be a super-rabbit, which is really what he is.

What you do is multiply your own weaknesses, I guess, in a character like Daffy. There was no problem after I began to understand what he was all about. My Daffy and Friz's are also a little different. Friz was the one, you might say, who kind of got him into that cowardly self-preservation. The minute he did it, I understood what that was; I knew how *I'd* feel. It's the awfulness, when you're on the battlefield, of realizing when your buddy is shot that your basic feeling is one of relief: that it wasn't you. Well, Daffy *says* that. He says, "I may be a mean little duck, but I'm an *alive* little duck." Or when he gave Bugs up to the Abominable Snowman, he said, "I'm not like other people: I can't stand pain—it hurts me."

When I'd go home, I'd tell Dorothy[2] a line like that, which just occurred as I was working. I'd say, "You know what that guy Daffy did today?" and I'd repeat the line, and then she'd look at me. She never got used to this. She'd say, "Well, you were drawing it, you did it." I'd say, "That isn't true! It developed! That's what he said. It was natural for him to say it!"

Of course it happens to anybody doing this sort of thing: it comes out of you because it's part of you. There's meannesses in everybody. In effect, that's what [Stanley] Kubrick was doing in *A Clockwork Orange*. He was multiplying the evil within us to gargantuan proportions, like fireworks, beyond belief.

I was drawing some Daffys, and I thought, "I love that character." And I was just getting a hold on him when the damn studio shut down. He's a marvelous, marvelous character! And at the very end, Porky was beginning to develop into something interesting. When we first started him, Porky was a Boy Scout kind of character. But in *Robin Hood Daffy* and *Rocket Squad* and some of those, he was *interesting*.

Adamson: Daffy always gets incredibly involved in these things, but Porky never does.
Jones: I always felt that Porky Pig was the subtlest of all the characters because he was consciously playing a part. He's obviously putting Daffy on, but it's a very subtle thing. In *Duck Dodgers in the 24½ Century*, he was playing the space cadet, but he was *aware* that he was playing it. He was like I would be in a class play—in which the hero really thought he was the character. Daffy Duck was like Lew Ayres, making the Dr. Kildare films just before the war, and he got so deeply involved with the thing that he actually volunteered for the Medical Corps. Really! And in *The Scarlet Pumpernickel*, when Daffy's trying to convince J. L. Warner that this great script is perfect for him, I'm sure that he always thought that everything in there was possible, that he *was* Super-Duck, or whatever.

---

[2] A reference to Jones's first wife, Dorothy Webster Jones.

We're basically working in terms of human dignity, which is true of the Coyote, or Daffy, or anything. *Robin Hood Daffy* is one of the best parodies I ever worked on. Daffy is Robin Hood, and Porky won't believe that he's Robin Hood because he's such an idiot—he keeps running into trees and all that kind of thing, and Robin Hood obviously wouldn't do that. But Daffy is concerned. He's not trying to achieve anything except to get Porky to believe that he's Robin Hood. That's a natural thing, in my opinion.

This is contained in the idea that the opposite of love is not hate, it's indifference. The opposite of hate is also indifference. We can stand either love or hate, we can survive them, but I think it's almost impossible to survive continuing indifference. And the other thing we can't stand is humiliation. So the preservation of dignity is the avoidance of humiliation or indifference, isn't it? If you understand that, you don't have to write it out.

Chaplin was always trying to avoid humiliation. In *The Gold Rush*, the terrible, terrible thing that happened to him was where he was rejected at the party. Jesus Christ, it's just too much. And when the Coyote falls, he gets up and brushes himself off; it's preservation of dignity. He's humiliated, and it worries him when he ends up looking like an accordion. A coyote isn't much, but it's better than being an accordion. But the director must *believe* that; you can't just make a thing, you've got to be really involved in it. So hopefully, I was always sympathetic to my characters.

Adamson: I notice *Summerhill* and *Education and Ecstasy* here on your bookshelf. Do these concepts in education affect what you're doing on *The Curiosity Shop*?[3]

Jones: I don't consciously use any precepts. I read everything, and the result is that some of it sticks, and since I'm supposed to be the executive producer, part of it probably will show up in the show, but it's not conscious. God, when *Summerhill* first came out I got very much interested in it. It's a startling, marvelous book. But nobody can run a family the way Summerhill is run. You can do it if that's all you're doing—and that's all Neill and all his people were doing, and they had a whole bunch of kids—but to try to run a family that way is impossible.

I have gone on the supposition that for any subject, it is worth trying to get stimulation, education, and entertainment. Those seem to me to

---

[3] ABC television series from 1971 to 1973, for which Jones served as Executive Producer.

be the three basic factors. If you can get any two of them, you're pretty good. Entertainment is probably the strongest of the three by itself. And by entertainment I mean that marvelous term that Groucho Marx used about television—he called it the chewing gum of the eye. He also said that television is very educational: "Whenever it comes on, I go in the other room and read a book." He's a pretty witty bird. His philosophy I enjoyed very much because he had a very clear-cut attitude toward comedy. He once said that comedy isn't so much what you do, it's what you *don't* do. That's typical to me of all great humor: the tendency to narrow down the areas in which you work so your disciplines are clearly established. You do become conscious of the need for those.

Adamson: I've noticed that in all your films. They're very carefully set up. Some of them are completely silent, with no talk at all. Some of them are talk fests, constant verbal exchanges.

Jones: That's right. We tried a lot of variations; like we'd use a lot of dialogue at the beginning, or dialogue at the end, or I'd use "Morning Ralph," "Morning Sam." And then in *Go Fly a Kit*, which I always liked, about the eagle that raised a cat so the cat could fly, we used dialogue at the opening and never used it again. So there are various ways that you can do it, but again you have to make up your mind this was what you were gonna do and do it. When the Road Runner first started, I had a few disciplines that I understood, but the longer I worked with them, the more I got, so I ended up with maybe ten or fifteen disciplines. The worst pictures were the ones that had the least disciplines. The narrower you got, the better you got. Just look at Chaplin—when he first started, his costume was rather wild and kind of nondescript, and then he got very precise.

Adamson: In terms of discipline, the Road Runner cartoons are funny because all the humor comes from the same thing; it's the same gag with twenty million variations.

Jones: It's based on ineptitude. It's based on the failures of the (in this case) anthropomorphized coyote and the fact that he makes mistakes. To me, he's everybody that works in a home workshop. When you think about it, with all the tools bought and all the garages and basements involved in making this stuff, no matter how well a man makes it, it isn't gonna be anywhere near as good as he can go out and buy! You feel that somehow the Coyote is his own worst enemy. I remember that George Santayana said that a fanatic was one who redoubles his effort when he's forgotten his aim. And that's what he is.

Adamson: You said that you understood the series better the longer you worked with it.

Jones: Well, some of the early ones were rough because I didn't really know what I was doing. As far as audiences were concerned, of course, none of the Road Runners ever did badly. But the first one I did as sort of a parody.[4] And then no one was taking it as a parody, so I said to hell with that, I'll just go back to making them funny again. So there was a little experimental area in there, and I wasn't sure what the build-ups were. For instance, I felt it was necessary to establish how hungry the Coyote was by having him catch a fly or eat a tin can or something.[5] That's Chaplin. The idea of a coyote chasing a road runner seemed a little more obscure to me than a cat chasing a mouse, or a hunter chasing a rabbit, which is a natural (though it may not be desirable) course of events. After a while it became obvious that it *wasn't* necessary.

Adamson: Don't coyotes chase road runners as a rule?

Jones: I doubt it. Road runners are not as fast as coyotes, but I think they're probably too elusive. A coyote can do about forty miles an hour, and a road runner can do maybe twenty miles an hour.

Adamson: [Thunderstruck] Is that really all?

Jones: Twenty miles an hour is as fast as a man can run.

Adamson: But you show him at two hundred miles an hour!

Jones: Or two thousand if you like. They're pretty damn fast all right, but not that fast. My opinion, in looking back on it—I didn't think about it too much at the time—is that the Coyote probably started chasing the Road Runner during some time of incredible famine. There are rabbits and gophers and all kinds of goodies in the desert, but obviously those animals disappeared for a short time, as they do, and the Coyote had to search around for something else. Somewhere along the line he started chasing the Road Runner; then when he no longer had to chase the Road Runner, he'd still never caught him, so he continued to chase him.

Adamson: After a while, catching the Road Runner becomes unimportant. What's important is the next contraption he's going to set up.

Jones: Precisely. And that's what brought the Acme Company into being. I felt that to improvise things was not nearly as much fun as it

---

[4] *Fast and Furry-ous*, 1949.
[5] *Stop, Look and Hasten*, 1954; *Guided Muscle*, 1955; *There They Go-Go-Go*, 1956.

was to send away to the Acme factory, and get half a mile of railroad track, or a pair of jet-propelled tennis shoes, or a fifth of bumblebees, or something. After a while I didn't use a letter or anything. As far as I know there's no money involved. There's just a factory someplace that supplies coyotes! That's one of the disciplines, but it has to be based on a certain kind of logic. There are factories that do supply people with things, so it's perfectly logical. The only difference there is that you never say where the money is or how he ever gets in communication with them.

Adamson: The Acme Company is a running gag that goes through everything.
Jones: In some of my early pictures I used different names and then I settled on Acme.

Adamson: The people who did the later Road Runners ignored all the disciplines.
Jones: That's Bob McKimson and the people over at Format Films. There were eight or ten pictures made there, but they ignored all that. All they had to do was ask. I was here; I could have told them. In one of them there was a dismal improvisation. They needed a costume, so they had a truck go across the desert and the back door flew open and a costume fell out. That's so stupid! Why do that when all you have to do is write to the Acme Company? They'd have as many costumes as you wanted!

Adamson: There's a very strong Laurel and Hardy feel about the Road Runners—not at all in style, but in the sense of frustration. Laurel and Hardy would do a whole film about something *not* getting done. And it doesn't take long in a Road Runner film to know that he's not going to catch him, and you just watch things go wrong. Very often there were gags that wouldn't be funny, it seems to me, without the inevitability of disaster. In *Whoa Begone* he goes through a whole elaborate routine, balancing on the wire, and then the wire breaks!
Jones: There we used the drum rolls, as you would in a circus. But God knows what he thought he was doing there. What the hell he wanted to put the damn thing on his head for, I haven't any idea.

Adamson: I was going to ask you about that. . . .
Jones: I don't have any idea what he was doing there. Even if he was successful, I didn't see how he'd catch the Road Runner. But that's the point, you see: the more frustrated you get, the more wildly inventive you become.

Adamson: But it seems to me it would be a cop-out gag, because it's just complete coincidence that the wire would break. And yet I know that thing always gets a big laugh.

Jones: It does, because I don't think they really expect that particular aspect of it to fail, not right then. You see, one of the tricks of this kind of humor is to anticipate where the audience is going to expect something to happen, and then either to *not* do it then, and let them relax a little bit, and then hit them; or to do it *before* they're quite ready for it. And that's what happened here. That's why he tried to get his balance over and over again, because you didn't know the wire was going to break.

Or when he's got that rocketship hanging by wire from that tower: the exhaust from the rocket burns the tower down. I don't know if anyone would anticipate that out of it. Or when he pulled up the iron ball on the crane. Did you see that one? It was just a crane, with one of those iron balls they use to knock down great buildings. And he's down there in the cab, and he's got a little engineer's cap on, which he's obviously taken, and he pushes the levers. This thing comes up the way it's supposed to, and it gets to the top, and it just rolls on over and rolls right down and lands on the cab and crushes it. And that's all!

Adamson: But you know something is going to go wrong somewhere. There's another one like that with the cannon. The build-up is so elaborate, and he goes to tamp down the cannon, and it blows up while he's tamping it.

Jones: That's right. I had half a dozen cannon gags like that. One time the cannon went off and left him in mid-air. And just *left* him there. And one time it went *ka-poomp* and plopped him out on the ground. And, as you say, one time he put the ramrod in and it blew him off the screen.

Adamson: You sort of do variations of the same thing, as if you were making it for an audience who had just seen the last Road Runner cartoon.

Jones: Well, I never depend upon them having seen them. But I think it was an advantage. Today, when they're seen over and over again, people are nice enough to say that these are connoisseur's gags—just like Laurel and Hardy!

Adamson: In *Gee Whiz-z-z*, he puts on a Batman suit. That is a specific case of simply the *drawing* of him standing there in a green suit being funny; that gets a big laugh before anything happens.

Jones: Yeah. That was a marvelous piece of animation that Ken Harris did—the flapping and then almost hitting the ground and coming up again. Dick Williams over in England thinks this is one of the greatest pieces of action ever done.

Adamson: Part of what makes that funny when he gets to the bottom is the way those black rocks are drawn—it looks so terrifying.
Jones: Yeah, I told Maurice Noble I didn't want any fruiting around with that. I wanted *saw teeth*, so that somehow when he missed them, you should have a little shudder. Ray Bradbury says that kids like to be scared, and you do. Psychopathic or psychological fright is one thing, but being scared is fun.

Adamson: I noticed that's something you have a lot of fun with—in films like *Claws for Alarm*, where the humor comes out of being scared for Porky. *Claws for Alarm* has this fantastic Hitchcock feeling about it: it really is terrifying, and it really is funny.
Jones: Yeah. I believe in that. I believe in what a magician friend of mine once called "reely." He said that whenever you were doing magic for children, if they looked at you and said, "Reely?"—you got it made. That's the way I feel about pictures. I think you should be involved with them, and you should really believe it's happening. If you're going to do a comedy about terror, it should be *reely* terror. I don't see much point in doing it otherwise.

Adamson: Joining them, though, would seem to be a very difficult thing.
Jones: Sure it is. You remember that in the "haunted" pictures any of the good comedians do, the monsters, the evil scientists, and so on were pretty evil. They didn't try to get humor out of the evil scientist.

Adamson: In *Claws for Alarm* and *Jumpin' Jupiter* you modified Sylvester's character enormously. Freleng always kept him in the role of the evil cat.
Jones: Well, Sylvester was a well-drawn cat, and I enjoyed working with him. Sylvester for me was a cat. Friz used him in quite a different way. I used him as a sympathetic character. Usually he was working with Porky, and he knew what was going on, but Porky the Innocent never knew what the hell was happening. He was trying to protect Porky, and Porky was picking on him. I always felt, why should there be the Noble Dog? Noble Dog was always a chauvinist in Walt Kelly's *Pogo*. In my case, I thought, "Why not have a noble cat?" I did one, which had to do with a

cowardly, sneaky, sly dog and a very noble cat,[6] and it was surprising the kind of response. People wrote in and said it was about time the dogs got their comeuppance. I think a dog is kind of a bond salesman, anyway. I have nothing against them, but if you're running into perilous times, a dog will kiss your foot and a cat will leave you. A cat says to hell with it. I had a friend who was a salesman, and he had one of these bond salesman dogs. He said every time he'd come home and he'd had a bad day and was feeling bad, his dog would kiss his hand and kiss his foot and all this, and he said, "I really became a very bad salesman, because we'd both sit down and kind of moan together. So finally I realized what I needed was someone to sneer at me." (He was a bachelor.) "So I got a Siamese cat and gave my dog to my girl, and that cat could tell within ten dollars what I'd sold during the day. If I were lower than the day before, then he'd look at me with an upright attitude, and he'd sneer at me. A couple of times I actually went out at night so I could come home with an easy conscience."

Adamson: When I talked to Freleng, he said that he used a layout man who was strong on character and that you used one who was strong on background.
Jones: That's right.

Adamson: He was trying to say that the emphasis in his cartoons was on character and in yours it was on graphics. But I haven't found that to be true.
Jones: No, I don't think that's what he meant. Friz is a brilliant cartoonist, and he was badmouthing himself all the time. He always said that I drew better than he did, which isn't true. He always had Hawley Pratt clean up his drawings, and I never did that; my drawings went directly to the animator. But his stuff, all the characters and everything, was great. All the funny little things he did with Sylvester and Tweety Bird and so on were really his original drawings.

What he meant was that I did like to get different kinds of design; we went in a lot more for unusual staging. That is mostly Maurice Noble, although I had John McGrew first as a layout man; he was the one who did *The Dover Boys* and *Unbearable Bear*. He was kind of a nutty man. After the war, he went to Paris to live. He didn't speak French but he was determined he wasn't going to speak English anymore, so he started teaching jazz piano, and for a year he never spoke English until he

---

[6] *Fresh Airedale*, 1945.

learned French. And he's lived there ever since; he just disappeared. I think he's taken a French name, I've never been able to find him since the war.[7] He was a great designer. Then Bernyce Polifka and Gene Fleury, who teach at Art Centre, were also layout people and very influential in setting some of our styles.

But Maurice was the most important, because he worked with me for so long and because he had this great variety to his approach. He's a brilliant guy; as far as style is concerned, Maurice was the most versatile. He had great staging techniques, and he understood what very few background men do understand—and actually very many live-action people don't seem to understand it in the graphics area: that the purpose of a great designer is to design an arena where the actor can perform. Or the animator can perform. And where the action shows itself to its best advantage. Now this doesn't mean you can't have high design. You remember *What's Opera, Doc?*—the thing would have been cluttered, except that it was so *well* designed. On many of them, we used pretty high design.

UPA was interesting and important because it got away from the old Brindle kind of backgrounds—although we had done a lot of experimenting in flat background treatment, and of course Disney had too. The "Toccata and Fugue" in *Fantasia* was long before UPA. The UPA supposition was that animation was dead and the thing now was graphics, which turned out not to be completely true. Where we work with deep space, the depth is identified by the movement, not by perspective lines. The fact that the character diminishes off into the distance is what determines how deep the background is. There's no way you can possibly get the same effect out of a still drawing of a background.

Adamson: Throughout your films, you've used basically the same animators. You've had Ken Harris since at least 1942.
Jones: Ken started with me; he was an animator with me from my first picture, *The Night Watchman*. Phil Monroe is another one I've had with me for many years. Rudy Larriva was an assistant, and then he became an animator. Ben Washam was an assistant, but on the first picture. Yeah, the same group all the way through.

The Phantom Tollbooth was a superb animation breakthrough for Ben, who had been a very solid journeyman animator, really the equivalent in

---

[7] Much to Jones's delight, he reestablished contact with McGrew after his return to the U.S. in the 1990s.

animation of William Holden as an actor, just like a solid journeyman. When you had someone like that, you didn't care what they did, they're believable, and that's what Ben always was. But I never knew that working inside of him were all these Lethargians. When that came along, why, all of a sudden he came to life and brought these characters out, and it was like nothing he had ever done. He was forty-five years old, or something, and all of a sudden these things came leaking out of him. I think you'll agree it's an astonishing bit of virtuoso performance in animation.

Adamson: How much responsibility does the animator have for the action that is finally seen on the screen?
Jones: The best way, of course, to understand the animator is to see that he parallels the actor. He has the same responsibility a fine actor has. Peter Sellers is an extremely versatile actor who can move in any direction; that's what a Ken Harris is. Who is the real Peter Sellers? There isn't any. With John Wayne, you've got John Wayne. Period. (And there's nothing wrong with that.) But with a Peter Sellers, you've got extreme versatility, and there is no true Peter Sellers. Harris didn't have a basic animation style; you see, he could do anything. But he was an animator, and not a graphic artist. And there are a great many mistakes in this area. Even the people who write about animation just don't seem to understand that when you have a drawing, you don't have a character. It's like seeing a photograph of an actor, and then saying, "We're choosing this actor." I don't understand these casting directors: what do you know when you look at him? OK, he looks the part, but until I see him move, I haven't any idea whether he *is* the part or not. If it's anything, it's the bodily style, bodily movement, gestures, mistakes that you make, that identify you, not what you wear, or the facial movements, or even the voices. The same thing is true in an animated character: "This is the first Bugs Bunny" has no meaning. It's how Bugs came to stand and move and act, and what his feelings were, and his thoughts, and what kind of personality he was. That developed over a period of time. And you need fine animators to do that. Bugs Hardaway can safely say that he did the first Bugs Bunny that was called Bugs Bunny.[8] The name "Bugs" came from Bugs Hardaway.

Adamson: Ben Hardaway—you called him Bugs?
Jones: Yeah.

---

[8] *Hare-um Scare-um*, directed by Ben ("Bugs") Hardaway and Cal Dalton, 1939.

Adamson: Why was that?

Jones: He was an old newspaper man and that was the kind of name people had: Prunes, and Bugs, and names like that. Here is the first Bugs Bunny model sheet. You'll notice down there that it says "Bugs'"— possessive. The reason why is that Bugs asked Charlie Thorsen to make a drawing of a rabbit, and when he sent it back he sent it as "Bugs' Bunny." And when they saw the "Bugs' Bunny," why, they decided that would be a great name.

So the director does three or four hundred drawings for a cartoon, character layouts, with key positions, and from that the animator works. But mine are *still* drawings; the animator's not beholden to use any of them and shouldn't even try. There are animators who always work between my extremes, and that wasn't what I wanted. Ken Harris would change it. He'd use it as an idea, but the action would flow through and go beyond it. He might forget it completely. But it would indicate what I had in mind.

Adamson: Were different animators better at different things?

Jones: Oh, yes. In his early days, Ben Washam was not a flowing animator; he tended to work between extremes. He would draw, and then he would in-between to the next pose, and it was like a series of telephone poles. That isn't what you want, you want flowing action. But, of course, you want strong hesitates. When you think about it, in animation, and in acting, the hesitates are what make great acting. You'll see Gene Kelly or Fred Astaire, each one of them has those little things. Fred Astaire's is more elegant and graceful, Kelly's is kind of powerful and strong. Astaire works down his own legs, and he'll turn around and kind of push his hat out. Or you think of Maurice Chevalier; he'll move up to a position and then his shoulders come up—"I'm glad I'm not young anymore."

But people like Ken Harris or Bill Littlejohn or Ben Washam *developed*. Ben became really a fine personality animator; he could do lovely things. Dick Williams adores Ken Harris. He worked with him on *A Christmas Carol*.[9] Williams is the sole person I know who is completely capable in every facet of this business. He's a good director, he's a fine animator, he's a hell of a designer, and he can draw like mad. On *A Christmas Carol*, he was sitting at the desk, and Ken was sitting on a

---

[9] Television version directed by Richard Williams in London, for which Jones served as Executive Producer, 1971.

stool behind him; Dick would make a drawing, and then Ken would tell him how to change the drawing. They were working as a team, Ken sort of directing Dick in action. Ken animated most of Scrooge, but he couldn't draw him. So Dick acted as clean-up man. Ken is an animator in the truest sense. There are animators who could not draw, in the sense that they couldn't make a single drawing; they made a *flurry* of drawings. Norm Ferguson was a marvelous example of this at Disney's. He was an animator who just didn't draw well, but he was an *artist* as an animator.

Adamson: Wasn't he the one who drew ovals and lines, and somebody else would have to come and finish the drawings?
Jones: That's Fergie. That's the way he drew. He just drew a line, then a head, and then a couple of things showing.

Animation in itself is an art form, and that's the point I think always needs clarification. True animation exists without any background, or any color, or any sound, or anything else; it exists in your hand. And you can take it and flip it. That is the difference between this particular form of creativity and any other form. Regardless of UPA's approach, or any of the rest of them—all of them contributed, but peripherally, because what they were doing was design, and other things. Even the dialogue adds to it, but that isn't the reason for it. It was very much like what happened on the stage at one time. People forgot they were actors and started making great stage designs, and great music, and great lighting. Okay, all this is important, but the only reason you're doing it is to embellish what the actor does. The actor depends on the director and the writer, but the actor is the key. The thing that makes a stage play is somebody standing up before you and doing something; that's what makes acting, whether it's good or bad, that's what it is. What makes animation is the fact that you have a series of drawings that move. You don't even have to have a camera, you see; animation exists without it. If you want to broaden your audience, or make it more colorful or add music, then you put it under a camera one frame at a time, and then you run it at the same speed as you flip it, and then you have animation. If it depends basically upon soundtrack, or basically upon music, or color, graphic design, or anything else to sustain itself, then it is not unique to animation. God! I don't know if you've ever taken any of the great Disney animation, a big thick scene, and held it and flipped it. It's so beautiful, you can't believe it. That Pink Elephant sequence in *Dumbo* is a marvelous example of this; there were no backgrounds in that. Everything was accomplished by the elephants turning into pyramids and camels. When they were skating, you knew they were skating because they were reflected. When they turned into boats, you knew they were boats because of the splashes around them. There's a perfect example of animation doing everything—no backgrounds, no nothing.

Saturday morning television is really what I call illustrated radio. It's a radio script with a minimum number of drawings in front of it, and if you turn the picture off you can tell what's happening, because you hear it all. In our stuff—even the talkiest things, like the Bugs Bunny–Daffy Duck stuff—even if you turned the sound off, it was interesting, and you could truly tell what was happening. I never recorded a film until I'd completely laid it out. I'd just make the drawings, and then I'd time it, but I always wrote the dialogue right on the drawings—I didn't write it as a script. I worked out the whole thing visually, and then when I'd finished, I'd go back and I'd type the dialogue off the drawings, so it always related to the drawings. Because if the writer wrote the dialogue, then you recorded it, and then you tried to make the drawings fit the dialogue, it was bound to suffer. In my opinion, the dialogue should never be redundant. Bob McKimson would have a character say, "There he goes." My opinion is that if he was going, you didn't have to say it.

And everything on Saturday morning moves alike—that's one of the reasons it's not animation. The drawings are different, but everybody acts the same way, their feet move the same way, and everybody runs the same way. It doesn't matter whether it's an alligator or a man or a baby or anything, they all move the same. You certainly can't imitate them. That's why I don't think the public has taken any of those characters to its breast.

Adamson: The odd thing is that most of them *are* imitations of W. C. Fields or Cary Grant.

Jones: All the voices are stolen—I mean stolen! And many times those people are alive and could certainly have used the residuals.

Mine is not a criticism. I'm sorry that people who were as good as Bill Hanna and Joe Barbera once were are not doing the kind of thing they're capable of doing. I'm sorry that Friz isn't doing the kind of things he's capable of doing. I'm sorry *I'm* not, for that matter, but at least I'm not doing that kind of crap.

Adamson: What is your feeling about the Jay Ward stuff?

Jones: I think Jay Ward would be lost if he used full animation. I think his stuff is extremely funny, with that clever humor that they have, but he has a reverence about his own style that inhibits him. They stick by that old Terrytoon kind of drawing. He has a thing about it. Bill Scott understands, I'm sure, that there's no reason why they shouldn't go high style, if they're going to use a very restricted kind of animation, but Ward insists upon staying with that Farmer Alfalfa sort of drawing. Jesus!

Adamson: I was wondering what you thought of John Hubley's films.

Jones: A few years ago they had a Hubley Retrospective at one of the houses in New York. They played to sold-out houses for about ten days, and then you could hear crickets in there. Apparently, everybody who was an *afficianado* of John Hubley had then seen the Hubley Retrospective, and when that was done it was all over. Hubley's done a lot of lovely things, but many people don't realize that in nearly all of his notable pictures there's been a lot of dialogue. *The Hole*, *The Hat*, *Moonbird*—Hubley's stuff is basically a soundtrack. I don't think in his lifetime Hubley has contributed anything to the art of animation.

We didn't do experimental pictures—very seldom, anyway. We did all our experimenting in the arena. All of our laboratories were within pictures. I think that's where all the fun is—to accept the idea that you've got certain problems, but never to let those diminish you, in the sense of keeping you down.

It's my opinion that eventually every motion picture maker must face the crowd. That goes for Ingmar Bergman and it goes for me. And every film director, actor, cutter, or anything else that has ever been great, eventually has had to face the large audience. It doesn't do any good to tell the Plight of Man in a theatre that shows it only to people who know it already. I had a terrible emergency call from Charlie Jenkins in London the other day: He was saying, "Please come, I need help," because all of a sudden the advertising agencies in London are demanding Road Runner/Bugs Bunny animation, and nobody in England knows how to do it. Nobody in *Europe* knows how to do it, for that matter.

Adamson: No. There tends to be an idolization of the kind of abstract things that they do in Czechoslovakia.

Jones: Yeah, but strangely enough if you go to Czechoslovakia you'll find out that they really want to know how to animate. When Gene Deitch went to Czechoslovakia, he found the guys were animating pretty well, but they didn't use exposure sheets. And he was startled. They put all the information that would go on the exposure sheet on the drawing—as to what other drawing worked with it, and how long it should be held—and then they traced that onto the celluloid. And the camera-man just looked down and saw that it was held for so many frames, and so on. See, they could study American animation on the moviola, which is the way everybody learns from everybody else. (Dick Williams completely rotoscoped at least two of my cartoons to find out how they worked; he actually traced off all 4000 drawings. But Ub Iwerks and Walt Disney did the same thing with the early Terrytoons.[10]) They could see how to animate, but they couldn't figure out the process. And there have been some great things done in those countries in terms of exploration of the medium, but by and large those things play art houses.

Adamson: You did one cartoon in 3-D, *Lumber Jack-Rabbit.* Did you do it differently from any other cartoon?
Jones: Johnny Burton was the one who figured out how to do it. It's based on a solid principle, which is that if you hold your finger in front of your face and look at your finger, you'll see two of everything behind it. And if you look at everything behind it, there are two fingers. So he figured out how to do it so that you use a double image in the foreground, which would be a green image and another one would be a single image—I don't know how it was done, I just went ahead and did the cartoon, and then he figured out how to put it on the screen. Actually, of course, the animated characters didn't come out three-dimensional. They couldn't be drawn round; they came out as a series of overlapping flats. So Jack Warner—who was making all that money off *House of Wax,* and that dreadful, dreadful African thing that Arch Oboler did in three-dimensions, where they threw spears at your face[11]—figured that everybody would be wearing multi-colored glasses until the time when they were adapted, and everybody was *born* with a green eye and a red eye. So he shut down the animation plant. I was under contract, but didn't want to work when the people weren't working, so I thought I'd work at Disney's for a while. I couldn't stand it. He asked me what kind of job I wanted, and the kind of job I wanted was his. But I got to know him and liked him very well, which is curious because I was one of the leaders of the strike against the Disney Studio in 1941.

---

[10] "Aesop's Fables" series.
[11] *Bwana Devil,* 1952.

Adamson: But you weren't working for the Disney Studio in 1941 . . .
Jones: No, but the whole industry was striking. We had a strike at Leon
Schlesinger's, and Schlesinger settled it in about three days. Then the
Disney people had fired Art Babbitt and a number of other people for
union activities, so the union called a strike and everybody in the business went out on the picket line. That went on for a long time. It was
acrimonious and kind of too bad, because it wasn't Walt. Somebody'd
gotten the idea of paying people six dollars a week, which was one thing
we couldn't very well sit down for.

Adamson: I've gotten the impression that through the thirties, everyone
in animation considered themselves to be trailing behind Disney.
Jones: We all did. The strange thing is, that was probably healthy for all
of us. As we weren't paid very much, we tended to experiment a lot,
because we were young and in the business, and because we had the
Disney group running ahead of us, and they had set up a pattern of
good animation which is really what made all of this possible. An animator at our studio was supposed to do thirty feet a week,[12] which we considered enormous; the average guy at Disney did about five feet. When
you think of it right now, thirty feet seems like nothing, because at
Hanna-Barbera, they do two or three hundred feet a week. And it looks
like it. But our stuff was still damn good animation.

Adamson: Into the 1940s and 1950s, you didn't think you were still
trailing behind Disney's, did you?
Jones: Well, yeah—because their character development was still astonishing to us. We *knew* we were trailing behind them. And of course
there was almost no interchange. Very few people left Disney's and went
to other studios. When they did, they usually fell on their faces because
they couldn't deliver the footage. Jack King left Disney's in 1933, and
he was a fairly good director and animator at Disney's, but he had no
imagination, so he needed support. As you know, the Disney directors
didn't have the authority that we did. The short subject directors had
the most authority, but very few of them drew or attempted to draw;
they had character layout men who worked for them. Jack Kinney and
Jack Hannah were probably the best of them, and Jerry Geronomi, and
so on. But their job was to get the work out, to see that it was delivered,
and it was more administrative.

---

[12] At 90 feet of 35mm film per minute, 30 feet is about 20 seconds of screen time.

Adamson: But there was a whole influx of people leaving Disney's right around 1942.

Jones: Yeah, that's right, because of the strike. Bill Tytla was one of the greatest animators. He did "The Night on Bald Mountain" [sequence from *Fantasia*] and Stromboli [in *Pinocchio*], things like this. He left. He wasn't part of the strike, oddly enough. He left in sympathy, just because he wouldn't cross the picket lines. And, of course, Art Babbitt, who was very deeply involved in the union. But very few of the experienced animators or directors or anybody else left the Disney Studio before the strike. The top people, the big animators or the big layout men, were always paid well. It was the bottom people where the problem came in; that's why the union came into existence. Disney loved animators. Today, after his death, they're treated with great reverence over there: the so-called "Nine Old Men." Disney felt, and rightly so, that he was a better writer than any of his writers. He couldn't animate, and he never made any pretense to animate, but he adored and respected what the animators did.

Walt called me in when he was going to underwrite the Chouinard Art Institute and the all-new California Institute for the Arts. I got very close to him in his latter years. I know that Richard Schickel's book *The Disney Version* is one of the most atrocious misrepresentations of personality that anybody's ever done. Schickel probably made as many errors as anybody could make in one book. You read it all through and you get the idea that Walt Disney was a businessman. You could go through it and pick out areas that make it sound like Disney was purely an artist. Yet Schickel was determined to prove that Disney was a businessman. It's the difference between a scientist and a non-scientist: A non-scientist will pick out an idea that he likes, and then he will go to work to try to prove it. And he'll select only those things that will add to it. A scientist comes up with a thing and then he'll spend seven years trying to *disprove* it. Darwin spent years trying to figure out what was wrong with his theories, right? Sure, that's the whole point. So Schickel comes up with the idea: "Disney's a businessman"—and he spends a whole goddamn book trying to prove it. It just isn't true. To call Disney a businessman is about like calling Adolf Hitler a humanitarian. He was the *despair* of the business. Anybody who would have made *Fantasia* in 1939 at 3½ million dollars, when I think all the money that was in the studio may have been 2½ million—that practically broke it! He kept doing things that nobody believed were right. Only now can people look back on Walt and say, "Hell, he was a commercial man." He wasn't anything of the kind. They didn't even pay a dividend until he died.

Walt was a man who really enjoyed what he was doing. He enjoyed working in pictures. He loved some of those special effects they got in *Darby O'Gill and the Little People*. He was something of a child, but with an enormous toy. Disneyland drove those people over there, like Roy Disney, insane. There'd be one of those rides that was making an enormous amount of money, and Walt would have something else that he liked and he'd say, "Tear that out and put this in, 'cause I like it."

They'd say, "You can't do that. It's making money."

He'd say, "I don't care if it's making money or not, I want this one in there. It looks better." He'd do things like that on features: you'd animate maybe three or four people doing something, you know, a very expensive thing to do, and Walt would look at it and he'd say, "It would be much better if you were animating it from this viewpoint. Turn 'em around." And, Christ! The amount of dough they put in things like that! And yet, in the long run, as far as general audience entertainment was concerned, he probably had the best touch of anybody in the whole industry—probably in the whole world.

Walt was a strange kind of guy, but he's still by all odds the most important person that animation has ever known. Not necessarily because of the artistry (but the artistry was *there*, nevertheless; a dozen of the best artists in the world are still working at Disney's), but because he created a climate that enabled all of us to exist. And his breakthrough was similar to the breakthrough at *The New Yorker* magazine: It changed the entire face of animation. Anybody who knows anything about animation knows that the things that happened at the Disney Studio were the backbone that upheld everybody else. *The Three Little Pigs* was the real breakthrough as far as all of our animation was concerned, because it was the first time it was proven that you could bring characters to life: the three pigs looked alike, and each had a different personality. It's really kind of astonishing when you think it was made forty years ago. So when we came in, you could look at it and say, "No matter what we do, they're going to be a little ahead of us, particularly in technique." So without thinking, we evolved a kind of style.

Adamson: When you talk about that whole period in the late 1930s and early 1940s, the sense I get is one of real enthusiasm. Avery talked about it and so did Freleng—everybody was excited about this young art form.

Jones: One of the important things is that we never thought of ourselves as artists. We never used the term. They now say that Laurel and Hardy are great artists, and that's true. But they never thought of themselves as artists. The same with Chaplin. When he started thinking of himself as an artist, he stopped being a good comedian. As a young man, he was primarily interested in money and in having fun doing his films. And it showed. These men were just as innocent, in a way, as we were—innocent in the sense that they were simply trying to make funny pictures, without pretense, and without recourse to the Plight of Man. Chaplin, who is now noted as the person who was most concerned with that, wasn't concerned with it at all in those days. He tried to make funny cartoons—I mean, funny pictures. ("Cartoons," that's good.)

Adamson: I always got the feeling that Chaplin said the most when he wasn't trying to.

Jones: Of course, but we all do. If you have anything profound to say, it'll come out in your work. If you don't have anything profound to say, starting to be *profound* won't help you!

I must say that I was completely smashed by Laurel and Hardy and the Marx Brothers—and all I could see of Keaton, of course, and Harold Lloyd was delightful. But they all—Larry Semon and even Fatty Arbuckle—had qualities about them that were special. I learned a great deal of my timing from those people—although I never analyzed one of their pictures, or timed it out, or anything like that. In my opinion, it isn't a good policy. You tend to end up imitating them, and that's not a good idea. But if they come to town, you see them. To me one of the greatest films ever done is that Christmas tree sequence of Laurel and Hardy's.[13] I'd never seen anything like that, little Jimmy Finlayson just rolling around. There's nothing left of the car at all, but he's rolling around in an agony of rage. I can feel that, because as a kid you get to the point where you just can't take it anymore and all you can do is lie there and scream and yell and pound. Finlayson was so perfect!

Somebody is always saying to me, "How come there is so much violence in your cartoons?" I just don't know the answer to that. Taking that Christmas tree sequence—Jesus, they broke a house to pieces, they beat each other over the head, they destroyed automobiles, they just

---

[13] *Big Business*, 1929.

destroyed property all over the place—as an example to the young, it's about as bad a thing as you can do!

I have a feeling that adults react more to the destruction of things than of people. I have never heard a shock wave go through an audience as in that James Bond film where they crunch that automobile![14] The audience went, "Oooohhhh!" Here's this brand new Lincoln, and there's no warnings—down the thing comes and crashes it— BONNNNGGG! They had already killed forty people in the film—nobody cared about them. One guy's thrown into a mess of piranhas, and he disappears, and the burbling blood comes up on the surface, but *that* doesn't matter. But you tear up a new Lincoln Continental, and the *audience* is torn to bits.

Supposedly, those films are not meant for children. Well, my films are not meant for children either. They were made for me—they weren't made for children. If you think they're too violent to show to children, don't *show* them to children!

Adamson: Weren't you thinking of children as your basic audience?
Jones: Never.

Adamson: Not even when you were doing Dr. Seuss?
Jones: No. Dr. Seuss[15] told me that he's never written a book for children in his life.

Adamson: There's something I always wanted to ask you about your childhood, and that was if you got a "C" in arithmetic.
Jones: At different times. I'm not very good at math, but I wasn't too bad.

Adamson: It must be hard when you've got to make out those complicated exposure sheets.
Jones: It isn't really complicated. I had to devise a specialized kind of arithmetic that worked for me; it's really translating arithmetic into visual terms. If I wanted to know how fast a character was moving on a panorama shot, I would simply pull a piece of background at a half-inch, or an inch, to see how he related to it—not just arbitrarily write down a blanket speed, because I found out beyond a certain point there was no sense of movement. Anybody who's ever ridden in an airplane knows

---

[14] *Goldfinger*, 1964.
[15] Theodor Geisel.

that you get beyond six hundred miles an hour, and you can't really tell how fast things are moving past you.

The only thing that makes motion pictures possible, as I understand it, is that the eye retains images at the rate of a tenth of a second. When we look at something, it registers and takes a tenth of a second for the impact on the rods and cones of the eye to be translated into chemicals and then into electricity, and then to pass the word on to your brain. So we have a series of tenths of seconds hitting us, and if we get something within that tenth of a second, we retain it.

Adamson: That's about two and a half frames.

Jones: Something like that. A single frame is apparently very difficult to retain. I found you can get an effect in four frames: a sixth of a second. Those are empirical theories; they were just things I tried, and they seemed to work.

Adamson: The reason I asked that was that it keeps being mentioned in your Ralph Phillips series; I just wondered how autobiographical those things were. At the beginning of *Boyhood Daze*, the boy appears at the window at the very minute your name appears on the screen: "Directed by Chuck Jones."

Jones: Yeah, I would say there it's reflecting a kind of general boyhood thing. At the end of that particular picture, when he's up in his room, and you hear those voices downstairs, I can remember that very well. You know, my mother saying, "Mmmmphrrblewrthg! Charles?" "Wrrrbrblrrrrtrbgrfrb." "Mmmmphbrlgrfthbrgr?" "Wwwwthglfrblthrgrwrprb." Then my father coming upstairs. That's what I tried to get in there: the heroic prisoner. I have a lot of material on that which I didn't use. I could make five or six more of those because they're really quite easy. He's like Mark Twain's Tom Sawyer when Tom was treated badly by his Aunt Polly. He thought about how it would be if he died and they brought his body in, and the wet curls, and everybody'd be sorry for him. Everybody has dreams of glory.

I still feel that twelve-year-old girls are the most frightening creatures in the world, because when I was nine years old, that's the kind of sister I had. My sister could lick any kid on the block. She always wore a midi and a skirt, and she always wore skates. As far as I know, she wore them to bed. I never saw her with them off for about two years.

When I was a kid, we lived down here on Sunset Boulevard, right opposite Hollywood High School, and we knew the Keystone Cops.

They used to come in front of our house and shoot those things. When I
grew up, I wanted to be one of those characters. By the time I grew up,
they were gone. There was only one place to go, and that was into
animation. I just fell into it—it was the only place I could get a job. The
people who went to the Chouinard Art Institute out here constituted the
basic supply of the industry. So I went to work with Ub Iwerks, when he
was away from Disney's, on Flip the Frog. I washed cels and inked
things—everybody started that way—and I became an in-betweener
and then slid gradually into animation. When you think about it, almost
everybody in animation came from either New York, Kansas City, or
Hollywood.

Ub was a brilliant animator, and a very bad story man, and of course
a fantastic technician. He was really Walt's key animator when they first
came out here. Well, I worked for Ub for a while, and then I worked
maybe a few weeks for Charlie Mintz out here, under George Winkler,
and then I went over to Universal and worked for Walter Lantz. I had
more variety in the first year than I had later!

Adamson: You didn't get fired all those times?
Jones: I don't know; I guess I did get fired. I went back to Ub Iwerks
when he was in Beverly Hills, and then my wife fired me. (She was Ub
Iwerks's secretary. It was his order, but she did it.) Then I went on a
cruise for three months, and I was shipwrecked—which gave me all the
romance I needed. Then I came back and sat on Olvera Street drawing
caricatures.

Adamson: Why was it you went to Chouinard?
Jones: Well, my father was in despair over me—there was nothing I
could do properly; but he did know that I drew a little, so he sent me to
Chouinard. My sisters drew, so they went to Chouinard too. A lot of
people from Chouinard went into animation, and then so did I.

Adamson: You say you "drew a little": you weren't one of these prolific
prodigies?
Jones: I guess I was prolific, but I didn't draw very well. Pretty crude,
compared with people like Bob Givens and Freddy Moore. Bob Givens
had a fantastic loose way of drawing, and when he was nineteen he'd
been at Disney's for a little over a year. He drew well to start with, but
then he saw the Freddy Moore/Norm Ferguson kind of animation style
that was so effective. He drew better when he was nineteen than I do

now, but unfortunately he doesn't draw as well now as he did when he was nineteen!

I realized when I was much older that I had to do an awful lot of schooling, so I went to Don Graham's class and spent like ten years at nights working to develop my serious drawing, which is important because it gives you line control. From 1946 for about fifteen years I was learning and teaching and lecturing and stuff. I taught life drawing at Chouinard. Then I taught a life drawing class for two years at the studio, for people who wanted to learn to draw. I guess I've lectured at fifteen or twenty colleges.

Adamson: Your really distinctive style begins to grow in around the early 1950s.

Jones: That's when I began to be able to control what I wanted to do and what I needed to do in terms of drawing. That's the most important thing, when you get to the point where you can, without worrying too much, put down the line or the character or the expression that you want. You can put down what you're thinking, instead of having to worry about whether you can draw what you're thinking. You may play around with two or three expressions, but you don't have to play around with how to *get* those expressions.

Adamson: I've heard it said that you don't think there are any great animators left.

Jones: There aren't any that I know of. The people who came up in the 1930s and 1940s are now the heads of practically every animation studio in the United States. Jack Zander, who owns Pelican Productions in New York, Friz Freleng at DePatie-Freleng, Michael Lah and Adam Gillespie at Quartet Films, Hanna and Barbera, all the directors at Disney's and all the top animators, are all the same school. They're all the same age, actually. And twenty years from now, unless something happens, every one of them will be dead. Fellows like Fred Wolf are doing interesting things in their field, but if you ask them to animate *Three Little Pigs*, they couldn't do it. Fred has been doing two hundred feet a week, and I don't think he could ever put himself down to doing three or four, or even ten feet a week. Ken Harris is in his seventies. Abe Levitow is considered a young man, as animators go, and he's almost fifty. And since there's very little demand for that kind of skill, aside from a few places, like my studio and Disney's, and a few commercial houses, the men who can do a certain kind of thing are just disappearing. I'm not bewailing this; I'm saying it just because it happens to be fact.

Some people say, "How do you feel about not having any residuals from the things you did at Warner Bros.?" Well, rationally, I know that it isn't fair. It isn't fair for any of the people who worked over there not to share the profits from the things that they did. It's kind of gross. Well, in this area I can avoid involvement, because if I did get emotional, I'd be spending all my time being involved and bewailing, rather than going ahead and doing things. You know, doing things is the fun.

Adamson: Did you complain about it at the time?

Jones: There wasn't anybody to complain to. If you asked them to share, they'd say, "Well, Jack Warner doesn't share with anybody." Which is like Stephen Potter's thing where two men are playing golf. One of them knocks the ball off into the rough; he goes over, picks up the ball, throws it back on the fairway, and says, "I *always* do that." Well now, what are you going to say? So Jack Warner says, "I do not share. These are my pictures, I own them." Until the unions came along and forced them to do it, they didn't do it. It was never done voluntarily. Jimmy Petrillo was damned by everybody as some kind of a fascist nut, or communist nut, or something, because he demanded participation for musicians. Everybody, even people like us, thought Petrillo was a didactic bastard. Maybe he was, but he set up ASCAP and these things, and the result is that all musicians who ever published anything know that they're going to get a certain percentage of the overall take. And then came 1948, and the actors went in. And they took away most of it. In my opinion, they were selfish.

To give you an example, Bill Melendez, who does Charlie Brown and was an animator at Warner Bros. for a long time, a very good man, did a commercial for Ford Automobiles called "For the Dog." A dog is polishing an automobile, and a voice comes on and says, "Are you a Ford owner?" And the dog says, "No, I'm a dog." Well, Bill Melendez probably spent a couple of weeks laying it out and animating it, and he was probably getting $250–$300 a week. That thing was run so many times that the man who did the voices got $40,000 in residuals. Sure, I can speak right up and say, "Those shitheads! They paid us low salaries and they didn't give us any participation. That's wrong!" I'm mad!

Okay, that's all of it. I'm over being mad now. That's where the fun of work of any kind is, I think—getting rid of it and going on to the next. If you linger over it, then you've diminished yourself.

Adamson: Did you ever use rotoscope for anything?
Jones: I think it's a good idea to study live action. Dancing and things like that are sometimes difficult, but we realized early that rotoscoping was not nearly as valuable to the animator as studying. In *What's Opera, Doc?*, we had a dance. It happened that at that time Warner Bros. had done some work with the Ballet Russe de Monte Carlo, and I wanted the dances to be authentic, so [Bob] Cannon and the other guys who animated the dances studied the action.

Adamson: When you say "study the action," what do you mean, exactly?
Jones: You look at the thing and you make a sketch. I usually went through it myself and I'd make a key drawing of Bugs in a good ballet position. And then Ken Harris studied it to get the feeling of the timing, just to see how long it took to turn an *entrechat*, how fast the legs went, or something like that. But you can't always guess at it, you have to work it out; so live action is useful, but more as a tool than as a model.

I did one about a squirrel once, *Much Ado About Nutting*. It's all done in pantomime, and it's a simple problem of a squirrel trying to break open a coconut. But I wanted it to be really and truly a squirrel, so we studied squirrels to find out how they work, what they did, and how they moved. I put footage on the moviola and counted the number of frames that it would take for them to scurry—the little head turns and things like this—then I would go ahead and do it. Then I studied the anatomy and changed it to fit my own feeling about it—which is really the way you develop a style. (I can't identify my own drawing. Most everybody else in the business can, but I can't. I believe that if you can identify your own style, you're doing something wrong.) The humor becomes much more apparent if it's real, in this case, than if it's an anthropomorphized squirrel.

Adamson: Your method seems to be the opposite of anthropomorphizing: you follow the very definite animal characteristics, and you exaggerate them. In *Two's a Crowd* and *No Barking*, you played on the familiar cat bit of landing on all four feet; you completely exaggerated the common cat characteristic, and it looked very lifelike.
Jones: Yeah, I feel that's important. I studied a lot of cat action to see whether they actually do that. They do a funny thing: they turn their head. In slow motion, if you drop a cat, his head turns, looking down; and when that happens, this thing they call "feedback" makes accents on the various nerve centers, and the body rights to meet the angle of

the head, automatically. He doesn't have to do anything about it; it's done by his feedback. I made a picture for the Bell Telephone Science Series on the human senses, and it also got into animal responses.

The same thing was true of *One Froggy Evening*, which was one of the best ones we did: It had to be a real frog or it didn't work. To have an anthropomorphic frog, like a man in frog's costume, would never do. Probably, of all my pictures, I like that one the best. Strangely enough, it was one of the most difficult. The thing that had to be funny was that the man would believe that a real frog was singing. The audience had to believe that too. So you had to think, well, how does a frog feel? I had to study frogs to make certain we had a real frog. He was built like a real frog, and he dripped like a real frog. You know, they're really just a blob, with those goddam legs hanging down, and kind of odd. Just a bony blob is what they are. So that's the feeling you have to get.

Of course, he could stand up on his hind legs, which most frogs can't do. But the only time he became humanized was when he sang; that was Ken Harris's too, that cakewalk. This meant that you actually had two ways of moving: one was as this nutty singer and the other was as a frog, with about as much interest as a frog has. I remember some men up at Princeton, I believe it was, were doing some research on frogs, and isolated the small part of its brain—you might call it the awareness area, the conscious brain in which the animal is supposedly aware of what he's doing—and blocked it off from the rest of the brain. And they said the only difference they could find was that it made a slightly better frog out of him. If there's any opinion a frog is likely to have, it sort of makes him less efficient.

And in an animated cartoon, the only way that you can make it a real frog is to make the man believable as a man. So what I did was kind of pattern the drawing after Sam Cobean, because his characters always looked to me more like life than life itself. He was a cartoonist for Disney, but then for years he did wonderful cartoons for *The New Yorker*. He was the one who originated the cartoon of the man seeing a girl walking by and envisioning her over his head as a nude, and then the girl looking at a man coming along and seeing him completely naked except for his wallet. That was Sam. But you had to make the man believable.

Adamson: The discipline in *One Froggy Evening* that I finally realized was so important to the way it works is that the humans never talk.
Jones: *Nobody* ever talks. See, you must never hear any voice but the frog's. And the frog is only heard by the man.

Adamson: Why was it that no other voices were heard?

Jones: I just wanted it to be that way. And I decided that the picture would be funnier if you imposed that discipline. For one thing, it had an explosive quality: You never knew when the sonofabitch was going to sing, but you always knew that nobody was going to hear it except the poor guy. The one exception was when the cop heard it, but he heard somebody singing in the middle of the park, in the middle of the winter; he figured it was the man singing. So there were many disciplines there. We did one scene outside the window, which gave us a lot of fun having the guy do the frog's act in pantomime, behind the glass.

Adamson: How did you pick the songs for that picture?

Jones: Well, we wrote one: Mike and I wrote "The Michigan Rag." We wanted that kind of ragtime thing, and Mike had always been good at that. He wrote that Italian music, too, for Charlie Dog in Italy— "Whattsamatta, whattsamatta, whattsamatta with you?"[16] Another of my favorite ones was *Bear for Punishment*, and Mike wrote a couple of the songs there. And he also had a lot of training—I don't know where he picked it up—in soft shoe, in dancing, and he'd work with the animators on that kind of thing. Ken Harris usually animated the dancers.

See, I was really lucky: I had such great collaborators! I seldom give enough credit to Mike Maltese or the others. The director takes all the risks; that's one of the reasons he tends to be a little egocentric in relationship to his past. The writer writes, and the writer thinks that what he sees on the screen is what he wrote. And it seldom is. A storyboard that any writer fed to the director was maybe one tenth of what you eventually saw on the screen. I don't mean that the essence of it wasn't there, but we didn't try to make the storyboard the staging device. Warner Bros. was a marvelous training lab for everybody, but particularly for directors, because there you had to do everything: you recorded, which they didn't do at Disney's; you did your own layouts, which they didn't do at Disney's; and you did practically everything. Hell, I never knew what was gonna happen. On the Road Runners I would just start where the Coyote had a bow and arrow, and then see what happened.

Adamson: The storyboard precedes your director's sketches, then, and the director's sketches are what you turn into the picture.

---

[16] *A Hound for Trouble*, 1951.

Jones: That's right—those are the feed sketches. Occasionally, you'd get a story that was complete, but very, very seldom; and you wouldn't want it that way, that's where the fun was. But I was lucky to work with Mike Maltese and with Tedd Pierce. Mike was brilliant at bringing up a gag; he was not really as much a writer as he was a great gagman. There's an important difference. Tedd Pierce, for instance, was a much better writer than he was a gagman. Warren Foster and Tedd Pierce were both good men in structure. But Mike has a great eye for oddities and he'll come up with these nutty ideas.

Adamson: Visual things?
Jones: Yeah.

Adamson: Then he wasn't strictly a verbal wit.
Jones: No, no. He has a marvelous, almost Grandma Moses cartoon style. It's really kind of terrible, and very effective. He gets his points over.

Adamson: What about the producers you worked with?
Jones: The first producer we had, Leon Schlesinger, was just lazy, and that was good for us. Schlesinger would come in and he would say, "What you fellath doin'?" Schlesinger lisped a little. His voice is where Daffy Duck came from. And it was also Sylvester—Daffy is just a speeded-up Sylvester. "Hey, fellath," he'd say, "Whatcha up to?" and we'd say we were doing a Porky Pig. He'd say, "That thoundth great." How great can that sound? And he'd say, "I'm off to the ratheth," and off he'd go to the races. And the only time he ever saw the films was when they were in test reel form (which are now called line tests) or the finished product. You could get fired for not doing the right pictures, but he never bothered you when you were working, so we'd try anything. And he had lovely terms—like he'd come in and look at a picture and say, "I ask for chicken salad and you give me chicken shit," or "I cast my bread on the waters and it comes back shit." He was a very big man on shit. Old Leon was one of the last of the robber barons. He was kind of like Collis P. Huntington, or William Hearst, or Jack Warner. He was that breed of cat, and there aren't many of them left.

Eddie Selzer came over from Warner Bros. He was a despot and thought he knew what he was doing. He was going to rule the roost and get all stories cleared with him before they went into production. But if he'd known anything about animation, he would have known that was ridiculous, because between the storyboard and the time the picture's laid out (at least at Warner Bros.) was when everything happened! You never had a completed script. You never even had a completed storyboard. But Selzer was going to demand that we present these things to him. He was sort of the model for Mr. Magoo. He looked like Mr. Magoo and was a very strange man. But by that time we had established our independence: we were really producer-directors. He would go up and take the Academy Awards for my films and keep them. I got only one of the three awards that I was given. I think that Friz was given five of them, and Eddie took four. And *kept* them. In the case of the first one I won, *For Scent-imental Reasons*, he fought me tooth and nail. He said there wasn't anything funny about talking French double talk, nobody would understand it, and he *forbade* me utterly to do it. I did it anyway, just because he forbade me. So, in a way, he was a sort of a gadfly on our rumps. If I thought he'd done it intellectually I'd adore him, but he didn't. He was just one of those people who spend their lives saying "No," which is a word anybody can use.

Eddie was a fox gnawing at my innards for twelve years. He's one of the two people in the world I disliked, and I can't remember who the other one was.

Adamson: Well, you must have found a lot of ways to get around him.
Jones: I didn't have to get around him, I just went ahead and did what I was doing, and he would scream and yell and threaten torture, and meanwhile the picture's gone out and proved itself, 'cause he was always wrong. And it's mighty hard to be that wrong.

Adamson: What about Mel Blanc? I saw Gloria Wood's credit next to his on *Nelly's Folly*, and it startled me that somebody else was getting voice credit. He was so much a staple of the Warner Bros. cartoons.
Jones: Well, Mel, for a long time, had a contractual agreement with Warner Bros.; nobody else got credit, whether they did voices or not. June Foray didn't get credit for a long time. She always did Granny, and she did Witch Hazel part of the time. She did most of the girls we used. Of course the Road Runners didn't have any voices, but the voice that was there, oddly enough, was not Mel Blanc's; it was a background man named Paul Julian. Let's see, Bea Benaderet did the Mother Bear in *The Three Bears*. That was one of my favorites. That was Billy Bletcher and Stan Freberg and Bea Benaderet; Mel didn't work on those.

Adamson: Which did Stan Freberg do?

Jones: He did the Big Bear: Duuuuuuh! And he does that wonderful terrible singing on *Bear for Punishment*. [Unable to control himself, Jones breaks into song]

> Who belongs with the stars above?
> It's Father, Father!
> Who's da bravest of the brave?
> It's Father, Father!

Adamson: I still think the Three Bears are about the funniest characters I've ever seen in a cartoon. I've never seen one of their films that didn't have me in stitches. Why was it that they died?

Jones: They didn't die. Jack Warner said he didn't want any more because everybody was making Three Bear pictures.

Adamson: But what does that mean? Was he thinking of Barney Bear?

Jones: I don't know what he was thinking of. He didn't know what he was thinking of, either. He may have just said it in passing. Anyway, Eddie Selzer took it for gospel because Jack Warner had said it. That's the way Eddie Selzer thought of the Warners. He believed there were three gods: Jack, Harry, and Sam. It was a shame. I'd like to make some more of those; I think they were enormously funny. To me, the finale on *Bear for Punishment* was one of the greatest pieces of action I've seen.

Adamson: What can you tell me about Carl Stalling?

Jones: He was really great. He was a strange little man, but was probably the most innovative and most inventive musician who ever worked in animation. He invented the tick track, which is used by everybody. He was the one who did the original *Skeleton Dance* [at Disney]. Brilliant musician. But the quickest way for him to write a musical score—and he did one six-minute cartoon a week—was simply to look up something that had the proper name. If somebody got in a cave, it was "Fingal's Cave." And if it was a lady, particularly in a red dress, he always did "The Lady in Red." Or if he were doing anything about eating, he'd do "A Cup of Coffee, a Sandwich, and You." I had a bee one time, and my god if he didn't go back and find a piece of music written in 1906 or something called "I'm a Busy Little Bumble Bee"—and *that* showed up in the picture.

Adamson: Was there ever a problem of rights for these things?

Jones: No. The original purpose for Merrie Melodies was to plug Warner Bros. songs. They owned four or five big music companies, so if he couldn't find it in there, he could find it in the public domain. But he was pretty good even at writing original music, although he seldom did.

Adamson: A lot of your great films seem to revolve around music of some sort: *The Rabbit of Seville* and *What's Opera, Doc?*, *High Note*, and I just saw *Nelly's Folly*. What is your music training, exactly?
Jones: Nothing. I don't have any music training.

Adamson: Well, you must have an interest in it.
Jones: Oh, I do, but it's just a question of what I like. I'm fascinated by it, and I know so little about it that a quarter note is very interesting to me, just in the shape. Or the shape of a whole note. They're not language. I still look at them as interesting graphic symbols—just like looking at an egg, or a bee, if you'd never seen one before; like looking at Chinese symbols. So when I work on musical pictures, I'm always kind of startled. I'm like a person who doesn't really know how to drive, with the result that I'm more aware of an automobile than a person who does drive. If you're learning, that's where the joy of the automobile is, because you're completely aware of everything about it, and it's frightening, and so on. I know enough about music to get it down.

Adamson: Do you go to concerts a lot? The Hollywood Bowl is always figuring in these things.
Jones: We used to live on Highland Avenue when I was a kid. We lived in an old house, and we could climb down the side of the hill and watch the whole Hollywood Bowl free. There was only one guard. He had a dog, and he always let us know when he was coming: he knew where kids were hanging out, and he'd whistle as he came up the side of the hill, or he'd run into things, so we'd know that he was coming. We'd just sort of fade back into the bushes until he'd passed, and then we'd go back and listen again.
    What's Opera, Doc? is probably the most difficult film I ever did.

Adamson: Why is that?
Jones: Because everything was done right to the music; it was all pre-scored. We took the entire *Ring of the Nibelung*, which runs, I believe, sixteen hours or something like that (it's a series of operas) and condensed it into a six-minute picture, a chestnut stew.[17] There were 104 cuts in six minutes, which is some kind of a record.

---

[17] Jones is oversimplifying somewhat here: *What's Opera, Doc?* doesn't literally boil down Wagner's entire Ring cycle to 6 minutes. He also fails to mention that the song "Return, My Love," for which Michael Maltese wrote lyrics, is based on "The Pilgrim's Chorus," a theme from Wagner's *Lohengrin*.

Adamson: 104 separate shots?

Jones: Uh-huh. I don't think it looked like it. It shouldn't look like it. I'm not one who believes that cutting should be seen. I believe if you're cutting properly, the audience is not aware of it.

Adamson: Who did your editing at Warners?

Jones: We had a brilliant guy, Treg Brown, who was the sound cutter. I got him in the habit of doing those incongruous sounds for the Road Runner and Coyote. In one of them,[18] the Coyote got his leg caught in a harpoon gun, and he was dragged along the ground: we used horns and bells and sirens and rasps and chain saws and everything *except* the right sound. And it was funny.

In one of the Sheepdog pictures,[19] there was a gag I always enjoyed where the dog was sitting on the edge of the cliff, and the Coyote, or Wolf, or whatever we called him (the difference was that when he was in the Sheepdog pictures he spoke a little bit and had a red nose, otherwise he was the same), put a boulder on one side and a boulder on the other side and the dog was sitting here in the middle. He put this big rubber band on the boulders and then drew it back, and obviously he was going to flip the dog off the cliff—but the boulders came loose. I didn't really know what was going to happen at that point. I knew he was holding the rubber band and these things were coming. But I realized that they have a way of moving apart from each other, and so they went past him. He just held the rubber band and looked at the audience, and then his head took off, and then his body took off, then his feet took off. Then his tail took off. So he's sailing along now with two rocks out here, and he's in the center. So I found a defiled cliff for him, with a break in the middle, the two rocks came down and went "Ka-Blonk!" and then he shot right through the gap, still holding onto the rubber band. Then I cut to him with the rubber band just stretched out and out and out and out and out, and there was a tree, and he came up to it and grabbed it and just held on real tight. And then you cut to the defile and of course that pulled the two rocks around so that now the two rocks were together and were coming right at him. And there wasn't any hope for him. It was a strange shot, because I liked that real strong perspective. The trick of the perspective is to keep the object way off in the distance for seven-eighths of the time, and then in the last eighth it comes

---

[18] *Zoom and Bored*, 1957.
[19] *Steal Wool*, 1957.

into the foreground and right up to the camera. That's a very subtle bit of graphics.

So Treg and I looked at it and he said, "What kind of sound do you want there?"

And I said, "I don't know." So he tried out several things, and we finally decided on the sound of a locomotive coming. And we put a crossing guard and a Doppler effect and everything on there. And when those damn rocks came, with that sound of the train and the roar of the whistle and the crossing gate and everything, hell, it all was enormously funny. He ducked his head, and the stones came through and went "Chonk!" and he just disappeared. But there was a section missing out of the tree now, so the top dropped down, and of course the rubber band now caught the top of the tree, and the tree came along. So now we had the Coyote and the two rocks and the rubber band and the tree all messed up together. And he finally hit a cliff, and they came and hit him one right after the other.

I felt that someday, if I'd stayed there another year, I would have made a Road Runner picture or a Sheepdog picture with just one gag. That one ran on for 150 feet, and I had one that ran on for 300, so it could have been done.

I learned an enormous amount from my parallel association with Friz Freleng. In timing, I think he was one of the most brilliant men who ever lived. And timing, of course, is the essence of comedy.

Everybody learned from Tex Avery. He had an exquisite sense of what you might call ridiculous timing. He's the only man I've ever known who can do things that I wouldn't even begin to try, and that includes the joke of panning up the barrel of a gun, and just going and going and going and going and then come to a sign that says, "Long, isn't it?" and then going on and on and on and on, as if "I told you so," on and on and on and on and on and on. He used to go on and on with things like that. And his timing always worked, he knew exactly what he was about. It's a very subtle thing.

Tex ran out just before the war. When you think about it, Tex was there at Warner Bros. for only a few years. He was there from 1935 to 1941—about five years. But he had an immense effect. He didn't have anywhere near that effect on MGM.

Of course Bob Clampett is a very strange bird; he's a different breed of cat completely. His approach to Bugs Bunny, for instance, didn't involve the disciplines that we would put in. He used Bugs Bunny like Woody Woodpecker, which I always felt was wrong.

I learned a great deal from Tex and a great deal from Friz. I think those two were the most influential, and they were masters of timing. And if there's one basic thing wrong with all motion-picture making today, it is a failure of timing.

Adamson: All motion-picture making? It's definitely a key problem in animation.

Jones: But it's also a key problem in features, and in student filmmaking it's almost endemic. I have a way of making money at student film festivals: I can bet anybody 50-50 that a student film will have somebody walking within the first three hundred feet—just walking. Some lonely young man or some lonely young girl walking in New York. Usually I can add to that bet by saying that he'll be walking along a beach or along a railroad track, and he'll pass an abandoned railroad station, and the cameraman for some reason will feel that he must climb a telephone pole and look down at him as he passes the station. If there's any kind of an overpass, the cameraman will go down and look *up* at him, and maybe there'll be a seagull up there, but there's gonna be a seagull within the first three or four hundred feet. If you find a hawk, that's fine, but a seagull is better. And one of two instruments will be used on the soundtrack, a guitar or a very lonely, lonely harmonica. And you can safely say that whatever it is, it'll be three times too long. Not twice, three times. And most features, *Easy Rider* and things like this, are too long, and they spend too much time on each thing. One of the difficulties is if you get a camera and start it running, it seems so authentic. The fact that you've taken a picture of somebody, it seems so damned *authentic*.

Our pictures were exactly 540 feet long, and we got to the point where we could lay out a film, starting from the beginning or wherever you felt like, and by the time we finished timing it we were probably within ten feet of 540. All of us—Friz and Tex and I, particularly—got to be pretty good at that. I think it was an economic necessity to do it that way, but it was also some damn good training.

Adamson: How restricted did you feel about following this set pattern?
Jones: You must understand, our budgets were around $30,000. They were upped a little bit after the war, but not much. They got up to 32–35,000, but the budgets didn't change a great deal. We compensated for that by making the cartoons a little bit shorter. Originally they were seven minutes, and they eventually got down to six-minute pictures, and that's cutting them by 15 percent in length. Strangely enough,

a 540-foot cartoon is much more difficult to make than a 600-foot cartoon. That's what developed that real sharp timing—there's no dead wood. My early things, like the Sniffles things, a lot of them were long. If I had the extra time, I'd tend to make the pans too long and the movements too slow. But when you came down to 540 feet, it seemed to be some kind of optimal length. And I believe that most films have a correct length. That goes for features or anything else. I think you can tell any feature story in between seventy-two and ninety minutes. Now, most pictures run two hours. The result is that most pictures are draggy or showy.

I used to think that this wasn't true of other forms, but strangely enough it is. I thought all Broadway plays were different lengths until one day I woke up with the sudden realization that every time I went to the theatre, I came out and couldn't get a cab. And it stood to reason that one theatre couldn't keep me from getting a cab for twenty minutes. I suddenly realized that everybody was letting out at the same time. There are some exceptions, but not many. Everybody pours out, the restaurants all fill up, and everything, within a few minutes of each other. It goes from 8:30 to about quarter to 11, so it must run two hours in length and a fifteen-minute intermission. It usually starts a little late, so let's say two hours approximately, and the goddamn things fit into that time period. And that goes for musicals, or dramas, or whatever.

I fell into a trap when I talked to people about making films, I'd say "We made it in 540 feet," and they'd say, "Yeah, but in drama or in books, you don't have to do that." But even books fit into a certain shape, about three hundred pages, the average book is probably within twenty pages of all other books and novels. But it's no different from Michaelangelo having to work on the Sistine Chapel. He didn't demand that this shape be changed, "Because I want to paint the other side of the wall." He did it, and that was the discipline that was enforced on him. When you think that a popular number runs two minutes and forty-two seconds because it has to fit on a 45 [rpm record], everybody from Hank Mancini to the Beatles seems to manage to do it in that length. And it really staggered me; all those years I'd been going to plays and didn't realize that—it was so obvious! And the reason I recognized it was because I couldn't get a cab.

Adamson: Did you ever run the pencil reel for an audience the way Tex did?
Jones: I never thought that way, you know. I never cared what the public thought. I never previewed anything because I found out that

people who did preview would usually go around from theatre to theatre until they found an audience that agreed with them. It's very confusing—that's why I don't like Nielsens.

I don't think Tex paid much attention to it either. I think he would run a test reel because he would maybe detect something that people would laugh at that he didn't expect. I don't think he paid attention to whether they laughed where he expected them to laugh, but if they laughed at something he *didn't* expect, then he'd go back and think about it; he might develop that gag and do it in the next picture. I never did that; I usually waited until the answers came back. For one thing, previews scared the hell out of me. It just destroyed me even to go in to see the films run for the studio audience, which I always had to do. I was considered a coward if I didn't. But I was a coward if I did!

For another thing, if your audience laughs at places you don't expect, then you try to pattern your behavior on their response from that time on. But of course, the laugh doesn't necessarily come at the point where you hear it. They may be responding to a cumulative thing, you never know; all my stuff tends to accumulate. There are a lot of gags that grow, like the earthquake pills. If you went and listened, and tried to figure out just exactly where it started growing, you might come up all wrong. What I would do, because I'm basically a coward about these matters, is wait until somebody came and told me that the picture was going well, and then I'd go see it. Otherwise I would have been way off.

I never understood the Inki and the Minah Bird pictures, for example. But they always got laughs. And it was strange because *nobody* understood them. They took them over to Disney's (this was in the early 1940s), and Walt brought his writers out. He showed them this thing, that stupid bird walking around, and he'd say, "Why don't you guys do things like that? What in the hell is he doing right?" Because he'd seen them with audiences; the audiences died over them. I could never understand it. They didn't seem particularly funny to *me*.

Adamson: Once you found they were getting laughs, you kept doing them?

Jones: Yeah, but the terrible part about it was that after I made the first one, I was dragged in by my hind legs to look at it being shown to an audience. And I just couldn't figure out the audience, because when we did the soundtrack mix they just sat there. We showed it to the studio audience, and there wasn't a laugh. It was the most dreadful experience. We sent it to New York, and New York said, "Yucch! We don't want any more of these." And then the damn thing went out and started knocking them over in the theatres, and they said, "We want some more." So I made another one, and the same thing happened. The mix was dead, the studio audience was dead, New York said "It isn't as good as the *other* one." And so it went out and did better than the first one did.

I ended up doing a few of them, then I finally went to Schlesinger and said, "No more! Absolutely no more! I'm not going to put myself through that kind of agony." So he asked the other directors if they would do one, and none of them could understand it. I said, "It isn't surprising, I didn't understand it." If Walt Disney didn't understand it, I don't know who the hell ever *did* understand it—except that people laughed at it, so there it was.

Another picture I didn't understand was *Now Hear This*. We kind of went out into—I don't know if it was left field; it was somewhere else I didn't understand. Jack Warner wasn't the only one who didn't understand that picture. I called it "Chuck Jones's Revenge," because it was one of the last pictures I made, and I was trying to find some way of infuriating him. So I made that picture and a couple of others, like *I Was a Teen-Age Thumb*.

Adamson: Why would that infuriate him?
Jones: Well, because it was so different from anything else. When things happened that he didn't understand, he usually got mad. And since I was leaving anyway, I figured I might just as well have the fun of trying out a few things like *Now Hear This*. So I did try them out, but I didn't succeed: he didn't get mad. Maybe he didn't see them, but if he did see them, he didn't get mad. It was too bad, because I kind of depended on them to get him mad.

My attitude about these matters is that if your pictures do well, accept it; then you're in the right business. If not, then you're in the wrong business. It's just that simple. What I try to do is continue to make pictures that *I* think are funny. Or interesting. And I suspect that's probably the only way to make anything. I know [Alfred] Hitchcock seldom goes to see pictures. He said that isn't the proper place to learn about films: You don't learn about films from films, you learn about films from other things.

Joe Adamson wishes to thank Mark Kausler, Lindsay Doran, Rulon Dempster, and Patricia Eliot Tobias for their assistance in preparing this version of his interviews.

Chuck Jones

GREG FORD AND RICHARD THOMPSON / 1972

From *Film Comment*, January/February
1975. Reprinted with permission.

Chuck Jones: Kansas City is where Ub Iwerks started, and Bugs Hardaway,
and Hugh Harman and Rudy Ising and Walt and Roy Disney . . . all
those people worked for that one little company, Kansas City Film Ad.
And until it kind of petered out, they actually made commercials, commercials for theatrical showing. Walt then came West, and then Friz,
Ham Hamilton, classic animators, and they all got established with *Alice
in Cartoonland* at Universal. I came up with the next generation—well,
generations were separated by about eight or ten years then. Those of
us who had gone to Chouinard Art School in Los Angeles, where could
we work? We could go into commercial art or we could go into animation. So I worked with Ub Iwerks, who had split with Disney at the time.
I worked for Universal, and then Charles Mintz, and . . . hell, in those
days you jumped from studio to studio. But eventually I came to Warner

Bros. Meantime, I worked as a sailor for a while, went to South America or someplace.

Q: And as a lumberjack, and a cowboy . . .
A: I was *called* a lumberjack by Disney people who thought I was a communist.

Q: What does a lumberjack have in common with a communist?
A: Well, they used to say that the communists took "little hairy Jewish people" along when they had a speech to make at a union meeting. When I spoke at a meeting, one of the Disney animators said, "How come they're using these big pink lumberjack types now?" and pretty soon everybody was saying it. So I went home and took a look at myself—I was twenty-five—and, sure enough, I was a big pink lumberjack type. And I was a *fat* lumberjack—two hundred and five pounds.

Q: In *Positif* magazine, they say that Chuck Jones, before he went to Warners, was a lumberjack and had a big blue ox named Babe.
A: That was true. That was a sexual relationship. But anyway . . .

Q: Somehow, we've got your chronology all screwed up. Did you do that before you worked in any animation studios? Or in-between?
A: I don't know . . . Anyway, I did it.

Q: Your first cartoons, starting from about 1938, seem to make a much greater effort to approximate realistic shape and movement than your later cartoons.
A: That really was an effort, learning how to make things move. One of the things I think is basically misunderstood about easel art is that, say, Andy Warhol, Claes Oldenberg, de Kooning, Robert Motherwell can all draw beautifully. They all had line control. They had to learn that, and then they branched out. It's hard to think of an artist that is worth anything who didn't have this ability. They started with the basics. With those early cartoons, I was learning the basics. What the hell, I started directing when I was twenty-five, so I had to learn the language, and so did my animators. We had classes—for years, we had at least two classes per week, at night. And we were working a five-and-a-half-day week, about fifty-six hours a week.

Q: Who conducted the classes?
A: I did. And I had to learn at the same time. I went to the lectures that they were having at Disney's with Don Graham. We also went through

a whole series of classes from the Art Students League, conducted by Kimon Nicolaides, who did those edged drawings, marvelous things, which kind of caught the character. He laid down the law that if you ever want to learn to draw, you have a hundred thousand bad drawings in you. And the sooner you get rid of them, the better you are. So we did thousands of drawings.

Q: This realism effects timing, too. An early cartoon like *Good Night Elmer* [1940] is rather slow—it seems obsessed with realistic movement, shape, and shading.
A: The shading was there because of the presence of a single light-source, the candle, which was very important. The story was just a tiny thing: a man attempting to put out a little candle. How can you make an entire story about that? Is it possible? That's what I wanted to know. I wouldn't say it was a particularly successful picture, but it was crucial in terms of what came afterward.

You have to stumble a lot, I can't think of any other way of doing anything. There are no short-cuts. And nobody had the time to do a scene and then throw it away—we *had* to use it in the final film. At Disney's, during the same period, they were experimenting with things and then *not* using them. They could afford to, but we couldn't. There was nothing wrong with that, but several of the pictures were experimental—some of them worked and some didn't. Some were slow, but I was attempting to discover things about timing here, and in the early Sniffles films. Besides, they didn't seem as slow then, basically because all cartoons weren't at such a fantastic pace. The pace thing started with *The Tortoise and the Hare* [1935] at Disney's.

Q: One aspect of *The Tortoise and the Hare* which you seem to have picked out and expanded in the Pepé Le Pew series is the "Slow and steady wins the race" idea of character action. Pepé maintains his steady pace, while the female cat Pepé is pursuing finally wears herself out with faster but more sporadic movements.
A: I did that even earlier in *Little Lion Hunter* [1939, Jones's first cartoon featuring the native African child Inki and the mystical mynah bird]. The mynah bird was that sort of steady character. I often have music dictating the steady pace. In the Inki series, the mynah bird would hop along to *Fingal's Cave* Overture. That was my first experience with Mendelssohn.

Q: The vocabulary of Carl Stalling, the regular composer for Warners cartoons, is unbelievable. He can even anticipate the audience's association with the image. For instance, in the middle of the chase in *Fast and Furry-ous* [1949], the first Road Runner film, you cut to an overhead perspective of this highway cloverleaf that the characters are running around, and Stalling immediately refers to "I'm Looking Over a Four-Leaf Clover." He seems to be able to relate to any kind of music.

A: There was a reason for that: he was a lead organist at some of the biggest theaters in St. Louis and Kansas City, where you had to have everything right at your fingertips. That was one of the reasons he tended to go toward visual titles. When a character was eating something, he'd play "A Cup of Coffee, a Sandwich, and You," even though it might not fit exactly. If it was a lady in a red dress, he'd always play "The Lady in Red," or if a bee, he'd always play "My Funny Little Bumblebee," which was written in 1906. Sometimes it worked and sometimes it didn't—that "Funny Little Bumblebee" thing was so obscure no one could make the connection. You had to be a hundred and eight years old to even know there was such a song.

Q: Around 1941 or 1942 your cartoons seemed to change—they began to present more violent and radical character-motion, and the backgrounds became more stylized. Do you think the war had any effect on this change?

A: I think as far as action and subject-matter were concerned, my cartoons actually *were* gentler before 1941 . . . so I'd agree with that proposition to a limited extent. But generally, no, I don't think there's much of a connection there. In terms of violent character-action, I suppose that I was affected somewhat by both Friz [Freleng] and Tex [Avery]. I always admired their sense of timing and sense of movement, and their gag structures—although they certainly worked differently. You see, after *The Draft Horse* [1941], I discovered that I could make people laugh—and not just be amused. And that's a heady thing. You get so you *want* to make them laugh, or at least make yourself laugh.

Q: *The Draft Horse* is still very funny today. To begin with, we're confronted with a superpatriotic plowhorse, flags in his eyes, who then of course is terrified when he's caught in the middle of some army war-games.

A: Well, at this particular time, very early in the Second World War, everybody was in favor of fighting. There were simple terms then. You have to be in contact with the idea of what Adolf Hitler was: he was an enormity, a giant black thing over the horizon. That was something you could see—he was an evil thing. It was the last of the great clearcut conflicts. Nevertheless, within the context of chauvinism, you could discover the idiocy of people just wanting to go throw themselves out in front of the cannon. At least you could be reasonable.

Another development is that after this film, and after the war, I worked more with the writer Mike Maltese. He was more of a gagman than Tedd Pierce, with whom I'd been working earlier. Tedd tended to be more of a writer. He was good at structure, and it was a humorous structure—but it wasn't gags. On the other hand, Mike Maltese was, and still is, a brilliant gagman. But whatever happened during that period, it probably wasn't due to the war. If anything, the war would have calmed it down.

Q: At any rate, we could say that in 1942 there suddenly was a decisive break from that over-awareness of realism.
A: Yeah, that's right. I think at that point the language began to be learned, and this group of people working together discovered that they were all reasonably facile. The team thing is very important. It gets to the point where you can snap your fingers, or make a single drawing to convey your idea. Whenever a new animator came to work for me, he was in trouble for a while, because on my exposure sheets, I would put down a notation like "BAL"—which was "balance"—or "ANT"—"anticipate." And all my animators had to know exactly what they meant.

Q: What *did* it mean—an anticipation before the actual motion?
A: Sure. Or "BAL" might mean that I'd want a particular character solid on his feet before he did something, so you'd know that there was a stability to the thing, before it moved into action. Of course, I used "holds," and animators learned that when I put down a twelve-frame hold, that didn't mean thirteen frames or eleven frames—it meant twelve frames exactly. When the Coyote fell off, I knew he had to go exactly three or four feet and then disappear for eighteen frames before he hit. A new animator would come in, and he would overlap that, and it would never work.

When we'd lay out dances, we began to understand that we could anticipate by one frame. If a step is supposed to come down on a beat, we found out that if you moved it up one frame, it would work, because the throw back to the middle of the theater, thirty rows back, would make the step appear to be exactly on beat. That's just one frame we're talking about, one-twenty-fourth of a second, but we found out it worked best for the entire theater if you were one frame ahead of the beat.

Q: How often did you use rotoscoping?
A: Almost never. Occasionally, when we had to shoot something like a complicated dance, we'd actually take live-action frames and study them, sketch them out and look at them to see where the feet would land. We did that for the leprechaun's little jig in *The Wearing of the Grin* [1951], where Porky goes to Ireland.

Q: There are so many disciplines just in terms of timing—the way Bugs Bunny walked must have been mathematically exact.
A: Sure, but the basic thing in animation is that you're talking about believability. You see, I was dealing with the idea of realism first, but then I realized that believability was much more important. So that with Bugs or any other character, it was the feeling of weight that mattered. One of the best examples of this is puppets or marionettes: they seem to work best if their knees don't bend when their feet touch the ground. Otherwise, they look all wrong, because there's no suggestion of gravity there. So I discovered that if you get the feeling of weight, you're all right—it doesn't really make much difference whether it's realistically drawn or not.

Q: In other words, the values become less literal and more abstract.
A: Sure. If you want it loose, if you want it buoyant, if you want it inflated like a balloon—well, go ahead and make it like a balloon. But if my decision is that it's a Bugs Bunny story—then Bugs has a particular weight. So I want him to feel, as he walks across a room, as if he has this given density, this given solidity.

Q: Unless he's pulling himself out of a hat, *à la Case of the Missing Hare* [1942].
A: Ah ha! But even then, pulling yourself out of a hat has a feeling of weight, as you lift yourself up. This feeling of weight and believability can even be offscreen, as in *Duck Amuck* [1953] and *Rabbit Rampage* [1955].

Q: Certain themes started emerging the very first year you began to direct. In *Doggone Modern* [1938], those two early dogs of yours, the boxer and his puppy pal, were pitted against the absurdities of technology, much as all those Acme devices would later backfire on the Coyote in his quest for the Road Runner. The two dogs got trapped in a modernistic house-of-the-future.

A: That's right. They wandered in, and the place had a robot broom that would sweep up anything, regardless of what it was.

Q: And the dogs had to dodge the robot broom, to keep from getting swept up themselves. You did a remake of the same film about a decade later, this time starring your mice characters Hubie and Bertie [*House Hunting Mice,* 1947], which seems to be such an incredible improvement on the original *Doggone Modern.*

A: Well, the style of background was completely different in the two cartoons. In the first few pictures I worked on, we used a man by the name of Griff Jay, who was an old newspaper cartoonist—and he did what we'd call "moldy prune" backgrounds. Everybody used the same type of thing back then—Charlie Johnston drew backgrounds for Tex Avery, and he was an old newspaper cartoonist, too.

Q: But the biggest difference between the two films is in the starring characters. The situation is the same, a pair of characters being victimized by crazy electronic house devices, but Hubie and Bertie in *House Hunting Mice* are active and fully developed characters, while the dogs are far too passive—they just don't have a chance.

A: No, they don't. The dogs don't really amount to anything. They just walk around and get mixed up in all the gadgetry. But they don't demonstrate any real human reactions, none that we can recognize anyway, beyond a sort of generalized anxiety. The characters aren't really established, so you don't care about them. You *do* care about Hubie and Bertie, though.

Q: They're real personalities. It's so much more exhilarating to see them respond to the machinery, occasionally react against it, and at odd times even triumph over it. There's a marvelous sequence where Hubie and Bertie succeed in temporarily outfoxing the robot, remember? Unlike the two dogs, they finally realize that this fucking broom is going to whiz out and sweep up the debris, regardless of purpose, and so this time, the characters make use of the fact and consciously try to wear the robot out. They turn on an automatic record ejector that shoots out discs and shatters them against the wall, the records fly and break into pieces, and

the robot invariably has to come out and sweep up, again and again. Also, there are shots, with simulated editing, of a missile sailing past intercut with a quick insert of a character just watching it go by.
A: That may have been generated from a fascination with tennis matches, and such intercutting effects would often make the scene work. It also demonstrates that you could get an object to look like it's moving a hell of a lot faster with editing. And eventually, I began to add shadows of the missile flying past; this happened very often in the Road Runner films.

Q: Most memorably, when you get an insert close-up of the Coyote, with a truck or train heading right for him, the shadow of it going over his face, and he's holding up a little sign that says, "STOP, IN THE NAME OF HUMANITY," or something like that.
A: Of course you realize that all our stuff was pre-edited; it had "simulated editing," as you say. The editing was all in the director's head. A lot of people don't realize that, so it's interesting and well worth emphasizing. This wasn't necessarily true of Disney, but we didn't actually *physically* cut our stuff at all. The directors here developed the ability to bring in a cartoon within ten seconds of its proper length. It's easier to do this on a spot-gag picture than it is on a story picture, of course. It was really mental editing, and I've never met a live-action director, or editor, who understood how this could be done. It's just like shooting these little clips of film in live action, at exactly their proper length, and putting them all together. And this was the *necessity* of the situation, since we weren't allowed any retakes. We weren't *allowed* to cut. We only had so much footage, and we had to do it right the first time. We did retakes in the sense that we'd re-animate something, if it was wrong, but we never re-filmed.

Q: One thing puzzles me: Treg Brown occasionally gets a film editor's credit. Usually he is credited as a sound-effects man.
A: Right, the film editor's credit also refers to sound-effects; he was a sound-effects cutter. He deserved his credit thoroughly, since he was one of the most brilliant sound-effects editors that ever lived.

Q: Your cartoons have more of this simulated live action–type editing than any other cartoon director's. In the middle of one of the Road Runner chases, the camera angles switch rapidly from pan shot to a close-up of the Coyote, to an overhead vantage, etc. Nobody at

Warners did this kind of thing more frequently, except possibly Frank Tashlin. Friz Freleng, on the other hand, seemed to opt more for an illusion of "stage space," as if the characters were performing live on a stage platform. You often revert to close-ups, reaction shots, and even very subtle uses of subjective viewpoints; Freleng goes for single-takes.

A: It sounds like an observation that you'd be able to make more accurately than I could. I don't see my old pictures too regularly, and I never think of them in terms of cutting.

Q: Another thing wrong with the two early dogs that appeared in *Doggone Modern* and a couple of other films at the time: there seemed to be some question as to what movements were defined for them. They were very naturalistically drawn, but their movements seemed to confuse human-like and canine actions.

A: That's why there wasn't any character, because what we were trying to do was to find out how the hell a dog moves. Just how he moves and nothing much beyond that. That's when I was fighting the anthropomorphic idea of movement. They were modeled with back-legs like dogs, but nobody really knew how to move them properly. The result was that they looked rather awkward.

One very pivotal film for me was *Inki and the Lion* [1941], where Shamus Culhane, one of the all-time great animators, finally got that lion to work—then Manny Farber wrote in the *New Republic* that he thought the lion looked like Robinson Crusoe. Anyway, we had to go through the process of anatomy first, in things like *Doggone Modern*, so that the later dogs still gave the impression of being dogs, but weren't drawn exactly like dogs and didn't move exactly like dogs. Marc Antony in *Feed the Kitty* [1952] and *Cat Feud* [1959] certainly appeared to be a dog, but he moved according to the anatomy we had established for him. He was over-weight in front and had a tiny behind.

Q: And the frisky puppy in *Terrier Stricken* [1952] and *Two's a Crowd* [1951] was a natural-looking, four-legged puppy. But his friskiness is just beyond the realistic. There came to be a very thin line for you, then, between the realistic and the slightly exaggerated.

A: Oh yes, a real dog might do other things than what this puppy does, but the puppy's basic characteristic is this fastness. So that's what I take off on and accent: that incredibly quick movement. He comes sliding in, barking like crazy, all ears, arms, and legs.

Q: And the squirrel in *Much Ado about Nutting* [1953] is also a natural-seeming squirrel.

A: Technically, that's one of the best pictures I ever made. I studied squirrels just to find out how they moved; they turn their heads in almost one frame and then they hesitate as they look—like a bird, they don't have binocular vision. I love those little hesitations when he's looking around and sniffing. If the surrealistic ending worked, it was because everything was so normal up to that time. The cocoanut was simply impossible to break, and when it did break, there was another one beneath it.

Q: Just one ordinary squirrel setting out to crack an extraordinarily uncrackable nut. And he tries everything: sawing it, exploding it, riveting it.

A: That was a difficult picture to do. It was such a simple gag; it's almost idiotic in its simplicity. No dialogue, of course. But when he tried to crack the cocoanut by pushing it off the Empire State Building—that was the sequence that got me. He starts pushing the cocoanut up all those flights of stairs, and I'm so sad for him when he has to push it up each stair individually, then scramble up the next stair and push it again, and so on.

Q: What struck you as most impressive in Buster Keaton's repertoire of physical gags?

A: He often moved like he was being pulled away—he'd doubletake as though someone were yanking him by the back of his collar. The classic scene of all is where he actually *was* dragged off—in *Cops*, I believe. There were these hundreds of cops chasing him, right behind him; a streetcar goes by, and Keaton just reaches out and grabs it and it pulls him off-screen.

Q: There's a gag like that in *Zoom and Bored*, where the Coyote's foot gets caught in the rope of the harpoon that he's just shot off. He's struggling to unsnarl his foot and finally succeeds, but then realizes that he's left mid-air over one of those terrible thousand-foot drops. So at the last second he grabs for the end of the harpoon rope, still zipping by—and he's yanked off in the way you described that Keaton bit. It seems to me you were influenced even more by Keaton than Chaplin.

A: I would think so, because my stuff is a little broader than Chaplin's, although the early Chaplin is quite broad, too. Chaplin originated those

funny little hoppy runs and turns where he bounces up and down a bit
while rounding a corner. I'd use that a lot; I thought it always looked
funny and strange because it wasn't at all necessary, physically. It was
redundant. Similarly, Chaplin's surprised reactions were always comically
over-elaborated. He'd jump up into the air and then come down and
then start to run. The jump is solely a method of registering excitement
and realization. He'd look like a human exclamation point, calling attention to his surprise—like saying, "Ah! I'm surprised!"—and then he'd run.
Since they had no other means to express it, they'd do it with physical
action, and it was beautiful to watch.

Q: You seem to have a special interest in eyes.
A: Oh yes. That's another thing I picked up from Keaton—those little
eye-flicks toward the camera, which I'd use, say, whenever the Coyote
realizes that something is inevitably going to fall on him and the action
stops for a moment. Of course, that was always used in the early
Tom Mix westerns, too, during a tense poker game—everything would
be stockstill in the frame except that the eyes, in close-up, would be
flickering back and forth, left and right. I found that you could get a
laugh from any of these minimal movements. Like in *Terrier Stricken*,
you hear the mistress off-screen telling the cat to take care of Frisky, the
little puppy. Claude Cat has a devilish smirk on his face, of course, but
we got the laugh from just his tiny eye-movement from side to side.

Q: Often you bring the whites together so that the two eyes are joined,
to indicate a character's surprise.
A: That just seems to make the surprise dramatically stronger. I might
take one eye up and even make the other one square under certain
conditions. I found that once they're accepted as eyes, you can do anything with them to get strong effects. Tex Avery used them so that the
eyes would shoot out approximately six feet, then fall on the floor, etc.
I never went quite that far.

Q: You did, just once in a special case—*Hopalong Casualty* [1961], when
the Coyote reads that Earthquake Pills aren't effective on road runners.
A: I usually use such extremes only for strong reactions, as when the
Coyote is amazed at the Road Runner's speed and his jaw drops straight
to the ground. But then he immediately picks it up and shoves it back
into its proper place. I wanted to get his startlement at the Road Runner's
speed.

Q: Those movements seem to suspend time, like when the construction worker in *One Froggy Evening* [1956] finds the singing frog in the cornerstone, and gives a prolonged look of disbelief at the audience, or when the Coyote is scheming and one of his ears simply flaps over.
A: I don't know how long those movements take, but when I use them, you see, it's simply a matter of conspiring with the audience.

Q: Sometimes you suspend all action for a moment as beads of sweat start forming on a character's forehead—like when the guy in *One Froggy Evening* is showing the frog to the agent and is worried whether or not it'll sing.
A: In the earlier cartoons, we'd have a heavier profusion of sweat for an anxious character. But in the fifties we learned that just one or two beads looked better.

Q: Another one of my favorite instances of this time-marking animation occurs in *Bully for Bugs* [1953] when the proud matador looks at the camera, doesn't move for a time, then simply flares one of his nostrils.
A: That's a caricature of Juan Belmonte, one of the great bullfighters. He looked like that and was every bit as vain. And then I put in him what I would feel under the same circumstances—that is, fear—once he's face to face with the bull. So he's dressed for the part, but he wasn't really the brave matador.

Q: But in terms of facial detail, I'd have to pinpoint *Feed the Kitty* [1952] for its gamut-running of facial expressions.
A: Of course, that was a very sentimental picture.

Q: The tough bulldog falls hard for a tiny black kitten.
A: The dog starts out pugnaciously with the cat but then runs the entire gamut of a relationship with anyone. It's like a girl, you know, when you first meet her: then you gradually get so that you can stand her, and then you fall in love with her, then you become obsessed with her and fear she's going to die or something. And that is what the dog went through; he was a very protective character. I got involved with that bloody dog, Marc Antony: his panic when he thinks the cat is going to die, his efforts to look nonchalant when he's trying to cover up for the cat. The drawings in that cartoon were a lot of fun.

Q: What are your favorite effects to show, say, the force of gravity in cartoons? You often use those straight-on shots of the Coyote in the midst of a fall, and different parts of his body fall at different times.

A: Well, that was an old trick of mine to emphasize the *idea* of falling. A good example of this in actual nature—one that always infuriated me—is when a red light changes. Why doesn't everybody move at once? But they don't: the first car moves, then the second takes its movement from the first, and so on, and yet supposedly it is possible that they could all start at once. To me it was funny to apply the same principle to a living body, so that the Coyote's trunk would drop away, and then his face and stretched-out neck would still be there, then the head would drop, leaving the ears, and then the ears'd drop off.

Q: It prolongs the agony, too, having the Coyote involved feel each part of his body drop at different times, his expressions changing in the process.
A: And yet when he lands, you know, it doesn't seem to hurt him any. It's usually just the idea of falling, the idea itself, which seems to carry the emotional impact.

Q: Sometimes you have entire cartoons set up around the idea of gravity. In *Mouse Wreckers* [1948], for instance, you have a whole string of gravity gags, the *coup de grâce* being the upside-down room sequence.
A: An earlier gravity gag in that cartoon is when Claude Cat is pulled through the house by the rope, which is triggered by the mice pushing the heavy boulder off the chimney. And remember? Claude would get pulled into stacks of dishes, around bannisters, under tables. Gravity is the simplest thing to use if you don't happen to have any other tools at hand.

I have a running gag I want to do sometime—picking up on the image of the Big Spring and making an entire cartoon about it. The Coyote could just get caught up in the spring, then later it could just bounce him along, then he could get caught up in it again, and it would just keep going. Then he could fall off the edge of a cliff, and one end of the spring could catch on top of the cliff, and then he'd get down to the end of the spring, and there'd be an outcropping, and he'd grab the outcropping. And then he'd spring back to the top, and he'd pull the outcropping up and that would drive him down again. Because when something compresses, it has to go in the opposite direction—it's cause and effect. And so, you see, just this spring, combined with gravity, would be all you'd need in terms of motive power.

Q: How would that cartoon end, just in the middle of the action?

A: I don't know how I'm ever going to end it, but it would obviously end up in a situation that implies a continuum, where the action goes right back where you started from. That "Here we go again!" kitsch. We might even use a spring wipe for the ending, going off in the distance or just falling away from the camera.

Q: *Mouse Wreckers* seems to us to be a major cartoon because the controlling factors of the film are always kept off-screen. Your two mouse characters, Hubie and Bertie, are stationed on the chimney playing architectural mind-games on poor Claude Cat, who's alone in the house below. The mice reconstruct his entire room, and when Claude wakes up, he doesn't know whether these things are really happening or whether he's hallucinating it all.

A: In the later MGM remake, *Year of the Mouse* [1965], the cat finally realizes that the mice are provoking these disasters, and at the end he catches the mice.

Q: Yeah, it's a moral ending where the earlier Warners film has an immoral ending.

A: Oh, well, I like immoral endings better. Forgetting the Tom and Jerry, the purpose in *Mouse Wreckers* was that the cat never realized exactly what was happening to him. And it was based on an actual happening. This upside-down room did exist; some English duke or something has a weird sense of humor, and at his parties, when someone would pass out, he'd haul 'em in there, and everyone would look through the holes in the walls and watch them come to. And people would do exactly what the cat did: they'd try to crawl up the wall or something—particularly someone with a dreadful hangover, you can imagine how hideous that was.

Q: The second-to-last image of that cartoon is amazing. It's just Claude's eyes with the cat being driven totally insane, cowering at the top of a tree, and the leaves falling away just enough to reveal those eyes.

A: In that picture I used a different thing: the eyes were handled almost like a pair of animated breasts—did you notice that?

Q: Yes, the pupil came out of the ball of the eye, like a nipple. The fear registered in Claude's eyes in amazing, as he looks from side to side.

A: Phil Monroe did a good job on that.

Q: When Claude is in the upside-down room, on the ceiling that he thinks is the floor, trying to keep his balance by digging his claws into the ceiling, the camera turns around and goes upside-down with Claude; it's fascinating. I wonder if you were trying to show the force of gravity through motion alone, and without the standard visual presentation of what's up and what's down.

A: Well, Claude opened the bottle and the liquid flowed up, while if it were shown from your viewpoint it would naturally flow down. And I wanted to show what he felt. Actually, Charlie Chaplin used something like that in the opening airplane sequence of *The Great Dictator*, when he's piloting his plane upside-down. And the same series of gags are in the Porky Pig cartoon *Jumpin' Jupiter* [1955] when they lose their gravity. There I didn't have to turn the camera around, obviously, since it was in outer space. I just used a little sign that read: "You are now entering a low gravity zone."

Q: This brings us to another natural force. I was wondering about your means of expressing velocity on the screen. One of my favorite gimmicks is in *Bully for Bugs*: as the bull charges, it leaves dozens of hooves in mid-air behind it. Daffy's horse in *Drip-Along Daffy* [1951] leaves hooves in its wake as well. You often use dust, as when the Coyote is lagging just behind the Road Runner and is trying to pick up speed.

A: Well, there again I'm giving the viewer something to hold onto, something to register the speed. A bow and arrow is a good example from real life. You pull the string back, and release the arrow, but the bow is there—except in a Daffy Duck cartoon. But the bow is there with its string vibrating and so, with these two things in combination, you still have something on the screen after the arrow is gone. Here, what's important is what's left over: the catapults in my cartoons are shown the same way; they give you a reference-point.

Q: There's an early Daffy Duck cartoon called *Conrad the Sailor* [1941] which had very pronounced experimentation with ways of presenting speed. You actually had the running characters leave ghost-images behind them, which would then catch up with the solid characters. I also remember a prominent use of matched cutting in that cartoon.

A: Well, we used a lot of overlapping graphics on that particular cartoon so that one scene would have the same graphic shape as an earlier scene, even though it would be a different object: first we'd show a gun pointing up in the air, then in the next shot, there'd be a cloud in exactly the same shape. It gave a certain stability which we used in many of the cartoons after that. John McGrew was the artist responsible for that sort of thing. *Conrad* was also the one where we used the first complete 360-degree turn, when the characters went up through the air.

Q: Conrad and Daffy are being chased through the air by a torpedo, and they go around full circle.
A: The fields themselves did not turn all the way around. The field only made a partial turn. The effect was accomplished entirely by changing the shape of the clouds. The clouds were the main thing. So when you saw it, it looked like you made one complete revolution—we started at one end looking down on a battleship, and at the other end you were looking down at the same battleship again. It was a very tricky problem; I'm not sure it was worth it.

Q: You've used the same basic technique since, as when the camera seems to do a 180-degree tilt. In *Mouse Wreckers*, when Claude is being pulled through the drain-pipe, you must have drawn the drainpipe so that it bulged out in the middle and tapered off at either end, to allow for the perspective-change during the camera movement.
A: Yeah, that's exactly, what we did. We used it before in an early Sniffles cartoon. In fact, that's one of few tricks we originated that Disney took from us—remember the perspective trick when the alligator comes slithering down that pole in "Dance of the Hours" [from *Fantasia*]? Anyway, John McGrew was a great student of film techniques. And oddly enough, much of the staging in *Conrad the Sailor* was taken from Eisenstein's writing. It had mostly to do with matched dissolves, with the relation of one shot to the next—so that one scene, formally, might be exactly the same as the previous one, even though the subject would change.

Q: You have a transition like that in *Hold the Lion, Please* [1941], one of your earliest Bugs cartoons, where this weakling schnook of a lion is claiming his status as "King of Beasts," and all the other animals in the jungle are laughing at him. The laughing animal faces in the first composition dissolve into shrubs, flowers, and foliage that serve as the background for the next shot. In regard to technical facilities at Warner Bros., did you have a multiplane camera, or anything like it?
A: No, we faked it a lot, but we never had any such thing. I don't think any studio did except Disney's.

Q: Sometimes, the Warners cartoons have at least *two* layers, moving in perspective during a shot.

A: Well, we could do that all right. Johnny Burton, who was in charge of production, was pretty damn good at maneuvering things around to get a three-dimensional effect, but all three layers would actually be on the same level as we were photographing them. He was very clever at working out the speed at which foreground material should go in relation to a second layer. I've used as many as three layers to achieve certain effects.

Also, one of the reasons you'd use a foreground object, if you weren't cutting in the middle of a pan shot, is that your background drawings would have to repeat—otherwise, they'd be on a mile-long sheet of paper. So you'd have to use a telephone pole to cover up the break between the first background and the duplicate field. But finally, with the Road-runners, say, this type of perspective didn't seem to count. We dropped it, since it just didn't seem necessary. The pans were so damned fast that the audience could never look at them too closely; other times, you'd get your speed and perspective effects just by having a diminishing body in space. You see, if we couldn't achieve the idea of intense speed through the character drawings, there didn't seem to be much point in using added mechanical means.

Q: In the later cartoons, you seem to use completely "slanted-over" backgrounds to accent the speed of the character.

A: Well, that was Maurice Noble's idea. And he'd always take this opportunity to use a lot of interesting shapes—abstract curves and things of this sort, which gave a sort of depth feeling to it. But for the most part, we were trying to avoid forced or Italian perspective, which you'd establish by having the various buttes get progressively smaller into the background. Except for the road itself, we used almost none of this forced perspective. The buttes and desert landscape backgrounds were flattened out, more Japanese.

Donald Graham, the dean of all art teachers for cartoonists, always said that cartoons were unique in the way they established space by movement. And he said that the Road Runner series was the only case that he knew in which a form moved in "pure" space, where the space was achieved *entirely* by the form moving it.

Q: That's certainly evident when you get those overhead viewpoints of the Coyote falling off a cliff. He falls straightaway from the camera,

isolated against a completely blank background, diminishing, then disappearing for a time until—poof!—he's been reduced to a puff of dust on the ground below. Are there any antecedents to that? In *Super Rabbit* [1943], Bugs Bunny is flying along and is about to "recharge his batteries," but then accidentally loses all his fortified, super-vitamized carrots, and he falls to earth at that point—a beautifully animated fall. In style and camera angle, it seems to anticipate the Coyote's later falls.
A: That was animated by Ken Harris, and it was very similar to all the Coyote's later falls. Ken added that "loose-limbed" feeling to the action.

Q: In one case you used the same background in two cartoons: the "Electric Eye" that was in both *Duck Dodgers in the 24½ Century* [1953] and *Rocket Squad* [1956].
A: Yes, that giant mechanical bloodshot eyeball suspended from the ceiling. I liked the shape of it, and it went so fast that I thought it would be fun to use it again. It was designed by Maurice Noble. He created most of the space-age gadgetry for those films. Maurice also invented that *Rocket Squad* "Evaporator": the character would step into a weird test-tube glass contraption and ZAP! disappear and rematerialize somewhere else. In that case, Maurice worked ahead of me on the story and originated that contraption.

Q: There is always a very marked contrast between foreground and background in your cartoons. Would you say that you generally gave more leeway to your background artists than other directors might?
A: Yeah, I did—you see, what I did was draft a very rough plan, just to show the layout man what I wanted. Now, if I put in a doorway, say, all I wanted was room for the character to exit; I didn't care what the doorway looked like beyond that. Maurice would take my layouts—let's say there'd be ten layouts for the scene—then he'd make a sort of *mise-en-scene* that defines the limits of the character action. He'd find the layout that goes the furthest to the right, the one that goes the furthest to the left, the deepest one, the closest one, and generally planned where most of the action would have to fall. He'd take all these separate layouts and put them all in one drawing, and then design the background around it. He'd also take into consideration what was happening in the story—which very few background men ever do. Generally speaking, the foreground characters were all mine, but Maurice would also often design background characters that were visually very strong,

like those Baroque-looking French bystanders in the later Pepé le Pew cartoons.

Now, in the Road Runner series, we almost never used color for emphasis. But in a more overtly experimental picture like *From A to ZZZZ* [1954], we had a scene in a boxing ring—we flashed to a completely red background at the punch, which then quickly diminished. There was a lot of high contrast stuff in that cartoon. But the most outstanding example of Maurice's acheiving mood with his backgrounds was *What's Opera, Doc?* [1957].

Of all the people I've worked with, Maurice was probably the most influential. Maurice was a brilliant designer, but very often people give Phil DeGuard credit for design, since the credit roster would say "Backgrounds by Phil DeGuard." Phil was an excellent follow-up man, certainly, and he's a fine painter, but he bears the same relationship to the layout man, in preparing a picture, that a contractor does to an architect in constructing a building.

Q: What about John McGrew's style and approach, as compared with Noble's?
A: John McGrew didn't really have a style; he was experimenting all the time. Maurice *does* have a style. John McGrew, you might say, was more of an intellectual. You could be intellectual, and get away with it— but if you're solely intellectual as a director, you weren't going to get away with it. The result was, however, that he goosed me into thinking that it might be worthwhile to try some different things with back-grounds and so forth. And later on, I would find this kind of thing very useful, in that often it would make your gag work, and sometimes you wouldn't even know why. Like that little abstract background at the end of *Duck Amuck*, with the sharply angled lines going off.

Q: There's a similar design in *The Aristo-Cat* [1943], where abstract lin-ear shapes serve as an expression of the character's mood—an almost laughably superabundant expression. This silly patrician cat is helpless when his butler walks out, so the cat goes running terrified through the mansion, screaming out "Meadows!" in a series of takes, each one with a new wallpaper design in the background, directly reflecting the cat's feelings.
A: That was McGrew. He was deeply interested in the emotional effects you could get from those jagged red and white lines in the wallpaper.

It's quite jarring. So, even though we were working with just a silly little cat, we wanted it to appear as though he were really in a state of panic.

Q: I love the monumental prelude of *Caveman Inki* [1950], your last cartoon with Inki and the Mynah Bird. It's crazy how the Mynah Bird, a tiny creature, is associated with mountains crumbling, the earth shaking, natural catastrophes that terrified all the larger animals.
A: Oh, they weren't terrified of the Mynah Bird, but they were terrified of the natural condition that arose from the Mynah Bird's appearance. The mountain split right in half, remember? Everyone expects something pretty tremendous, and then this little thing comes out.

Q: Isn't this a recurrent theme? You frequently show these violent contrasts between very small characters and their environments. It's visible in your early *Tom Thumb in Trouble* [1940], which features little Tom taking a bath in his father's cupped hands. It's also operative in your early Porky cartoons—*Porky's Ant* and *Porky's Midnight Matinee* [both 1941]—that co-star an African pygmy ant. Then in *To Itch His Own* [1958], years later, there's your flea, the Mighty Angelo, who wants to settle down on some nice quiet dog in the country. A lot of directors have used size deformation, but differently. Clampett's tiny characters are often designed to convey smallness and cuteness, with heads and rumps large in proportion to the rest of their bodies. Similarly, when Avery magnifies his characters in *King-Size Canary* [1947], their shapes change to convey largeness—their stomachs distend grotesquely out of proportion. But when you shrink or enlarge a character, their anatomies retain their original proportions. It's less like a biological nightmare and more like a sort of absurd displacement. Your pugnacious flea, the Mighty Angelo, looks like a perfectly proportioned circus he-man.
A: As a sort of lay physicist, I've always been fascinated by the peculiar perfection of tiny things. When I was a kid, there was a general assumption that things which were very small were imperfect. Large houses were fine, while a grain of sand was nothing. But the more I became acquainted with this, by reading Sir James Jeans and Isaac Asimov and other popularizers of science, the more I realized that it wasn't a matter of perfection or imperfection. Long after that, I finally got along to the DNA molecule. The most perfect thing and the most misunderstood thing is the DNA molecule. And then, on the other hand, you have infinities that no one can possibly understand either.

So you begin to wonder if there isn't some kind of big loop that hooks them together—perfection/imperfection, small size/large size, microcosm/macrocosm. Each "opposite" is really the same thing looked at from a different viewpoint. If I'd been a physicist, I would probably have hooked into it in another way; or if I had been a novelist, I probably would have tried to write something like O'Brien's *The Diamond Lens,* which was preoccupied with the same idea. I *did* read it when I was young, and it probably had something to do with my later work. At the time, the idea of a story like that seemed ridiculous. But now we know it's far from ridiculous. *Horton Hears a Who* [1971] was a good example of a microcosm/macrocosm relationship, and it also contained the "person's-a-person-no-matter-how-small" idea, which, I agree, is also represented in things like *Porky's Ant.*

Q: It's interesting how long you've kept this concern, and how images from your earlier films spring up again in the later ones, in altered ways. Your early black-and-white *Joe Glow the Firefly* [1941] has a firefly scooting around the face of a sleeping camper, walking the part in the guy's hair; and the camper's mouth, twitching in sleep, creates a major earthquake for Joe. Years later, you do this again in *Beanstalk Bunny* [1955] with the same kind of immense close-ups on a human head, as Bugs and Daffy are running around the Giant Elmer Fudd's ears, nose, and mouth. It's a weird, almost Swiftian image.
A: The Swiftian connection is exactly right, because I remember those descriptions of enormous pores and things that Gulliver saw; the enormous size of the hairs, and how gross it was when he was on a woman's breast.

Q: The humor of these change-of-scale effects seems to be based on taking a character who's tailor-made for largeness, whose very drawing style and body-structure suggests largeness, and shrinking it—like the tiny bulldog in your late Tom and Jerry cartoon *The Cat's Me-Ouch* [1965] who had those wild flashing teeth that tore through all the other characters.
A: Yeah, that little piranha dog! He was really a shrunken version of the big bull-dog, Marc Antony.

Q: Or, most especially, your miniature elephant who "terrorizes a large metropolis" in *Punch Trunk* [1954].

A: That had to be a real elephant; it couldn't even be a cartoon elephant. It wouldn't have worked at all unless it was a real elephant. You had to establish it as a perfect miniature—and the people who see it as real people—or else their response wouldn't count. If we had used an anthropomorphized elephant, there wouldn't have been any shock value to it, and you wouldn't have believed it.

Q: Not all the people who see the elephant are surprised by it, though.
A: No, but that's the idea. Some people live with fantasy every day of their lives. The drunk, you remember, staggers out, sees the elephant, and takes it calmly—just looks at his watch and says, "You're late!" The little girl who lives in the penthouse accepts it as a new toy, while the people who trade on "sanity"—such as the parents of the little girl or, later on, the psychiatrist—are terrified.

Q: Technically, the movements of the elephant are so fluid. It's as if you were using the same number of drawings that you would if you were animating a large elephant.
A: Yes—in fact, I would say we used *more* drawings. We used a real elephant cry on the soundtrack, too. The same thing, in a different area, is the bull in *Bully for Bugs*. The bull had to be believable as a bull: he had to present the same terror and probability of injury to Bugs as he would to you. And that's why I showed that first man facing the bull, the Juan Belmonte caricature, before Bugs even got into the story—if *he's* afraid of the bull, well, poor Bugs. But that's the trick, I think, if you're going to do miniaturization: you've got to make your audience really believe that such a thing is possible. Of course if you'd ask Eddie Seltzer, our producer, he'd say, "You should use *fewer* drawings for a god-damn little elephant!"

Q: The same thing seems to work, in reverse, with that little puppy you had in *Terrier Stricken* and *No Barking* [1954]. His motions and anatomy are tailor-made to convey smallness and friskiness. And yet, with the same type of funny perverseness, you took *that* character, in the 3-D cartoon *Lumber Jack-Rabbit* [1954], and made him into a giant—casting him as Paul Bunyan's dog.
A: Right, his movements are frisky. When you look at a puppy, at the time he first stops being an infant and becomes what you'd call an

adolescent puppy, well, his movements *are* very quick. They stand there posed, ready for action, looking at you and trying to provoke you—so their movements are very cleancut and sharp.

Q: I'd like to talk about your attitude toward Disney. Not only the person of course, but all the associations one has with the Disney name. In your cartoons Disney seems to be a simultaneous inspiration and exasperation.
A: Well, I know I exasperated him a lot. You see, the *Three Little Pigs* established the whole idea of character animation. Before that, there wasn't such a thing. The cartoon with the grasshopper and the ant, and others they did in the thirties were the progenitors of the whole idea of character animation. And Bugs Bunny, of course, is finally the offspring of Max Hare from Disney's *Tortoise and the Hare*—that was the first pure speed cartoon as well.

Q: It certainly seemed to influence you a great deal.
A: And it's still pretty hard to beat. And *Band Concert* [1935] was superb, but it wasn't quite as strong a development as *Three Little Pigs*. The three pigs looked alike, but had completely different personalities. You might say that they were the beginnings of the Seven Dwarfs, who all looked similar but all had different personalities.

Q: *The Band Concert* expresses character conflict in terms of musical conflict in the same way that your *Long-Haired Hare* [1948] does. Donald plays "Turkey in the Straw" on his fife, interfering with Mickey, who's trying to conduct the *William Tell* Overture. You have Bugs Bunny strumming a banjo, and belting "What Do They Do on a Rainy Night in Rio?," while your opera-singer, Giovanni Jones, is trying to sing an aria.
A: I don't know if there was any conscious relation to the Disney picture, but in general you'd have to say that in terms of the tools supplied to those who followed him, Disney was to animation what Griffith was to live action. Almost all the tools were discovered at Disney's; they were the only ones who had the money, and who could and did take the time to experiment. Donald Graham gave lectures to future animators at Disney's. There was one on distant action and one on secondary action—secondary action being those instances when a character comes to a sudden stop and his hair moves out on its own, without the volition of the character. A primary action is when you

move your head, and a secondary action is what happens to your hairset.

Q: That's certainly very evident in *Fantasia*.

A: In "The Sorceror's Apprentice" sequence there was a tremendous amount of secondary action because Mickey was fitted in such a big costume that when he stopped the suit would swirl around him. Of course, I used this a lot in the Road Runner series as the bird stops and the dust continues to go by.

Q: Despite the obvious influences that Disney has had on your cartoons, many of them seem to be satires or parodies of Disney.

A: Right. Well, Disney himself never went in for satire. I don't think he understood it very well. *What's Opera, Doc?* can be looked upon as a satire of *Fantasia*. I never made a cartoon that didn't contain some flick-of-the-wrist at the establishment of the day; the Disney people seldom did that, of course.

Q: *Broomstick Bunny* [1956] changes the concept into who's the ugliest one of all instead of who's the fairest one of all, à la *Snow White*.

A: The witch in *Broomstick Bunny* was so afraid of getting pretty, and she tried to get rid of Bugs's ugliness.

Q: It has a great deal of abstract variation on Bugs's usual character shape. At the end he looks like a stick with a head stuck on top, and the head is almost nothing but eyes as Bugs makes that ultimate pathetic expression.

A: My characters often used the exaggerated "soulful eyes" with the gooey, oversized centers—the "old soulful eyes routine"—to get themselves out of a jam. I think I first used that in a Charlie Dog cartoon, *Little Orphan Airedale* [1947].

Q: I'd like to talk about the rules and disciplines you applied to individual series. You said in *Psychology Today* that the more rules you applied to the Road Runner series, for instance, the funnier the films were.

A: Well, if you sit down to paint a picture, and you spread out on a table every color you can buy in a paint store, you'll find it very difficult to select *the* color that will be of any use to you. But if you take arbitrarily, say, yellow or green or a particular shade of blue, you can paint a pretty good picture—because the fact of painting a picture depends more on you and not so much on the tools available. You can paint a very good picture of a green meadow without any green paint. You might substitute white for green and then surround it with brown, using colors very sparingly. It will still look springlike.

Everyone I've ever respected always used restricted tools. The greatest comedians were the ones who wore the simplest costumes and worked in prescribed areas—such as Chaplin. So it just became evident after a while that the narrower the discipline in the Road Runner series— for instance, that there was no dialogue, that the Road Runner wouldn't hurt the Coyote, and that the Coyote would be victimized by his own ineptitude—the better it got.

Q: Could you compare the Road Runner series with the Tom and Jerry series which you took over in 1964? They seem similar enough that there might be some overlap in concept.
A: I wasn't really at home with the Tom and Jerry characters. Hanna-Barbara handled those characters beautifully, much better than I did. Jerry was a much more charming character in their best cartoons than I could ever make him, simply because I could never understand him. And I couldn't really draw Tom very well; I had to turn him into a different cat really. So I purposely said, "The hell with him." And I tried to keep Jerry attractive personally, more like the Road Runner, in that he never really hurt Tom in my version. Bill and Joe's Jerry would sometimes cut Tom into slices. It became sort of half-assed with my Tom becoming a combination of the Coyote and the original Tom. It's difficult to work with someone else's characters.

Q: You've used the same Coyote character in many different ways— which way do you think he operates best?
A: The Coyote really represents three different characters: he's one character in the Wolf and Sheepdog series . . .

Q: His name's Ralph, Ralph Wolf, and as he and the sheepdog pass each other on the way to work, they punch in together at the timeclock . . .
A: And they say, "Hello, Ralph," "Hello, Sam." So in the Sheepdog series he's one character, when he's working with Bugs he's a completely different character, and when he's working with the Road Runner he's a completely different character. He *looks* the same, I admit. I don't know, I liked the shape of him. It's like the same actor playing three different parts in live action films.

Q: Of course, there are elements of personality that overlap from one series to another. The Coyote who works with Bugs Bunny *is* different because he has a voice and dialogue, but he's like the Coyote who chases the Road Runner in his obsession with his own machinations. In *Operation: Rabbit* [1954], the Coyote draws up various inventions at a draftsman's table—"Plan One: Pressure Cooker; Plan Two: Explosive Decoy; Plan Three: Flying Saucer." He's obviously hung up with himself in a smug, self-congratulatory kind of way.

A: The last scene in that was one of my all-time favorite gags. The Coyote is in the munitions shed, filling up Bugs's carrots with nitroglycerin, complimenting himself on his idea, while behind him, through the window in the background, you see the train coming toward him. But the Coyote doesn't pay any attention; he just continues screwing the carrot-tops back in place, and thinks he's so smart, saying to himself, "'Wile E. Coyote: Super-Genius.' I like the way that rolls out—'Wile E. Coyote: Super-Genius.'" This Coyote's a type of very shabby egotist, because he has that exaggerated self-confidence that he refuses to lose.

Q: But isn't this trait carried over from the Coyote in the Road Runner series, that same love for his own schemes and devices?

A: Oh yeah, but the whole thing is changed. In the films with the Coyote and the Road Runner, the entire situation is more desperate. The Coyote here isn't merely an egotist; he's almost possessed; he's a fanatic. And now I realize, it was only in the earlier cartoons that I made much of a point about the Coyote wanting to eat the Road Runner. Later on, even that didn't seem to matter any more, and the Coyote's motivation became even more generalized: all he wanted to do was get him, or something, because his dignity was shot.

Q: And eventually, in the last of the series, even the Road Runner bird himself seems superfluous to the series. For example, he hardly makes an appearance in *To Beep or Not to Beep* [1964], as the Coyote spends more than half of the film trying to operate one single catapult, an instrument which was originally *intended* to get the bird.

A: Right—the catapult itself achieves a sort of perverseness, a personality of its own.

Q: There's a general difference between the "spot-gag" cartoons and the narrative cartoons.

A: The difference is in the relationship of timing, pacing, and hitting the proper length for the film without going over the budget. If a spot-gag film was too long, you could just lift out a gag and save if for the next film.

Q: But the Road Runner films, though spot-gag films, are definitely *structured* works. They don't have a narrative structure, but they're far more than strings of unrelated gags.

A: I evolved a kind of rhythm to them, which sometimes had to do with planting a gag which reappears in a "poster ending"—in *Zoom and Bored*, for example. I'd have three or four of the Road Runner's nerve-wracking "beep-beeps" at the opening, in rapid succession to prepare the audience for more. But by the end of the film the Coyote, poor bastard, was so shaken that I didn't have the heart to let the Road Runner send him off the cliff. So when the Road Runner comes up behind the Coyote, he holds up a sign saying "I DON'T HAVE THE HEART." Then sometimes, in other Road Runner films, I'd use a different kind of running gag, a cumulative gag, like the dynamite cartoon . . .

Q: You mean *Lickety Splat* [1961]? That one has the Coyote in a balloon, toward the beginning, unloosing these hundreds of flying dart-shaped dynamite sticks . . .

A: Yeah, then at the end of every scene that followed afterward, one of the little darts, left over from this first gag, would come in and explode. Or sometimes I'd go through a number of very simple visual jokes, fast-like, saving a very long gag for the end, like when the Coyote swallows the Earthquake Pills in *Hopalong Casualty*. But there is a structure. It isn't, as it may appear in the beginning, a series of spot-gags without relationship to one another. I'd alternate, say, a gag which would let the audience in on what was going to happen, where the surprise might be in *how* it would happen, with a scene that would get a laugh from something that the audience couldn't have the remotest idea would happen.

Q: Explosions seem to be very important to you. There is a use of explosions in your work, more so than in the work of other animators, that releases a lot of the tension which results from the extreme pacing.

A: That's probably true—I got to a point where I needed something to release all this tension. But also, to me, an explosion is best used not as a dramatic device in itself but as a point or an idea in the comic sequence.

An example is the cartoon where the Coyote built a fantastic, long trough up the side of the mountain [*Zoom and Bored*]. You didn't know what he was going to do with it, but the camera panned up and you saw all the work he put into it and how delicately the trough was balanced on the rocks. By the time the camera finally got to the top and the Coyote lit the fuse to the dynamite, it wasn't even proper to let the fuse burn down. The second the Coyote lit the match, the whole thing exploded. BOOM!! Immediately. The humor is not in the explosion at all, but in the fact that the guy obviously worked for hours and hours and weeks and weeks on the damn trough.

A. C. Gamer, who did some of the best special effects we had, concocted a big, beautiful explosion with curlicues and stars splaying out. It was a marvelous thing, and it was based on a discovery we made around the time of *Draft Horse*: that there were mechanics to an explosion we hadn't known about. Before, we always supposed that an explosion would go out fast, so we'd make a small drawing, and then a bigger one, and then a bigger one, taking maybe three frames to spread out. Well, when you think about it, you realize that it couldn't conceivably be that way, because each frame was one-twenty-fourth of a second. This meant that it would take three-twenty-fourths of a second to get the full effect, which was far too much time. So, by studying some live-action explosions, we discovered that the brightest frame was the very first one. That became evident to everyone later, of course, with the documentary footage on atomic bomb explosions, which actually went all white at first, and then faded down a little bit until you began to see the mushroom. So what we would do was to take the explosion to its furthest point at the first frame and then take a few frames to diminish. I later applied that principle to more minor, less violent actions: if someone simply got socked in the jaw, the most extreme drawing would be the first one, and then we'd diminish it.

Q: I'd like to know more about the less known but very remarkable Wolf and Sheepdog series.
A: I got the idea for that series at about the same time I made a one-shot film with Mike Maltese called *Go Fly a Kit* [1957]. There were these large-scale arguments going on, as to which was the more important conditioning factor: environment or heredity. Well, I would guess that both of them are important, and nobody really knows. But it got to the point where it was so idiotic—the young people were rearing

their children either with *all* environment or *all* heredity in mind. I felt that, OK, it's absurd, so let's make it really absurd and go on the supposition that an adopted cat raised by an eagle would obviously be able to fly.

The same thing would hold true for the Wolf and Sheepdog series, I thought. Just as human beings go to work, punch their cards down, and become at that point, say, bus drivers—a bus driver isn't a bus driver on his way to work, he's only a bus driver then he gets in the bus. And I thought, if that's true of human beings, why can't it be true of animals? A snake isn't a snake until he goes and punches in in the morning. And a wolf and sheepdog could be very good friends, real buddies, up to the point that they punch in, the factory whistle blows, and they do what they're being paid to do.

Q: Once you mentioned that the Road Runner series began as a satire on the usual kind of character-conflict in cartoons, the Coyote being a purely intellectual and motivated character, while the Road Runner bird is completely unmotivated, a natural or nearly supernatural character. You have a similar classic dichotomy here, with the Wolf and Sheepdog. And then there's the fact that the Wolf and Sheepdog are antagonists only after the whistle blows, which seems to indicate a satirization of typical cartoon character clashes.
A: It may have been an underlying thing. Although in this case, you have one person with the object of protecting the sheep, and this is the major difference in the series. You have the Wolf who wants to gather up the sheep, and the Sheepdog who wants to keep the sheep together. This is quite a different thing from protecting yourself, which is the con-cept that the Road Runner series dealt with. To me, it's a more sympa-thetic situation, and therefore the means of protection could be a little more dramatic, a little stronger. And visually, come to think of it, the Sheepdog is the exact opposite of the Road Runner bird, who is very fast, while in this case the dog, who takes the same part, doesn't move at all.

Q: He just appears on the cut, from no-where.
A: Yes, with an almost magical quality.

Q: And in this series, the Sheepdog actively clobbers the Wolf all the time—it can get pretty severe. In *Steal Wool* [1957], for example, the Wolf is squished pancake-flat and gets punched in the nose, leaving his snout accordian-crinkled.

A: Maybe the fact that there was little action otherwise indicated that there should be stronger pieces of dramatic business than there would ever be in the Road Runner-Coyote cycle, where you always have plenty of action, even when nothing's really happening. A lot of my explanations are dependent on the stylistic problems that I was trying to solve at the time.

Q: I find these cartoons very moving. They always suggested to me a kind of duplicity involved in jobs, an alienation-from-self, the necessary compromises that people must make in certain jobs—that sort of assumption of a disguise within a disguise. The climax of this occurs in *Sheep in the Deep* [1962], where you pictorialized first a wolf in sheep's clothing, which turned out to be a sheepdog in wolf's clothing, which turned out to be a sheep in sheepdog's clothing, and so forth.

A: Yes, I enjoyed that. It just kept going forever. But that really is always true, and in a way, I suppose, it's a sort of satire on the idea that working people experience a great difference between life as it is socially and as it is when you get to work. For instance, if two people walk into a room and one sits down behind a desk, the one person becomes the power and the other person becomes the subject of that power.

Q: This relationship is completely arbitrary—and how much did they change over the years? Not much, except that you eventually added a lunch-break for the warring characters.

A: That's right. The beginning and the end of the cartoons remained the same, but employee conditions improved in the interim.

Q: How do you see Porky in relation to the other characters?

A: Porky began as a child, and grew up along the way. But to decide what the disciplines were with the Porky character is impossible. He tended to change with each series he appeared in. He was kind of square, I suppose; but you always felt, in a movie like *Duck Dodgers in the 24½ Century*, that he had his tongue in his cheek. There was always some sly awareness. For instance in *Duck Dodgers*. Daffy is so caught up in his crusade—his assignment to find a supply of Aludium Phosdex, the shaving-cream atom—that by the end, he has succeeded only in obliterating the entire alien planet and goes on to claim the remaining crumbling mound in the name of Earth. Then we pan down to Porky, hanging off the edge of the thing and saying, "B-b-b-b-big deal!"

Q: More often than not, you've used Porky as supporting-player rather than star. He's an "eager young space cadet" to Daffy's "Duck Dodgers." In the Westerns, he's even subtitled a "Comedy Relief" to Daffy's "Western-type Hero," with little absurdist labels resembling the Latinate captions you always use for the Road Runner and Coyote.

A: I thought Porky was at his best as the Fat Friar in *Robin Hood Daffy* [1958]. I did hundreds of layouts on that—I got so infatuated with that fat-assed character. That whole picture I enjoyed very much.

Q: And it's very well designed. You once told me that you knew Eugene Pallette.

A: Oh, yes, Pallette was a good friend of mine—he used to stay and live with us all the time. Of course we'd also see Fairbanks occasionally, and the mannerisms of these people would affect you; they were such strong personalities. I guess that helps, unconsciously. Actors like Flynn were really holdovers from that earlier era. Flynn wasn't quite an original. Daffy was really parodying Fairbanks there, more than Flynn. Daffy's swashbuckling poses were exaggerations of the way that Fairbanks moved. His body had strong, dramatic actions to it.

Q: Pallette is very strongly evoked as Porky falls over laughing at Daffy's buffoonery, out of control, with that great animation of his jelly-like stomach bounding, thumping up and down.

A: And Daffy says, disgustedly, "How jolly can you get?" That stomach *was* good. Abe Levitow animated that. I'd say that that was his first really good piece of animation.

Q: I'm very fond of the horror-show-type series with Porky and Sylvester, where the character construction seems to be one of Sylvester's paranoia versus Porky Pig's complacency. My favorite is the second, *Claws for Alarm* [1955], where Sylvester is terrorized by these rascally mice armed with axes, chopping blocks, nooses, guillotines, but Porky remains entirely unaware and, through blindness or dumb luck, always emerges unharmed.

A: There you have a very logical Porky—he's not a dope, but he's certainly very naive in the sense that he doesn't see what's happening. The cat is determined to protect him and victimizes himself in the process. You might say that this is a variation of the "singing frog" situation, in that whatever happens, there's no evidence of it. This one guy had the privilege, or the curse, of seeing the singing frog, but when other people looked at it, it stopped doing its song-and-dance.

In *Claws for Alarm*—as well as in the first in this series, *Scaredy Cat* [1948]—this poor cat is trying to save Porky's life all the time, but he always appears to be taking Porky's life, poor devil. The lights go on, and there's Sylvester, caught in the midst of a protective act, but seeming to be the guilty party, holding the knife or razor blade to Porky's throat, while the guilty mice are hidden somewhere. Somehow the funniest thing is that Porky isn't even alarmed by this—he doesn't believe Sylvester has the courage to do it. He sees Sylvester holding the razor, but he doesn't really take it seriously. He just says, "You psychopathical pussyca—you psychopa—you manic-depressive cat, you." Porky's voice always drops at the end, I don't know why, so when you say "you cat, you," that little "you" at the end drops down about three notes.

Q: In *Jumpin' Jupiter*, the last of the series, Porky and Sylvester are threatened by a fantastic Martian: a Dr. Suess-like bird, consisting entirely of smooth, curved lines. There's another Martian, in *Duck Dodgers*, with a Roman Legion-type helmet, tennis shoes, and just a black circle for a head—no facial features at all except two large oval eyes.
A: That was one of the first times I discovered you could get on easily enough without mouth action. You can convince people that the little Martian is speaking simply through the way he moves, and with that funny, meek Richard Haydn kind of voice—innocent, harmless, and saying things like "I'm going to blow up the Earth, as it obstructs my view of Venus."

Q: It was a Porky cartoon that introduced Charlie Dog, that very aggressive mutt who feels that he has to ingratiate himself to a master. He continually finds unwilling masters, but keeps going to great lengths to find a home. In one cartoon, *Doggone South* [1950], he tries to befriend a plantation owner and so adopts a Southern accent, eats chitterlings and cornpone, the whole works. In *Little Orphan Airedale*, he actually fakes pregnancy to win over a master, even though the dog's name is Charlie.
A: Right. Porky finds out the dog is male, throws him out, then Charlie pops right in again to testify: "Well, there *was* such a case in Venezuela." I loved that line. Then there's the one that takes place in Italy, where Charlie tries to break into a pizza parlor, trumping up an Italian dialect.

Yes, I always liked that dog, that eager dog. He's kind of a chauvinist dog, or a salesman dog—always trying to sell himself, advertise himself. But that's really what dogs are. They'll butter you up, lick your foot, die on your grave.

Q: What would you say the basic discipline is in the Pepé Le Pew series?
A: That was miscegenation, obviously. After all, what's a mule but a hunk of miscegenation? This is involuntary miscegenation, which is a slightly different thing. Pepé thought the girl was a female skunk while in reality she was a female cat, and she could never understand why she was being followed, you see. I mean, from her viewpoint, it was miscegenation, while from his viewpoint, it certainly wasn't.

The other thing is that Pepé always represented the other side of my personality, because he represented what I *wanted* to be, and what I think every man would like to be: irresistible, at least in one's own eyes. You don't have to be irresistible in women's eyes if you *think* you are. As for Pepé, he got plenty, you might say. But it never occurred to him that he had offended anyone. He was never fazed, under any circumstances.

In the first cartoon [*For Scent-imental Reasons*, 1949], there was a pantomime sequence where the girl is hiding inside a glass case and Pepé is outside, and she is saying [imitates female cat's pantomime of disgust, holding hand to nose] and he goes [imitates Pepé's soundless, shocked/upset reaction]. So he pulls out a gun and walks off, the cat quickly running out, feeling bad about this presumable suicide. It turns out that Pepé is completely all right, of course, wasn't the slightest bit deterred. He just takes the girl in his arms again, saying, "Fortunately for you, I meesed." It's that complete self-assurance. With the Coyote of the Road Runner series, I understood him because he made so many mechanical mistakes, which is natural for anybody, particularly for me. But Pepé was the super character, a super sex-job, and he knew it. And he never gave up.

Q: Where do you suppose the audience identification goes in those cartoons? Toward Pepé or toward the female cat?
A: I've never been able to discover that, because all the girls I've ever known adore the Pepé character as a sex-object, you might say—he was really irresistible.

One of my favorites was *Wild Over You* [1953], because there Pepé's mistaken desire was this enormous wildcat, and the situation furnished some good remarks—"Acres and acres of her, and she's mine, all mine." I liked the end-line. The wildcat is ferociously fighting Pepé off in a balloon floating away into the distance, and she's clawing the hell out of him. You can't quite tell what was going on, just a big mess, a big brawl in the distance, and then we cut back to a close-up of Pepé, looking up at the viewer and saying, "Eef you haff not tried eet, do not knock eet."

Q: At times, Pepé Le Pew is pretty overt, as far as sex goes.
A: Well, he's overt, but that's an honest love for a woman . . . I can't see anything wrong with that.

Q: Something one can respect, something one can understand.
A: That's what I thought, anyway. The entire cat-mouse cartoon cycle, the chase cycle, might be called "oral" today. But in those days, it was a matter of eating somebody, like a cat eating a mouse. Nourishment. Sustenance. Survival. Today, if you say that a character is going to eat somebody—well, it has a different meaning. But the skunk Pepé was unique in chase cartoons of the period in the sense that he was after the cat, well, to screw her, I suppose. He says, "She theenks by playing hard-to-get she can make herself more attractive to me—*how right she eez!*" And "Not, every man would put up with thees—lucky for her, I am not any man."

Q: Are all his feminine foils cats instead of other skunks?
A: They had to be. Another skunk wouldn't make any sense, because the other skunk would go for him, so where's the comedy? So there always had to be a ploy of getting a white stripe accidentally down a cat's back, which, I can tell you, got a little tiresome trying to figure out. It was strange since the audience never objected to the implausibility of having it happen again and again, film after film.

Q: It's very graceful in *Cats-Bah* [1955], where the guy is painting the hull of a ship, and a lady passenger comes down the gangplank with her pet cat on a leash, and some of the paint sloshes on the cat. It's also the film where the seduction story is structured with an "As Time Goes By" *Casablanca*-like flashback. But why, if Pépe is irresistible to other skunks, would a cat resist him?

A: Because he *smells* bad! When I was a kid, I worked on a boat that carried creosol piling, and I don't know if you've ever been close to creosol piling, but it has a terribly strong smell. But strangely enough, in about four or five days, you forget, and everything resumes its normal smells again, except that everywhere *you* go, you notice the people reeling—*you* smell. As far as Pepé was concerned, it really came down to that simple level of misunderstanding. Do you know what he once said? In one film he daintily sniffs his wrist and says, "Do I offend?"

Q: Pepé's one moment of self-awareness.

In *One Froggy Evening*, much of the humor seems to be derived from a sharp break between anthropomorphized movement and natural animal movement.

A: It was anthropomorphic when the frog was singing and dancing and completely natural otherwise.

Q: Did you actually use a frog as a model for that?

A: I studied a frog, but I didn't actually get a real frog as I did with the squirrel in *Much Ado about Nutting*. I was more interested in the action; I knew I could draw it. It was obvious, the way the frog had to move, from the way he was drawn.

The trick was that the audience would never hear anything but the frog's singing voice. The rest is entirely pantomime. There are a lot of ways of doing this, and they all seem obvious once you look at them— putting the characters behind the plate glass window in the theatrical agency, for instance. There the timing had to work interestingly, because when the protagonist went back to get the theatrical agent, once the frog had started singing the rag, we kept the music going, but you couldn't hear the voice. The phrasing works out so that when the frog starts to sing, his owner runs back inside in a hurried fashion, trying to tell the agent what's happening. Subconsciously, the audience knows what he's telling him even though there are no words spoken, because the music is still being carried over. Then you cut back to the frog; as the frog is finishing the song (" . . . that lov-ing rag!"), PLOP!! the door opens, a guy points, the frog looks up, croaks, and the theatrical agent gives that tiny look at the audience which I often use—it's one of my favorite gags. Then you cut to the street, and the frog and his owner are thrown out. By the way, did you know that Mike Maltese and I wrote "The Michigan Rag"? We needed a ragtime piece, so we wrote one.

Q: The whole cartoon seems to be in a parable structure. It's like an excessive punishment for one man's greed—for his desire to exploit the discovery of the singing frog and make millions.

A: That's right, the guy wants to join the establishment, enjoy the fruits of the establishment. And that was also one of the first of my continuing, or cyclical, cartoons, like *Horton Hears a Who*, the endings of which imply that what's happened will happen again and again in the future.

Q: That certainly existed in cartoons like *I Was a Teenage Thumb* [1963], which ends with the narrator saying " . . . and he had a son the size of his thumb, etc."

A: Getting back to *One Froggy Evening*, it would have been easy to keep on using the Lubitsch trick, implying the action going on behind closed doors or barricades. I wanted to see if I could find other ways of conveying the same thought—as when the frog is singing in the park, and the cop is behind the wall. The cop can hear the frog. In this case, it's simply that the cop's eyes are behind the wall; by seeing the top of his head you know that he's a cop. The cop's activities are determined by the actions of his hat. And then there's the terrible time that the owner of the frog has in the theater: first getting the people in there, then having the rope to the curtain break. You have to feel sorry for the guy; he's stuck with that frog, and somehow the only place he can get rid of it is back where he got it—back in the cornerstone of another building. It was really an exemplification of frustration, and it continued.

Q: Getting back to the idea of individual disciplines for characters, what about Bugs Bunny?

A: Well, I always underwrote the idea of Bugs never being a heckler—he's minding his own business, and then somebody comes along and tries to disturb him, hurt him, destroy him. But when he fights back, he becomes an anarchist, rather like Groucho Marx.

Q: It takes a butt from a bull to antagonize him in *Bully for Bugs*, as Bugs goes sailing over the arena declaring, "Of course, you know, this means war!"

A: That's the old Groucho Marx line, and it certainly became basic to Bugs's character. A cross between Harpo and Groucho is what he'd become at that point: he had the intellect of Groucho combined with the zaniness and oddity of Harpo, which I never understood—I'm sure

Harpo himself never understood it. In other words, Bugs's behavior would often surprise himself. He never knew what he was going to do next. Another important rule was that we always started him out in an environment natural for a rabbit.

Q: With or without banjo, *a la Long-Haired Hare?*
A: Well, that was a slight exception—but he did have his feet in his rabbit-hole and he was out in the woods, remember? Sitting there playing the banjo the way *any* rabbit would under the same circumstances. And that, to me, was always very important. Next came the provocation, and the provocation is always based upon a guy who is minding his own business.

Q: In *Long-Haired Hare's* musical language, Bugs Bunny, on the one side, seems to represent the popular, singing pop songs or folk songs, while the opera-singer, on the other side, represents the classical, or in this case, the pretentious. Where did you find the voice for the opera basso?
A: We found a young singer with a terribly strong voice. And remember Bugs's revenge on the opera-singer? The singer's performing at the Hollywood Bowl and Bugs is perched on top of it. Bugs tests the Bowl first, saying, "Hmmm . . . acoustically poi-fect!" Then he causes the whole thing to vibrate, bouncing the singer down below. We had to do something similar to our actual singer. We told him, "We're not going to hurt you, but something may happen to you while you're singing. Whatever happens, keep singing." So while he was recording at the microphone, we snuck up behind him, grabbed him and shook him. His voice did just what you hear on the soundtrack.

Q: I think *Super Rabbit* holds up very well among your earliest Bugs cartoons.
A: In fact, it was one of the first cartoons where I got a real feeling for Bugs, which I had some trouble doing for a little while. That was one of the first times I got a hold on the character, and on the way he would later develop, for me at least. You could see he was really *enjoying* himself, which I enjoyed.

Q: Well, he certainly seems to enjoy himself during that great scene where the villains try to blast him with the cannon. And this, too, is a Marx Brothers bit, in the way that Bugs imposes a completely foreign discipline on the ominous situation: staging a basketball game with the cannonball, turning the hunters into a rooting section.

A: The only reservation that I might have about *Super Rabbit* was that it had an ending that only related to that particular time and that particular war effort in 1942 when Bugs goes off to join the Marines.

Q: What sort of disciplines would there be in Daffy Duck cartoons?
A: Well, Bugs and Daffy actually started out very similarly . . . they both began as raving lunatics. Daffy eventually became a self-preservationist. It was really his job to save his own life.

Q: But he's always showing off so much.
A: Well, he's a show-off too, but basically he was concerned with taking care of himself. Friz Freleng and I used a competition between Bugs and Daffy throughout the *Bugs Bunny Show* TV series. All through it, Daffy was trying to get to be master-of-ceremonies, but Bugs got all the applause. This sort of thing would drive Daffy nuts. Daffy always wanted to be triumphant in whatever he did, but in some cases all that meant was having to survive, and he was always apologizing. He'd stand there and say: "Pain hurts me," "I may be a cowardly little black duck, but I'm a *live* little black duck," or "What a shitty thing to do." We often wrote Daffy's dialogue with four-letter words, and then we'd abridge it later.

Q: It seems that Daffy is often cast in ambitious parts that he's always unequal to, Errol Flynn-type romantic leads.
A: I don't know why *Robin Hood Daffy* worked so well. But there you have a straight parody. There he did not act, as usual, the part of a self-preservationist, but he did want people to believe he was Sherlock Holmes, or Robin Hood, or whoever, so he was still trying to establish the fact that he had a right to be there.

Q: Would you say that role-playing, then, was central to Daffy's character?
A: That's certainly one important aspect, but then there are many pic-tures where he plays just the part of Daffy Duck. The very early ones don't really count, since he had yet to completely develop his character. Just as you think of Jack Benny as being a very miserly person, so Daffy is miserly regarding his own life. Of course he can't stand loss of dignity; that's another aspect.

Q: There's a brilliant sequence in *Robin Hood Daffy*, very sad in a way. Daffy has a heroic line to deliver before he performs some athletic feat of derring-do, screaming "Yoicks, and away!", swinging on a vine, and smashing right into a large tree. He keeps saying, "Yoicks, and away!" over and over, crashing into a new tree each time, his voice getting more and more tired. Wasn't this the cartoon where Daffy's beak kept springing up?
A: Yes, it was. Manny Farber called it "a token of Daffy's ineptitude," or something.

Q: Genre-parodies often come up in Daffy Duck cartoons.
A: Very often. I liked to do that. I did one on Jack Webb; sort of a Dragnet-in-Outer-Space cartoon, called *Rocket Squad.* I would say the basic discipline there was to be as true to the original style as possible, accenting the comic qualities of the particular genre all the while. As in *Rocket Squad:* "Thursday—4:05—P.M.—I struck a match—Thursday—4:05 and a quarter—P.M.—I lit a cigarette."

Q: In *The Scarlet Pumpernickel* [1950], you exaggerate, to just the right degree, the Michael Curtiz-type grandiose set decoration and use of shadow, all those very romantic trappings of costume epics.
A: There were a lot of in-house jokes in that cartoon—mostly in the casting. We put on the Mother Bear from those earlier Three Bears cartoons I did [*Bear for Punishment, Bee-Devilled Bruin*, etc.] and Henery Hawk appeared briefly as a messenger—it was an epic, so all my characters had to be in it. Everybody appreciated it except Jack Warner, and I don't think he ever realized we were talking about him in the cartoon.

Q: Daffy was trying to sell a script to Warner, the script providing the mockepic story, the cartoon-within-a-cartoon.
A: Daffy was no great writer, of course, so the thing had to end with one clichéd disaster after another: "Then, the dam broke!" "Then, the volcano erupted!" "Then, the price of food skyrocketed!"—while pictured on the screen was one kreplach with a pricetag of $1000. The ultimate catastrophe. We end it with Daffy shooting himself, saying, "It's getting so you have to kill yourself to sell a story around here!"

Q: And *Drip-Along Daffy* [1951] parodied the high-angle shots generally used for classic *High Noon* gundowns.

A: The thing that made that work was the distant sound the horse made. I used the distant spur-jangling sound too, even though the characters weren't wearing any spurs.

Q: It seems to me there's a great deal of *From A to ZZZZ*'s Walter Mitty-ish Ralph Phillips character in Daffy, in his naive desire to actually live out these heroic fantasies.
A: That's right, Daffy's an innocent; he's an ingenuous character. Not only when he is playing parts, but in a straight situation: all he wants to do is survive, and be triumphant, without having to do the work that was necessary, and without having to be particularly nice.

Q: In *Drip-Along Daffy*, Daffy first rides into the Western town, sees the sign that a sheriff is wanted, opens his coat, and has an all-purpose selection of badges: "Chicken Inspector," "Junior G-Man," etc. He's ready to impersonate any given role at any given moment.
A: I like the way he pulls out his guns, and his chaps come off along with them. "Time out, whilst I adjust my accoutrements . . ."

Q: Daffy seems to be very consistent with those self-conscious asides of his, sent straight to the viewer off the screen. You've said that you didn't preview your cartoons, but one verbal bit in *Rabbit Fire* [1951] *must* have been previewed. Elmer Fudd is stalking both Bugs and Daffy—this is the first fully developed cartoon that features all three of them together—and Bugs keeps engineering it so that Daffy is the one who gets blasted by Elmer. Daffy angrily takes Bugs by the collar and says, "You're despicable!" This line always brings down the house . . . and then, as if you *knew* it would get a terrific laugh, Daffy proceeds to soliloquize on Bugs's despicability, elaborating on the line.
A: No, I actually rewrote the line on the soundstage when Mel Blanc *said*, "You're despicable!" The way he said the line was so good and so strong that I immediately rewrote the line and said, "Look, I want you to play with this thing, draw it out as much as you can—You're despicable, and not only that, you're pickable, and not only that . . ." And Mel just kept going.

Q: It does appear very spontaneous.
A: It *was* spontaneous . . . I just let Mel go, let him run out of gas on the idea. We used that in one of the Westerns, too . . .

Q: Yeah, Daffy's great mouthings-on. There's a lot of rambling speech in the Charlie Dog cartoons as well.
A: They were both pretty noisy characters. Those Charlie cartoons were real talk-fests. I probably prepared myself for *not* talking, in the pantomime cartoons, by talking a lot in these. And I enjoyed it.

Q: From your very first cartoons, you made a great effort to find those plots and situations that are so basic that there's no need for dialogue—so often, you've opted for pantomime cartoons. Is it simply a matter of your preference for visual rather than verbal wit? There must be more to it, since when you use dialogue, you use it in a special or unique way.
A: I could understand a person's inability to express himself more than I could his ability to express himself. Like Daffy saying, "You're despicable! And not only that you're pickable, etc."; he was always reaching for it. Frustrating verbal expression seems to me to be more effective because, well, that's what I know best.

Q: Friz Freleng's characters, on the other hand, were always more vocal.
A: Yeah, there's a classic example, when he has Yosemite Sam telling Bugs to shut up . . .

Q: And Bugs answers back, "Sure I'll shut up, of course I'll shut up, I'll shut up any time anybody says so. I'm the kind of person who shuts up whenever I'm told to, I'm the best shutter-upper you ever saw, I'm . . ."
A: And then Sam screams, "Shut up shutting up!!" Anyway, it *is* a different way to approach the character, and I guess I never used dialogue to that extent.

Q: I'd say that you had a more self-contained Bugs . . .
A: Maybe. I'd suspect that Friz's Bugs would be more of a scamp, and Tex Avery's more a controlled lunatic, a brilliant controlled lunatic. Bob Clampett's was a thoroughly amoral lunatic; with flashes of greatness. All these characters—Bugs, Daffy, Pepé, Porky—in a way are like the multiplications of our own foibles. And if they weren't, of course, they wouldn't be valuable at all, they wouldn't be funny. But I suspect that all humor is based on that fact: the recognition in others in a multiplied form, of something that we ourselves are capable of. It's like what Orwell said: "I've never met a person that was any worse than I am."

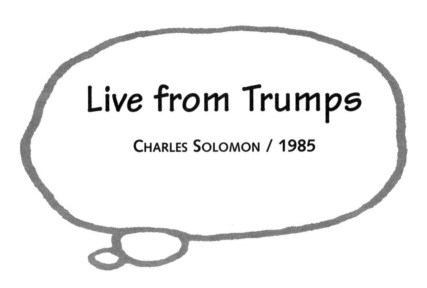

Live from Trumps

CHARLES SOLOMON / 1985

Radio broadcast, KUSC-FM, April 16,
1985. Copyright © 1985 Charles
Solomon. Transcript published with
permission.

Solomon: We have three guests with us this afternoon: Chuck Jones,
three-time Oscar winner, Peabody Award winner, the creator of the
Road Runner and Coyote and of Pepé Le Pew, one of the great Warners
directors, whose work can be seen this month at the Los Angeles County
Museum of Art. Commercial animator Bob Kurtz, also the winner of
numerous awards at festivals and of Clios for commercials, whose work
is on display at the Art Store Gallery in West Hollywood. And Bill Scott,
co-producer, head writer, and the voice of Bullwinkle, a stalwart of the
Jay Ward Studio, who never won any awards and therefore had to
content themselves with the devoted following of millions of *Rocky
and Bullwinkle* fanatics.
Scott: I'm happy to say that we have corrupted an entire generation.

Solomon: I think we might begin by explaining how the animation process is actually done, as not too many people are familiar with it.

Scott: You said this wasn't going to be a dull program, Charles, and here we are didactic from the first minute!

I guess the briefest way to say it is that animated cartoons are made backwards: they're cut before they're shot, and they're recorded before there are any actors; it's a very strange medium.

Jones: Someone once described it as engraving the Lord's Prayer on the head of a pin on an assembly line. That's about as close as you could come.

Solomon: Trying to play Alistair Cooke here . . . actually they begin with a script and storyboards. The dialogue is recorded, the designs are made, layouts are done, then the animation, then it's photographed—something live action directors find incomprehensible.

Jones: Have you ever heard of a script? One of our producers came to Warners, and he didn't know what an animated cartoon was. He insisted on seeing all the scripts. He said, "I don't know anything about animated cartoons, but I know a good story when I see one." You remember, Bill, you were there at the time. This little man looked something like Mr. Magoo or Grumpy with a shave. Remember the uniform he wore? Mao Zedong's tailor must have made it.

Scott: Only fingernails showing below the cuffs.

Jones: Yes, but dirty fingernails.

Solomon: Trying to keep some semblance of order . . .

Kurtz: Let me interrupt you again. Actually the script quite often is a storyboard.

Jones: It's always a storyboard.

Kurtz: Most of the time, it's a storyboard. We often get asked how can you draw and write at the same time, but that's usually what you do. You think in terms of words and pictures at the same time.

Solomon: One of the new trends we've seen is the film as gigantic commercial—the most recent example being *The Care Bears Movie.* Instead of creating characters, animating them and making them live, they're taking products and turning them into filmic characters.

Jones: I feel that it's proper—after all, that's the way *Alice in Wonderland* was written: the dolls were all made first, then they made the picture about the dolls, right? *Treasure Island*—they made the Long John Silver dolls first.

Kurtz: For *Treasure Island* they built this island . . .

Jones: That's right. Then they said, "That would make a great movie, wouldn't it?" They backed away and wrote the story.

Scott: I don't know why I despise the idea. It provides work for people in animation to make a living, and I think that's marvelous. But to attack a child, and that's what they're doing, with a battery that includes a character, a product, a cereal, a book, and everything—and it's with the knowledge that it's going to disappear within a year—it's tacky; it's just dreadful.

Jones: It's a thing that'll be taken care of by the Furies. They were there to take care of people whose crimes were unpunishable on Earth.

Scott: Does anybody at the table have anything good to say about the Strawberry Shortcake/Care Bears approach to animating the product.

Kurtz: No, it's hucksterism on the worst level, because the product comes first. This may sound strange from somebody who does commercials. But the product is so much more important than the story, and everything is to make money and very blatantly.

Scott: To pretend you're doing something else is what I find distasteful: *The Care Bears* was pretending to be a real movie.

Jones: I think there are several things that are grotesquely wrong with this. At the outset, how can anybody go along with the supposition that something can be good enough for children but *not* good enough for adults? Any film or any book or anything that's ever been worthwhile for children can also be enjoyed by an adult. *Peter Rabbit* is a wonderful book: it's beautifully structured, beautifully drawn and everything else. I was speaking facetiously of *Treasure Island*, but *Treasure Island* is a magnificent piece of writing that will always be read with pleasure by adults. Also, we find on Saturday morning television that group behavior is the only way that anyone solves any problems—everybody has to get together.

Scott: I have written perhaps five hundred commercials for the Quaker Oats Company about their cereal Cap'n Crunch. And Cap'n Crunch is a marvelous character—a funny little feisty guy who always made mistakes, but he was an eager guy, and eventually he won through. We were told a few years back that the Cap'n could not be important anymore; the Cap'n could not do anything. The children had to solve "The Problem." Because that's what kids identify with. Well, that reduced our feisty, funny Charlie Butterworth-voiced character to a wimp. He just wandered around; the kids had all the business, and it destroyed not only the character but the concept. Simply because some kind of research had been done about what they thought about people and how things were done. It hurt the character, it hurt the commercials, and I think it eventually began to hurt sales.

Kurtz: For the last ten years, I've tried to present original material to the networks for specials, and I keep coming across "Great, but I would like to have a pre-sold idea"—pre-sold meaning something we have seen before, probably in a comic strip. There's nothing wrong with the animated *Peanuts*, other than having been done too many times—you have *Peanuts, Garfield*, etcetera, and none of them are bad, but that's all there is. No one looks for anything original. Not on prime time and now not in features or on Saturday morning; there's nothing original. When I first got into the animation business in 1959–1960, I used to sit and watch Saturday morning. I loved it; I loved watching animation in every form. It was exciting; it was always an adventure. It's been many, many years since I could do that. How can I think about getting up in the morning to watch Mr. T—animated?

Solomon: And badly animated.

Kurtz: Not only badly animated, but if we hear what's coming next year on the networks, we could make silly jokes, but it's going to be on. We can't be any sillier than what's going on next year for "the children"—in quotes—as long as it's something that can be sold: G.I. Joe; Barbie Meets G.I. Joe. . . .

Jones: He-Man. Don't forget He-Man.

Scott: The ghettoization of animation on television has been a dreary thing for me to watch. I'd like to return to something you've said Chuck. The great cartoon characters, the characters that made American animation, the personality-animated characters, were never designed for children. They were designed for big, general theater audiences. It wasn't kids that made Mickey Mouse a star; it wasn't kids that made Bugs Bunny a star or a host of other characters. These were written for general audiences. And I'm fond of saying I have never known a writer in animation whom I respected who ever wrote for children.

Kurtz: That's correct. You write for yourself.

Solomon: When you were writing for Rocky and Bullwinkle, you weren't writing for children.

Scott: No, I was writing for me and Jay. If Jay fell on the floor and I chuckled, we had what I considered a reasonable story.

Jones: We never wrote for anybody but ourselves. We were forbidden to preview our films, because it cost money. Our producers were troubled at the idea of having to lay out thirty-five cents for each of us to have dinner and go to a preview. Since we weren't able to preview, we had only the supposition that if we were making each other laugh, perhaps we were making others laugh. Eventually the word would come back from the exhibitors, because all of our films were made for theaters, not television.

Solomon: Bob's most famous commercials are probably the blue Chevron dinosaurs.

Jones: They were broadcast and anybody who wanted to could enjoy them, just as our pictures were originally there for anybody who happened to go to the theater. But we didn't draw funny things like you do. Your characters are funny looking. Bugs or Daffy or the Coyote are not funny to look at; they're kind of ordinary looking. We hope the comedy arises out of what they do, not what they look like. Once a six-year-old boy was introduced to me as a man who drew Bugs Bunny. He looked at me, and he was furious. He said, "He does not draw Bugs Bunny; he draws pictures of Bugs Bunny!" Which is exactly the way I felt about Tom Sawyer. It never occurred to me that anyone was *writing* Tom Sawyer. He was *reporting* Tom Sawyer; he's writing *of* Tom Sawyer.

Scott: When I first started working at Warners, I went back to Denver. The relatives asked me what I did, and I said I wrote animated cartoons. There was this glazed look on everybody's face, "What do you mean you write animated cartoons?" I said, "You've seen Daffy Duck. Well, I write some Daffy Duck cartoons." There's another pause. Then a relative says, "You mean you write what Daffy Duck says?" I said, "Among other things, I write what Daffy says." The reply: "Well, you know, the things he *does* are funny enough."

Solomon: You put that Duck in front of a camera, and you've got a movie. I've argued in a couple of articles that the commercials that Bob is doing in this country—and Oscar Grillo and Richard Williams in England—are the real heirs to the Hollywood cartoon shorts. These days that's where the good animation is done, and most of the original writing and original designs, rather than in the programming.

Scott: I think that may very well be the case: commercials generally have much more of what animation is all about, because they must say something very quickly and very intensely. Animation is what Marshall McLuhan called a very hot medium. It uses up material like that! In doing specials, you have to keep piling up material, because the medium moves so fast. When you leave a commercial and go back to a program where the object is to use as few drawings as possible, to be as bland as possible, to be as cheap as possible, to do as little as possible in the half hour that you have to spend, there really is a world of difference. I am given to understand, however, that this is intentional: that sponsors in particular do not want a *hot* show that's going to be a dazzler, that's just going to knock the kids out of their socks, because they want the high points to be the commercials, which indeed, in many instances, they are.

Jones: In the beginning, when no one was paid very much, animated cartoons at Warners and other places ran seven or eight minutes, maybe even nine. Everyone was paid so little that the difference wouldn't even attract Leon Schlesinger's attention. But with an increasing demand for the talents, if you want to call it that, of the animators and directors and so on, the prices went up. Leon was no fool—well, he was a fool, but he wasn't that much of a fool. He realized the best way to keep the cost down was to shorten the pictures. So he kept pushing and probably would have taken it down to thirty seconds if he'd been allowed to. The pressure coming from underneath was the exhibitors. In order to make a two-hour program, which is what they wanted, a newsreel, a short subject, the coming attractions and the feature had to make a two-hour program. So it came down to six minutes.

Solomon: Leon Schlesinger was the first producer of the Warners' cartoons.

Jones: So we were pushed on the top by Leon and from the bottom by the exhibitor and were crushed into six minutes. We anticipated the problems that you run into, Bob, with commercials, because we had to make each cartoon five hundred and forty feet, which is six minutes. So we learned the most vital thing in comedy is timing. Without timing, the rest of it can go blah. The drawings may be great, the material may be great, but it you can't time it, it won't work.

When I was a little kid, my father had an orange grove on Sunset Blvd. One day, he came home and told me he'd watched Charlie Chaplin doing one of those choppy little runs he'd do around corners, and he wanted to do it on ice. He'd oil this piece of canvas, and he'd try to go around that corner on it. My father said he shot it one hundred and thirty-two times before he had it right, and you can imagine what shape he was in after that. But it instilled in me the importance of timing. People look at the drawings we do, and they don't realize that instead of overshooting, we throw drawings away. It may take seventy-five drawings to make one right.

Kurtz: People who are in animation realize how very close it is to dance. It's choreography; it's timing; it's sound. In the commercials I do, we're making miniature statements, very small, but it's with a rhythm that hits the audience. First of all, I try to respect the audience, assuming they're not watching, so you've got to grab them in the first five seconds and really have something unique, graphically, sound-wise, something. Then you turn it, and move it and you motivate them. I'm not interested in selling anything; I am interested in communication, in communicating an idea clearly, through design or comedy.

Going to go back to something you said, Chuck. I worked with a couple of the people from Warner Bros. at DePatie-Freleng. I was writing on *The Pink Panther*. I would be there writing by myself, and we'd have two weeks to write a five-minute Pink Panther story. It used to be six weeks or eight weeks for two writers; we were down to one writer and two weeks. The first week wasn't bad, but it was like a pyramid: the next week got harder and the next week . . . pretty soon, you'd be breathing real hard on Friday, knowing that on Monday you had to have a new idea. And you were always working with someone who didn't understand what you were doing.

Scott: You cannot write a five-minute animated cartoon in that length of time and have animation. You can write a story, but you can't really flesh it out and do anything with it.

Solomon: In Chuck's days at Warner Bros., there were three and some-times four units doing an hour of an animation a year. In one season of Saturday mornings, a studio may produce seventy-five half-hours of pro-gramming, and it's done in about six months—that's the time from the network approval of a project until they start delivering the finished shows.

Tex Avery once said he discovered if an object fell out of the sky in seven frames, that is seven twenty-fourths of a second, it would get a laugh. If it was six twenty-fourths or eight twenty-fourths, it wouldn't get a laugh. Chuck, you've said something similar about the Coyote falling off a cliff.

Jones: I found at least in my own mind, that if he fell off a cliff, he would fall for eighteen frames, then he would disappear, then fourteen frames later he would hit. It seemed to me that thirteen didn't work and fifteen didn't work.

Talking about time, it only took Mark Twain six or eight months to write *Tom Sawyer*. Then he tried to write *Huckleberry Finn*, and it took him fourteen years. And yet one of the studios here is quite willing to take on seventeen hours of *The Further Adventures of Huckleberry Finn*. When Mike Maltese was my writer, he did one picture every five weeks. When he went to Hanna-Barbara, he was asked to do a half-hour show a week. I don't know how you multiply things like that, but it's murderous. You were a high school teacher, Bill, maybe you can work out the mathematics.

Scott: I taught English. I don't even know if you know this story, Chuck, but it was your unit. Mike and Bob Givens were doing a story; Mike was writing it, and Bob Givens was the sketch man. Apparently they got on a roll and wrote and sketched a story in a matter of days. They finished the damned thing in about a week, but they would not put the sketches up. Each day they'd sit and throw push pins and tell gags and what not, and at the end of the day, Givens would pin up X number of drawings, and that was the day's work. And they finished exactly on time, in six weeks.

Scott: I talked with Bruno Bozzetto, the great Italian animator and director.

Solomon: The man who brought us *Allegro Non Troppo*.

Scott: He is feeling the pain the other way: he has nine minutes to fill. The Italian cinema will support him, he gets to do that, but he has to do nine minutes. He says, "I have some wonderful five minute stories, but I can't do a five-minute story; I have to do a nine-minute story." He has to make it nine minutes long. I have the feeling that may be what happens with the sleazier kind of filler that we see.

Solomon: Did you run into that kind of constraint when you were writing *Rocky and Bullwinkle?*

Scott: Oh goodness gracious, no. The wonderful thing about Rocky and Bullwinkle was that there was no ending. We'd just write 'til we had three-and-a-half minutes written; all we had to do was get to a climax and a little cliff-hanger then pick up the next one.

Actually, when we started writing Rocky and Bullwinkle, I only had one story in mind—I figured it would go on forever. I had no idea we would ever get to the end of it. In fact, I had an idea that we were going to be cancelled after thirteen shows, so it didn't matter whether I ever finished it. The first major story on Rocky and Bullwinkle ran forty episodes! Others ran four episodes or eight, but they generally would take about as long as the story would stand up. There was one we had to close out in a hurry. . . .

Solomon: "The Great Box Caper."
Scott: Boris and Natasha were counterfeiting box tops, cereal box tops. and our sponsor at that time was General Mills. They went, "AHHHHHHHH!!!! Counterfeiting box tops!" So we had to finish it up.
KUSC Announcer Dennis Bade: The voice of Cap'n Crunch was a good deal of the character, and it was Daws Butler. At Warner Bros. virtually all the characters were done by Mel Blanc. Voices like Daws Butler's would tend to indicate that the voice could become the character, and then you would draw somehow to match that. With Mel Blanc doing every voice. . . .
Jones: He didn't do every voice, and he worked differently from Bill—Bill draws and does voices. Mel implies that he originated the characters, and he didn't. We wrote a script exactly as if we were writing without any knowledge of what the character's going to be. We wrote the dialogue and did the drawings first, then we called in Mel; we used him a lot, and he's a very versatile guy. But the inference that he originated lines, originated voices as such and invented characters—he did not. I think all of us feel a little sorry that he feels it necessary to imply that he did; he's a brilliant man, but he's the only voice person I know who makes this claim.
Kurtz: Now, we have Bullwinkle here.
Scott (as Bullwinkle): Well you certainly do!
Jones: But you were drawing him *and* doing the voice.
Scott: I was doing the voice before I started writing. I had no idea I was going to do the character; I wrote things, and I would read the scripts. But I have some devastating news for you all.
Jones: Is it time to shut the show down?
Scott: I'm canceling all your contracts. I really am going to have to leave this happy board. I'm sure these two astute, fine and talented gentlemen will carry on. And perhaps when I am gone say something nice about me. And so I thank you very much for having me on the show.
Jones: If you've ever seen a moose leave with a cookie in his mouth. . . .

Solomon: We can happily report that Bullwinkle is back on the air on Sunday morning on Channel 7, and that the statue of Rocky and Bullwinkle on Sunset Blvd. has been restored to what Bill termed, "Its pinnacle of bad taste."

Jones: Speaking of bad taste, we have two programs on the air tonight, too.

In *Bugs Bunny's Busting Out All Over*, I have a sequence where Bugs and Elmer are about seven or eight years old. Elmer carries a pop gun, and I call it "A Portrait of the Artist as a Young Rabbit." But also I have a Coyote and Road Runner picture in which the Coyote finally catches the Road Runner. He catches him, but he doesn't win. If you want to find out what that means, take a look at eight thirty.

Solomon: I've often thought the relationship between Bugs and Elmer reflected that between the animators and the producers at Warners. The animators didn't like the producers who knew very little about animation. But they were the ones in power, as Elmer has the gun, which should give him the upper hand; the animators, i.e. Bugs, used their intelligence and wiles to outwit them.

Jones: That's so incredibly profound; I wish we'd thought of it, don't you?

Kurtz: Yeah, I wish I knew what he said.

Most of the producers in this day do not have any affinity with the artists. The animators, designers, directors, storyboard people all really get into the characters. Even when you're working for advertising agencies, the artists enjoy the work, and it really is a part of you. Even in commercials, you create characters—you feel part of them. Everybody relates to them as a part of you. As for conflict like Elmer Fudd or whomever, I just always think we're anti-authority.

Jones: Of course, we always are. How come you get two mikes, and I only get one?

Kurtz: They're multicolored for those who don't have color radio. They're colored like Easter eggs.

Jones: And mine, appropriately, is yellow.

Solomon: Getting back to the idea of being anti-authority, you started to say something and got completely sidetracked.

Kurtz: As opposed to semi-sidetracked.

Jones: Authority—semi, yes, that's the history of life. And my wife, too. Something we often misunderstand is that a gimmick voice means character, which it doesn't. You have to get a voice; you have to find

out what the character's all about. One of the things I think that makes
Elmer an appealing character, if he is appealing, is that when you pick
him up walking through the forest following the rabbit tracks, he says,
"Wabbit twacks!" then he turns to the audience and says, "Be vewy,
vewy quiet. I'm hunting wabbits." But he's about to cry, because he's
afraid somebody's going to interrupt him—that's character. The lisp itself
doesn't mean anything; he just happens to lisp. Leon Schlesinger inspired
the voice of Daffy Duck. He had a lisp, too. He'd come back when we
were working, "Watcha workin' on fellaths?" We'd say, "We're working
on Porky Pig." He'd say, "That's it boyth, put in loths of joketh. I'm off
to the raceth!"

Solomon: One of my favorite stories about a film of yours, Chuck,
concerns *Bully for Bugs*. The second producer of the Warner shorts
was Eddie Selzer, who apparently knew less about animation than
Schlesinger had.
Kurtz: Which is a tough thing to do.
Jones: But Leon didn't pretend to know anything. If the money came in,
he didn't care.

Solomon: Apparently Selzer told you you could make cartoons about
anything but bullfights?
Jones: He actually appeared one day, in his Mao Zedong uniform with
his little fingers sticking out, and he was mad. I couldn't figure out
why he was mad. He was standing there in the doorway, and Mike
and I looked up in wide-eyed innocence. We were wide-eyed innocents;
we still are wide-eyed innocents. Mike's dead; he's still a wide-eyed
innocent. We looked up, and Eddie glared at us and said, "I don't want
any pictures about bullfights; there's nothing funny about bullfights!"
Then he turned and walked out. There was a long pause. Mike looked
at me and I looked at him. He looked at his fingernails, and said,
"I never knew there was anything funny about bullfights, but Eddie's
never been right before." We didn't know there was anything funny
about bullfights, but we figured we could learn from other people.

So we studied bullfights and went down to Mexico City and saw a
bullfight. You see that little guy standing out there who weighs about
one hundred thirty pounds in the suit of lights. Then that door busts
open; here comes a three thousand pound animal who's never seen a
man. I made a caricature of Juan Belmonte, who was one of the great

bullfighters out of Hemingway's *Death in the Afternoon*. He looked like Juan Belmonte, but he acted like me—pure cowardice.

Solomon: "That gent in the fancy knickerbockers."
Jones: Bob, you've worked with agencies and gained their respect because your stuff is so wonderful, and these guys finally see the light. They do respect you; they respect Richard Williams and two or three others. I only did two commercials: one was for Gillette, and I worked on the original Charlie Tuna spot. There was one scene in the latter where I had a character snapping his fingers. Someone from the agency insisted I had him snapping his second finger instead of his third finger. I asked how he knew, and he said, "We put it on a movieola." So this is the kind of stuff you've had to put up with. But you've survived and you look remarkable—you don't look over seventy!

Solomon: Tell him the story about the sun.
Kurtz: We did a Sparkletts commercial in which we had a sun drying up in the sky. The scenery dried up, and the sun got so hot that it opened up its mouth, and its tongue fell out on the ground. A little truck drove up the tongue and dumped the water in, and Hans Conried—who I loved using—said something about, "We'll do anything to bring good-tasting water to a thirsty world." That was the spot, and it was on the air for six weeks or eight weeks, then it was taken off. I didn't find out until three years later the reason it was taken off was the client's wife was embarrassed, because the tongue was obscene. I've shown this film in every country I've traveled to—and never knew that.

The Chevron spots, which involve metamorphic dinosaurs coming out of the land, were one of my first attempts to do something like Winsor McCay. I consider him the father of animation; he did such wonderful things around the turn of the century.

Solomon: *Little Nemo* was 1911.
Kurtz: We were finishing the spot when I suddenly got a call. Then people from Chevron would fly down three times a week for meetings; we dealt directly with the Chevron people through their advertising agency. But this time, they said we have to stop the commercial. I loved the commercial; I knew exactly what I wanted to do in it. They said the reason is that oil isn't just fossil bones; it also comes from the flora, so it isn't scientifically correct. I said we'd make it scientifically correct, no problem. I made a flower come up and punch a dinosaur in the nose.

The scientists said, that's fine. I later showed the film at the University of Southern California, and someone from the geology department came up to me and said, "Do you know that your film is geologically correct?" I said, "Yes, I know." But it's geologically correct in a broad sense—let's call it an animator's way of looking at things.

Solomon: Something you started to get to talk about, Bob, was animation seems to be at its best when it's as far away from reality as possible. The closer animation gets to live action, the less interesting it becomes as animation.

Kurtz: Yes, I think so. I came up with a little line: we have live action which is the illusion of reality; animation is the illusion of fantasy. It's much more dream-like. The hardest characters to do in animation, even though they put some of the best people on them, were the princes in the Disney films. They don't breathe life; they aren't broad enough. Whenever you get believability in animation, strangely enough, it comes from broad strokes, not small strokes. It's a general statement, but it seems to work.

Jones: I don't object to that idea, but film graphics or animation covers such a broad scope. I think Bob belongs to the same area as Tex Avery. He exploits the wonder of things that can be done in terms of graphics. Bugs Bunny hardly looks like a rabbit—rabbits are big blobs; they look more like a wet. . . .

Solomon: Like a meatloaf.

Jones: Like a fuzzy meatloaf, if you like. But they also have a bad kick. We had a Belgian hare that broke my brother's leg by kicking it, so rabbits are not all the same either. To me, motion pictures are quite different than just graphics. Animation, the way I use the term, refers to the development of personality by the way the characters move, not by what they look like. Bob, you cross another boundary; you work in an area where the looks of something are probably as important as the essential character itself.

Kurtz: I think sometimes my drawings might be broader, but I really try to climb inside and say the character would work this way. Because I began as a writer—I love what you're saying, and I'm in total agreement about personality coming from within. It's a combination of drawing and character motivation and voice all coming together so it's believable.

Jones: That's right, although we never depended on the voice as much as most people think we did. We finished a film, and we always ran it silent to see if it worked or not. We never put the voices with it, although we did record the voices. Even with a Bugs Bunny picture, we'd run it silent to see if it worked without the background, without music, without color, or anything else. It was almost like flipping the drawings for the entire film. The kind of animation we did was there or it wasn't, and if it wasn't there, the picture wasn't going to work.

Solomon: When an animator finishes a series of drawings, he'll flip them the way you might flip through a book to see the images moving and gauge how correct the motion is.

Jones: I—pretty much everybody when they were in school marred text books or tablets by making little stick figures that would dance. You just multiply that by intricacy and you have animation in the sense I'm talking about. To me, one of the most remarkable things is we have three people here representing animation, and they're probably the only animation people in southern California who don't depend on Saturday morning children's programming or kid-vid—one of the most revolting terms that ever burdened human life.

Kurtz: You can't see it, but we all have smiles on our faces.

Jones: Smiles of hatred. But when you think about motion pictures and animation together, you realize that animation has much more in common with music than it does with any other form of graphic art. What we're talking about here is a series of impacts on the visual senses, just as music is a series of sounds impacting on the auditory sense. It's the memory of each note that makes music work, and the memory of each image that makes motion pictures work. Every single frame of a motion picture, whether it's Margot Fonteyn or Woody Allen, is a series of still pictures hitting the retina and going to the brain. Your single drawing might be funny, but it wouldn't be funny in sequence.

Kurtz: No, in fact, we throw out funny drawings to make funny films. The individual drawings may not always make sense by themselves, but they have to be funny in motion. When a designer tries to animate, it's often horrendous, because they tend to see good drawings instead of motion. There have been animators who drew beautifully, and animators who really didn't draw that well, but their drawings were alive. They could make something funny, or they could make something poignant. They made you feel for these drawings.

Jones: They were like Irving Berlin, who could only pick out his tunes with one finger on the piano. He couldn't play the piano, but the tune was there. Norm Ferguson, who animated Pluto, actually drew a skeleton of Pluto—it was a fluid skeleton that went from the tip of the dog's nose clear through to his tail. He'd draw single lines for the legs and just indicate where the feet were, then his assistant would come through to make a finished drawing.

Kurtz: Did he do the famous flypaper sequence—that classic mime sequence?

Jones: One of the great ones. He also did one of Pluto with a plumber's helper stuck on his behind—fantastic piece of action. But I think that's the point: what we're dealing with is different from any other graphic art, if what we're dealing with is an art.

Kurtz: I think it is an art. I like to think of animation as art on film and it can be any style of art. It's frame by frame filmmaking and it can be done in the style of Claes Oldenburg, Persian miniatures or Eskimo art. It can be humorous, it can make you cry, or it can scare you. I had recurrent dreams for seven years from the Witch in *Snow White*.

Solomon: I still cry every time I see *Dumbo*.

Jones: That's a magnificent piece of work. What's incredible is that you just have the elephants' trunks, for God's sake.

Kurtz: The two trunks when the mother is inside the cage and she reaches out and Dumbo tries to touch her.

Jones: Can you imagine describing that to an agency; this'll be poignant.

Kurtz: Or talk Saturday morning and poignant animation.

Jones: Poignant, schmoignant. They'll say, "Right. Get lost!"

Solomon: That animation was done by Bill Tytla, whom many people consider to be one of the greatest animators ever. He also animated Chernobog, the black god in the "Night on Bald Mountain" sequence of *Fantasia*.

Jones: He was the Michelangelo of animation.

Kurtz: And he did Stromboli in *Pinocchio*, which is still incredible animation.

Jones: The power and strength of that.

Solomon: We only have a few minutes, but one thought I'd hoped to bring up was that it seems to me that animators have given up the realm of fantasy. George Lucas, Steven Spielberg and Joe Dante are using live action for the kind of fantasies animation once provided, and animation has essentially turned into live action on Saturday morning.

Kurtz: Lucas and Spielberg are basically telling stories in fantasy.

Solomon: And doing it well.

Kurtz: And doing it well. They're good stories. One thing about animation that a lot of people don't seem to realize is that after about five minutes, it loses its uniqueness, and it has to have a story to carry it. All the good animated features and specials that we remember had wonderful stories. *Dumbo, Pinocchio*—those are wonderful stories.

Jones: With great characters. That's what story is: characters.

Solomon: We still have one minute.

Kurtz: Do I have to give these microphones back? I wanted to take them home; they go well with my colored matzo balls.

Jones: I'd like to close by saying that for me, and I believe this is also true of Bob, we are both extremely fortunate, because we've spent our entire lives being paid for what we enjoy doing. I don't know how many people are allowed to do that. I always thought somebody ought to shake me and say, "No. That's not true at all. You don't belong there!"

Kurtz: I love it. It's living a dream.

Jones: That was fun.

Interview with Chuck Jones

STEVEN BAILEY / 1988

Copyright © 1999 Steven Bailey.
Published with permission.

It's amazing what you can get in life if you only ask for it. We at the Cartoon Annex had admired the cartoons of director Chuck Jones (creator of the Road Runner and Pepé Le Pew) ever since we turned into those movie nerds who read credits. (For a quick take on Jones's greatest work, check out *The Bugs Bunny/Road Runner Movie* [1979].) The interview below was obtained after only a couple of calls to Jones's daughter's office (Linda Jones Enterprises now handles his cartoon-related work). Jones even did an original Bugs Bunny drawing for us.

This interview, conducted in February 1988, didn't set the animation world on fire, but it was certainly one of the highlights of Annex webmaster Steven Bailey's life.

Bailey: So how does it feel to have influenced an entire generation of filmmakers?

Jones: Well, I don't like to look at it that way. If you start to take yourself very seriously, you don't go very far. When one of my colleagues was given an Academy Award, he said, "What do I do now? I've earned the highest honor possible. There's nowhere else to go." And you have to think, well, it's just an award!

Bailey: But certainly you're aware of your influence, when you can go to a record store and buy a Leon Redbone album with your drawing on the cover, or you see a Mel Brooks movie [*Spaceballs*] where an alien sings the same song your frog sang [in Jones's cartoon *One Froggy Evening* (1955)].

Jones: I'd say I did a lot of good cartoons that were enjoyed by a lot of people, and someone else pegged me as an "artist." We certainly didn't regard ourselves as artists when we were doing them—we were making films that we thought would last maybe two or three years. We didn't know what the audience wanted. And it probably still doesn't know what it wants—this business of testing and marketing is pretty silly. We made the pictures for theaters, and for ourselves.

Bailey: Well, then, let's say your cartoons had an impact on people. Were you aware of an impact when you were making them?

Jones: Oh, no. In fact, when UPA [creators of Mr. Magoo] first came about, their P.R. man decided they needed an enemy, so he said, "Our enemy is Disney. We're doing 'modern' animation, and we're against fuzzy animals." Well, we never did fuzzy animals to begin with—you can hardly draw them. But people were impressed with UPA, so all the local schools hired people from UPA. They never bothered with us. We were recognized in Europe long before we were in the United States, and I think the Californians were the last to notice.

Bailey: What's the most surprising response you ever received to your work?

Jones: To be asked to lecture at Oxford is pretty startling. But then, they're all pretty startling. I don't know how many different languages we've been translated into. I saw a comic strip of the Coyote once in Copenhagen. It was a printed comic where the Coyote is falling, and as he fell off the cliff, he was saying in big letters, "HJELP!" I said, "What do you know? We can write in Danish!"

Bailey: What does an animation director do?

Jones: It depends on where he works—a director at Warners didn't work the same way as at MGM. At Warner Bros., you'd work with a writer, though you'd find you'd have to be about half of your own story department. Most of the writers at Warners didn't draw very well, and really, I didn't want them to—I wanted them for storylines and gags.

After we finished the story—and of course, it wasn't really finished, just like a director isn't finished just because he has a script—then I'd take the storyboard into my room. And I'd ask Maurice Noble [Jones's layout artist at Warners] to do "inspirational" sketches to see what worked visually. I'd do three or four hundred drawings myself, out of a cartoon with maybe four thousand drawings, and then I'd write the dialogue. Then I'd call in Mel Blanc [voice man for nearly all Warners characters] and direct him with the dialogue.

Then I'd time it before it went to animation. This is the part that amazes directors like Steven Spielberg. They can't see how we'd do it. We'd time it in our heads so that it would come out pretty close to 540 feet, the average length of a six-minute cartoon. We had to time it ourselves, because we didn't have the luxury of shooting something and then not using it, as was done at Disney. The director makes *all* the decisions.

Bailey: Is the humor in your cartoons based on your triumphs and failures?

Jones: Totally. Where else can you go for inspiration? You act on what you know. I'd like to think I'm Bugs Bunny or Pepé Le Pew, but in my heart I know I'm more like Daffy Duck or the Coyote. Or take the Grinch. [Jones directed the peerless 1966 TV version of Dr. Seuss's story *How the Grinch Stole Christmas.*] Everyone hates Christmas a little. Someone who hates Christmas a lot is a real character to find!

Bailey: What amused or influenced you when you were growing up?

Jones: Mostly reading—anything. My father always said, "If you read, you'll get in the habit." If you read *The Bobbsey Twins*, you'll probably throw up. But in doing so, you'll discover what *is* good. Beatrix Potter, on the other hand, is wonderful and can be read by children *and* adults, and that's the key. If you try to write just for children, you'll talk down to them, and I don't think that's the way to go.

Bailey: What sort of comedy do you find funny?

Jones: I loved Chaplin and Keaton. We didn't consciously copy them, but a lot of it got in there, I guess. *City Lights* and *Modern Times* are two of my all-time favorite comedies, but then Chaplin started regarding himself as an artist and tried to be profound. I'm not even sure *The Great Dictator* is good social commentary, much less comedy. Woody Allen was wonderful until he tried to become Ingmar Bergman, and that's a pity, because there aren't enough talented comics around.

Bailey: There seems to have been a resurgence of high-quality animation in the past few years. Do you think animation will ever return to the level it was at when you were working at Warner Bros.?
Jones: Well, it's possible—there are some great things going on. You have guys like Ralph Bakshi [*Fritz the Cat*] and Don Bluth [*Anastasia*] doing some wonderful things. I may not like a particular guy's style, but if he likes animators, I'll follow him to the end. But animation has to grow—we can't live in the past. I liked *The Duxorcist* [Daffy Duck's 1987 "comeback" cartoon], but it was rather imitative of the old style. You have to find something new.

Bailey: Your work seems to reflect your philosophies. Do you subscribe to any particular religion or philosophy?
Jones: Oh, no. As the man once said, I have some suppositions but no facts. I prefer to live with the questions.

Bailey: If you had a choice, would you do anything differently?
Jones: No, not at all. You know, I don't get residuals from my movies or videocassettes of my work, but it's silly to complain about not making money from it. All those years, somebody paid me for what I wanted to do!

Chuck Jones and the Daffy World of Cartoons: The Warners Legend Remembering the Glory Days in an Animated Autobiography

TOM SHALES / 1989

From *The Washington Post*, November 26, 1989, G1, G5. Copyright © 1989 The Washington Post Writers Group. Reprinted with permission.

Chuck Jones has breathed life into creatures great but small. He's not only drawn scores of wacky animals, he's worked for a few; the bosses at Warner Bros. didn't really know what Jones and his fellow animation directors were doing in the little shack they named Termite Terrace, and that may be just as well.

If they did know, they might have put a stop to it. And then where would we be?

"Harry Warner used to say, 'The only thing I know is, we make Mickey Mouse,'" Jones recalls, as he has recalled before, and as he recalls again in his warm-hearted and clearheaded autobiography

Chuck Amuck, just published by Farrar Straus Giroux. Mickey Mouse, of course, was made at Disney, another studio altogether.

Subtitled *The Life and Times of an Animated Cartoonist*, Jones's book tracks his life from his first set of drawing pencils as a kid through the years at Warners, when he created the Road Runner, Wile E. Coyote, and Pepé le Pew and directed cartoon shorts starring Bugs Bunny, Daffy Duck, Elmer Fudd, Sylvester, Tweety, and many other brash immortals.

Chuck Jones was still a kid then, really. He is still a kid now, though in his seventies, and with the addition of a tidy grey beard, Jones looks as though he could be a nuclear physicist or a law professor, or at least the way such a person might look if all the cartoon characters got together and drew him.

He has a voice like eggnog. Maybe like hot tea with lemon and honey. Maybe like molasses in May. It's a voice that wouldn't hurt a fly, unless maybe the fly became head of a motion picture studio, and apparently, some have.

Jones and his wife, Marion—his first wife, Dorothy, died in 1978—have been hopping down the book-tour trail in honor of the autobiography, which is named after a riotous Daffy cartoon, *Duck Amuck*. Before coming to Washington, the Joneses stopped in New York for the ceremonial inflation of the Bugs Bunny balloon that bobbed down Broadway in this year's Macy's Thanksgiving Day parade. In 1990, Warner Bros. will celebrate the fiftieth anniversary of the illustrious Bunny with a big Bugs bash. Jones says he may even contribute to a new Bugs cartoon.

"Warners is finally getting around to the idea that there is some importance to these things," Jones says. "Unfortunately, Friz and I are the only ones left of the old group. Friz is too mean to die, and I haven't had any practice." Friz Freleng is the other surviving director from the glory days. Tex Avery, Bob Clampett, and the others are gone.

In their zeal to be funny and in their resentment of the front office, the boys sometimes caricatured executives in their cartoons. Mel Blanc mimicked the slushy lisp of Leon Schlesinger, who first ran the unit, for the voice of Daffy Duck. Schlesinger never caught on. Occasionally, the likeness of an actual Warner brother would totter across the cartoon screen.

"Jack Warner was in *The Scarlet Pumpernickel*," Jones says. "But I made a picture before I left called *Now Hear This*, which I called 'Warner's Folly' because I was trying to insult the son of a bitch, and it's hard to insult somebody that uninsultable. But that's really true what I said in the book: Jack Warner sold those cartoons for three thousand dollars apiece in 1948. Incredible! I mean, how stupid can you get?"

Warners still owns the post-'48 cartoons. Ted Turner's are the little mitts into which most of the pre-'48s have passed. Jones doesn't get a nickel in residuals, but the cartoons already have lived more than nine lives and are still earning strong. They're a bulwark of ABC's dominance in the Saturday morning ratings race, and they show up on cable's Nickelodeon and TNT channels. Other packages are syndicated to local stations. CBS still shows prime-time specials patched together from scraps of old Looney Tunes.

Warners licenses tons of merchandise with likenesses of the characters, including copies of *Chuck Amuck* autographed by the distinguished zany who wrote it. In recent years, the rift between art and commerce, between the creators of the cartoons and the company that released them, has healed somewhat. The brothers Warner have died. Edward Bleier, now president of the division that includes Warner Animation, is a devoted fan, a veritable Chuckaholic.

Gradually, too, the public has become more aware of the people behind the wabbit, the duck, and the Fudd guy. Steven Spielberg, who wrote the foreword to Jones's book, excerpted a Warner cartoon in his feature *The Sugarland Express* and has acknowledged his debt to the masters. And then there's the feature-length homage *Who Framed Roger Rabbit*, directed by Robert Zemeckis. Last year's big box office hit, it is now inundating stores in its home video incarnation.

To Jones, however, *Roger Rabbit* is a tribute he could do without. He hated that dumb sloppy hare, and the coarse movie built around him.

"He's ugly," says Marion. "He's just plain ugly. He's not cuddly."

"I call it a successful *Tron*," says Chuck of the film. "You remember *Tron*? Well that was another tour de force of technical stuff. Roger Rabbit, after all the wonders of putting live action and animation together, presented the case for a very unpleasant character. Roger was not appealing in any way. And if you approached this thing as a motion picture, forget it! Could anybody believe that this guy was married to that dame? He'd need an alpenstock at the very least."

Alpenstock. "A strong iron-pointed staff used by mountain climbers." Thank you, Mr. Webster.

"Mainly this guy was frenetic and they were trying to imitate Bob Clampett. Zemeckis believes that the Clampett pictures were the best ever done at Warner Bros., so he demanded that this be done that way, and Richard Williams—to his shame, because he's a marvelous animator—decided he was Bob Zemeckis's pencil.

"I was supposed to be in on it too, at the beginning, and Dick and I started out with a storyboard and a lot of material with Donald and Daffy Duck playing dual pianos. I thought that was a very funny idea, and an historic idea, but they ended up with something horrible. No, I didn't like it.

"All that money wasted on that."

Jones says he's heard that about half of the $50 million budget for *Roger Rabbit* was spent on the animation. "And I figured out that that was about twice as much money as it cost to make *all* of the Warner cartoons. All of them! Now, which would you rather own—all the Warner cartoons or *Roger Rabbit?*"

That's an easy one. The Warner cartoons were crisp and witty. Some were charming, like the Jones classic *One Froggy Evening*, about a miraculous singing frog that vocalizes only when in a certain mood. But if the cartoons were great, it wasn't because studio executives were lavishing attention and accolades on the cartoonists. More often they were ignoring them or upsetting them.

"This book has no one to blame and very many to praise and to love," Jones writes in his introduction. If he doesn't precisely "blame" anybody, though, he does take the occasional blunt poke at an executive dunderhead from days gone by. Schlesinger's "sole method of determining the quality of an animated cartoon was how far it came in under budget," Jones writes, and Schlesinger's successor, Eddie Selzer, got the job "following a diligent search of the studio to find out who hated laughter most."

Selzer issued random dictums like "I don't want any gags about bull-fights, bullfights aren't funny," and Jones set to work on a bullfight cartoon. The result was *Bully for Bugs*, a hilarious 1953 gem. Selzer also said nobody would laugh at the fractured *Français* spoken by Pepé le Pew, the lovesick skunk. He was wrong. They did.

"Eddie, like the people in charge of network television today, hated and feared anything he had never seen before," Jones writes.

Hated? Anybody in his right mind could hate this stuff? "The New York office hated the first Bugs Bunny," Jones says. "They hated the first Road Runner. They'd never seen them before. And Eddie Selzer protested mightily when I was making the first Road Runner because he said, 'After all, we pay Mel Blanc a salary to do voices, and you don't have any voices in here.' Even the 'beep-beep' wasn't Mel. Oh, we had some lulus."

"But in a way, I've always felt that it was a vital factor to have people you fight against." Similarly, the fact that Termite Terrace was all but hermetically sealed—isolated from the rest of the studio—may have been an advantage. "It was probably a very, very good thing, you know. I mean, if you want to make an heroic allusion, so was Vincent van Gogh. He didn't know what the hell, if anybody would ever care about what he did."

Jones says the animators were protected, too, by the now-extinct practice of block booking. When exhibitors bought a movie, they had to take the short subjects with it. "That's one reason we experimented so much. And since we weren't paid very much, we figured, why don't we have all the fun we can have?" Sometimes the fun didn't make it into the finished product. Jones confesses he would sometimes insert a frame of Pepé le Pew in explicit amorous poses with a young female just to shock the executive reviewing the footage.

One reason the animation unit was isolated is that for years it wasn't even on the lot. It moved onto the lot in the '50s, Jones says. He is asked if he ever ate lunch in the studio commissary. He says only when all other options failed.

"There were three parts of the commissary, and one was the Green Room, which was more expensive, and the stars and the executives ate there, and there was one above that, the so-called private dining room where Jack Warner and his toadies ate." Not froggies, toadies.

"An honest person would never go in there, but we were dragged in to meet Jack and Harry Warner, fifteen years after I started directing. What they meant by 'private dining room' was the Sistine Chapel. Eddie Selzer was such a toady that Mike Maltese, one of our writers, said he measured everything by the private dining room. He'd be talking about his living room and he'd say, 'It's two-thirds the size of the private dining room.' Or he'd say, 'I bought my new Cadillac and it's maybe one and a half times the size of the private dining room.' "

Jones would saunter onto one of the vast Warner sound stages when it was time for Blanc to record the voices for the soundtracks. If it was a conversation between Daffy and Bugs, Jones would read Daffy's lines while Blanc recorded Bugs's, and vice versa, and then it would all be spliced together.

It was on those sound stages, too, that Carl Stalling conducted the sizable Warner Bros. orchestra in the musical scores for the films. Sometimes the song being played in the background is an added joke: In Jones's *Bunny Hugged*, Bugs and a wrestler grapple while Stalling conducts the band in "Cuddle Up a Little Closer." And so on.

"If we couldn't find anything else, Carl would do it by the title," Jones recalls. "One time I did a Three Bears thing, and it was involved with bees, and he went back and found a piece that was written around 1900 called 'My Darling Little Honey Bee.' Well, who the hell would know? It wasn't like 'Flight of the Bumblebee' or something like that. And he'd jam it in there.

"We tried desperately to avoid anything with people eating, because he'd always play 'A Cup of Coffee, a Sandwich and You.' "

But what an orchestra. When Jones made *What's Opera, Doc?* his magnificent Wagnerian spoof, he had an eighty-piece ensemble to back him up. "I think we had sixty pieces on *Rabbit of Seville*. Those guys, plus Johnny Green and his orchestra over at MGM, at night they were the Los Angeles Philharmonic, and during the day they were the MGM and Warner Bros. orchestras. So they were terrific.

"And they loved it, although they never saw the cartoon, because it wasn't finished by the time they were doing the music."

Jones's reminiscences about the men who ran the studios, and who headed the animation unit, are usually not fond. So, all right, let's say they were terrible people, ignorant people, philistines and vulgarians. Even so—would that we could bring them all back. Even the worst of them. Because under their daft tyrannies, Hollywood had its finest hours and, in the case of the great Warner cartoons, its finest six minuteses.

"I never accuse them of not helping us," says Jones. "They *were* helping. I didn't say that it was bad because of them. I said it was good because of them." He isn't complaining about those days; he is celebrating them. "The idea of anybody paying me just to draw never occurred to me," he says, still looking awe-struck at the thought.

They didn't pay him and his rollicking colleagues all that much, but they drew all that well. They put pens to paper and magic came out. They started jokes that started the whole world laughing. And while "the merry-go-round broke down," as the title of the Merrie Melodies theme put it, the laughter may simply never stop.

Chuck Jones: Animation Pioneer

ACADEMY OF ACHIEVEMENT / 1993

From the Academy of Achievement website, online at www.achievement.org, June 25, 1993. Copyright © 1993 Academy of Achievement. Reprinted with permission.

Academy of Achievement: We've been asking people that we interview "What person inspired you the most?" But in your case, I believe there was a cat.

Chuck Jones: Well, there was a cat by the unlikely name of Johnson, the only cat I've ever known who had a last name for a first. We were living in Newport Beach, California, this was around 1918, I was six years old. It was early in the morning, and my brother and I saw this cat come strolling over the sand dunes. He had scar tissue on his chest, and one ear was slightly bent. He had a piece of string tied around his neck, an old wooden tongue depressor, and in crude lettering, in lavender ink, it said, "Johnson." We didn't know whether that was his blood type, or his name, or his former owner's name, or anything, so we called him Johnson. He answered to that as well as anything else. Like most cats, he answered to food, that's what he answered to.

Anyway, he came to live with us, and he turned out to be a rather spectacularly different cat. He came up to my mother while she was finishing breakfast, and she figured he wanted something to eat. So she offered him a piece of bacon, a piece of egg white, and a piece of toast, all of which he spurned. He obviously had nothing like that in mind. Finally, in a little spurt of whimsy, which was typical of my mother, she gave him a half a grapefruit, and it electrified him. Suddenly, there was this flash of tortoise shell cat whirling around with this thing. Then he came sliding out of it, and the thing slowly came to a stop. The whole thing was completely cleaned out, and we looked at him in astonishment. He loved grapefruit more than anything else in the whole world. So each morning for a while we gave him half a grapefruit, and that was nothing to him. So we gave him a whole grapefruit. And he'd eat it until all the inside was gone. Sometimes he'd eat it in such a way that he ended up wearing a little space helmet, which is really the whole grapefruit, with a flap hanging down on one side like a batter's helmet. But when he had it on, he seemed to like it. And sometimes he'd walk out on the beach with this thing on his head, until it really bothered him, then he'd kick it off.

He liked to be with people, particularly young people. He was very fond of children. We'd all learned to swim early, and one day we were swimming and we looked around and here was Johnson out there swimming with us. I don't know if you've ever seen a cat swim or not. They can swim very well, but most of them don't seem to like it. He really did, but only his eyes would show above the water. He looked like a pug-nosed alligator with hair. For some reason they grimace like this, and his teeth were hanging down, and most of him was under water; all the oil comes off the fur and trails behind them, along with a few sea gull feathers and other stuff. When he got tired out there, he would come and put his arms up on our shoulders and sort of hang there for a while. It was all right as long as it was only people in the family. But unfortunately, it wasn't always, because if he couldn't find one of us, he'd approach a stranger. People would come out of the surf looking pretty disturbed, and you knew they'd had a social encounter with old Johnson.

At any rate, the great moment for Johnson (the cat) came one time when he had eaten his grapefruit and it was stuck on his head, and he came out and strolled down the beach. We were up on the porch of our house, a two-story house, looking down at the sand. And he started off toward the pier, and as it happened the Young Women's Christian Association was having a picnic there.

Well, not only did he have his helmet on, but somewhere along the line he had found parts of a dead sea gull and it had left a few feathers on his shoulders. So he was quite a sight.

He strolled down to where these girls were having a picnic. And they took one look at this thing with the feathers, and the whole business, so they screamed and jumped up and ran into the ocean. Well, that was a technical mistake, because of course, Johnson, being a gregarious sort, decided that he wanted to join the group. I don't know, maybe he was going to appeal to the Supreme Court that male cats were allowed in the Girl Scouts, or whatever it was. So he went in after them, and they left in various states of undress—not undress, I mean their minds were boggled. And I never saw so many girls that were so boggled. And they never came back to Balboa, or Newport Beach.

It was important to me, because it established once and for all in my mind that every cat is different than other cats.

AA: In your book you make it clear that Johnson provided a lesson for you about human nature.
CJ: You cannot take anything for granted. The basic thing about Johnson was the fact that he was different than other cats. He was not every cat, in other words, any more than any of us are really every man, or every woman. That laid the groundwork, so when I got to doing Daffy Duck, or Bugs Bunny, or Coyote—that's not all coyotes, that is the particular coyote. "Wile E. Coyote, Genius." That's what he calls himself. He's different. He has an overweening ego, which isn't necessarily true of all coyotes.

Mark Twain's *Roughing It* is a book that many people don't know about, but I highly recommend to anybody at any age. He and his brother crossed the United States in a stagecoach. How romantic can you get? They went from Kansas City and Independence, Missouri, and out across the Great Plains, with four horses, pulling them across the plains.

Mark Twain went on to start telling the first time he met a coyote. And his expression—when I was six years old I read this—and he said that the coyote is so meager, and so thin, and so scrawny, and so unappetizing that, he said, "A flea would leave a coyote to get on a velocipede (or a bicycle)." There's more food on a bicycle than there is on a coyote. And he said how the coyote always looked like he was kind of ashamed of himself. And no matter what the rest of his face was doing, his mouth was always looking kind of crawly. And there are some wonderful expressions about how the coyote exists in that terrible environment, but how fast it is. And he said, "If you ever want to teach a dog lessons about what an inferior subject it is, let him loose when there's a coyote out there."

Mark Twain's *Roughing It*. I've read it over and over again, and I recommend it to anybody. You can still get it. It's two volumes. He goes on to when he lived in San Francisco and Silver City. It's great history, and charmingly told.

AA: Do you remember when you first read it?
CJ: I was six, I think.

I started reading when I was about three, a little over three. My father felt it was best if we did our own reading. He said he had too many things he wanted to read himself to waste his time reading to us. He said, "You want to read? Learn to read." He said, "Hell, you learn to walk at two years. You can certainly learn to read at three." And so we all did. We all learned to read very early. And he helped us by seeing to it that we had plenty of things to read. In those days people moved a lot. And very often people left their whole libraries. You must understand—anybody living today, or the day of television or radio and stuff—that in those days there wasn't any such thing. Reading was what you did, that's how you found out things.

That was the way you learned anything. In 1918, when I was six or seven years old, radio was just coming into use in the Great War. Nobody had a radio. It wasn't until the 1920s people began to have that. Even a phonograph, or something like that, was pretty expensive. They were marvelous, but we didn't have one until the 1920s.

Although my childhood was stringent, we were hardly living in abject poverty at any time. But we were able to move to houses that were loaded with books. There were four children and two adults. We'd move into that house like a pack of locusts and go through all the books there. Then my father would go out and rent another one of what he called a furnished house. It didn't matter whether there was any furniture in it, but it did matter if there were books in it.

AA: How did your father feel about you becoming a cartoonist?

CJ: Actually, he was responsible for it, but he didn't know what I was going to do. When I went to high school I wasn't brighter than the other kids, I just read so damn much. I got good grades in things that I liked, but I didn't get along with the things that I didn't. Finally, when I was about to enter my junior year, my father took me out and put me in art school. He figured that I'd probably had enough general education, but I needed to learn how to do something, he didn't know what. There was a fine arts school there called the Chouinard Art Institute, which is now called the California Institute of the Arts. They have a fine animation division there now, probably the best in the world, which is a curious thing because a lot of the young people that went to Chouinard Art Institute became the backbone of the animation business when it was new. He didn't lead me into cartoons, he led me into learning how to draw in a practical way and not just drawing anything you wanted to.

I would say my mother had more to do with my education as an artist, if you want to call me that, than anything else. All of us drew, and all of us went into different fields of graphics. My sister is a fine sculptress, and my other sister taught painting. My brother is still a very fine painter and a photographer. All of us went into it. Why? Because we weren't afraid to go into it.

AA: I gather that your parents were not critical of your art?

CJ: No.

My mother said—and I didn't realize how well it works—when I'd bring a drawing to her, she said, "I don't look at the drawing. I looked at the child, and if the child was excited, I got excited." And then we could discuss it. Because we were bringing something that meant something to me as a child. And so she would join in my lassitude, or my excitement, or my frustration. She wasn't a psychologist, but she did understand this simple matter.

The only thing an adult can give a child is time. That's all, there isn't anything else. That's the only thing they need, really, is time. If you give them time, you'll have to be understanding.

AA: Who gave you your first break in the field of cartoons?

CJ: I came out of art school in 1931, right in the worst of the Depression, two years before Franklin Roosevelt came in. The whole United States was flat. To expect to get a job when three out of every ten people were unemployed was ridiculous, particularly for a kid without any experience in anything. I had worked my way through art school by being a janitor, but I never worked full time as a janitor, and I wasn't sure I was capable. I was certainly willing.

When I came out, one of my friends who had been at Chouinard with me had gone to work with Walt Disney's ex-partner, a man by the name of Ub Iwerks. He was the one who animated most of the Disney stuff. Disney was not a good animator, he didn't draw well at all, but he was always a great idea man, and a good writer. Iwerks was a great artist and a great animator. Somebody convinced him that he was the brains and the talent in the outfit, so he left and started his own studio.

He was hiring people, and he hired this friend of mine named Fred Kopietz. Fred called me up and asked me if I wanted to go to work, to my extreme astonishment, which has held for sixty-three years. I'm still astonished that somebody would offer me a job and pay me to do what I wanted to do. And to this day, that's been the astonishment of my life, and delight of my life, and the wonder of my life, and the puzzlement that anybody would be so stupid as to be willing to do that. I hear all these success stories of people, these captains of industry, these forgers of the world, and empire builders and so on. And they talk about all the money they've made and become presidents and all that, and I thought, jeez, but look at me. When I was offered a chance to be head of studios, I wouldn't take it. I like to work with the tools of my trade. The tools of my trade are a lot of paper and a pencil, and that's all it is.

AA: Tell us what your first job was.
CJ: I started out as what they call a cel washer. The cels are the paintings that go into the camera in animated cartoons. The ink lines are on one side and the color is on the other. In those days, they were black and white, but they were made the same way. In those days, those cels cost seven cents a piece. You used three or four thousand drawings in those simple days in a seven- or eight-minute cartoon. So after you finished a picture, you washed them off and used them again.

One of those black and white Mickey Mouse cels recently sold at auction in New York for $175,000. They were washing them off, too. Nobody thought to save them. Why should they? They weren't worth anything. So that was my first job, washing them off. Then I moved up to become a painter in black and white, some color. Then I went on to take animator's drawings and trace them on to the celluloid. Then I became what they call an in-betweener, which is the guy that does the drawing between the drawings the animator makes.

AA: You bounced around a good deal in the early years, from one place to another.
CJ: Yeah, for about a year. I worked for the Charles Mintz Studio, and then I worked for Walt Lantz, who later on did Woody Woodpecker.

AA: Tell us about how you came to work for Leon Schlesinger and Warner Bros., what that was like.
CJ: In 1933, I went to work for Leon Schlesinger and that's where I stayed for thirty-eight years. Leon had formed a company called Pacific Art and Title. To this day that company exists. It does a lot of the title work for various studios and independent producers.

Unfortunately, he was very lazy. All he knew was he made pictures that Warner Bros. bought. I think he was married to one of Warner's sisters, or something. There was a familial relationship of some kind there. He made pictures and sold them to Warner Bros. And he didn't care. As long as they bought them, that was fine. Warner Bros. didn't care what they were, as long as we provided the product. You had to have a feature picture, and you had to have two or three short subjects, which were aggregated into a two-hour program. So you needed a bunch of short subjects.

AA: Tell us a little bit about how Leon Schlesinger became one of the prime inspirations for Daffy Duck.
CJ: Well, Leon Schlesinger was very lazy, and that stood to our advantage, because he didn't hang over us or anything. He spent as little time in the studio as he could. He'd come back and ask us what we were working on, and we knew he wasn't going to listen, no matter what we said. So we would say something like, well, "I'm working on this picture with Daffy Duck, and it turns out that Daffy isn't a duck at all, he's a transvestite chicken." And he would say, "That'th it boyth. Put in lot'th of joketh." He had a little lisp.

So, one day, when he went out, Cal Howard, one of our writers, said, "You know that voice of Leon's would make a good voice for Daffy Duck." So he called in Mel Blanc and said, "Can you do Leon Schlesinger's voice?" And Mel said, "Sure, it's very simple." The one thing we forgot was that Leon was going to have to see that picture and hear his own voice coming out of that duck.

AA: Did you think you'd be fired?
CJ: Oh, yes. I expected to be fired. In fact, we all wrote our resignations, all of us that worked on the film. We figured we'd resign before we got fired. Fortunately, we didn't send them in.

Leon came crashing in that day, as he usually did, and we assembled all the troops to watch the picture. Leon jumped up on his platform and said, "Roll the garbage." That's what he always said. It made you feel like he really cared. So we rolled the garbage, and of course everybody in the studio knew the drama of the situation, so nobody laughed. He didn't care, he didn't pay attention to what anybody else did anyway. It was only his opinion that counted. So at the end of the picture there was this deathly silence, but old Leon jumped up and glared around, and we thought, "Here comes the old ax." And he said, "Jesus Christ, that's a funny voice, where'd you get that voice?" So, that was what it was, and he went to his unjust desserts, doubtless taking his money with him. But the voice lives on. As long as Daffy Duck is alive, Leon Schlesinger is there, in his corner of heaven.

AA: You've said we laugh at ourselves when we laugh at Daffy Duck and Bugs Bunny, and that laughter can be therapeutic because it makes people feel less alone. Do you have a sense of doing that for people?
CJ: It's a marvelous thing when it happens. I've never gotten used to the idea that I can do anything that way. When people laugh, and they respond, it's a gift. There's one rule that I feel is vital. It was set down by G. K. Chesterton, who said, "I don't take myself seriously, but I take my work deadly seriously." Comedy is a very, very, very stringent business. Jackie Gleason said it's probably the most difficult and demanding of any form of drama. Because you have an instant critic: laughter. You don't know if people are suffering enough or not in tragedy, but in comedy you know.

If you're making it for films, you don't know until you've taken it to an audience. I never had the courage to take any of mine to an audience. The first picture I ever made, I thought that it wouldn't even move when it got out of there. And they had to lure me out—I was in a terrible funk—to go out and see it in front of an audience. It scared the hell out of me. And I pretended like I wasn't there, you know. And so, we were sitting in the balcony in Warner's theater in Hollywood, 1938,

and the cartoon came on, and there was a little hesitation. And the little
girl sitting in front of me said to her mother, she said, "Mommy, I knew
we should have come here." You know, "I knew we should have come
here." The tenses get all mixed up. But I wanted to adopt her and take
her home, because she was laughing. At six or eight years old. She was
past that terrible age. If she had been five she would have destroyed me.

The remarkable thing, I think, about all creative endeavor, whether it
be music, or art, or writing, or anything else, is that it is not competitive,
except with yourself. And all business, and all manufacturing, and everything that's presented to the public is competitive. They are trying to
present the same object perhaps under a different name to supersede
the other person, and it's competitive, it's a foot race. But art can't be.
One thing is, you don't know what the other guy is doing. I'm talking
about good writing and good art. It can't be competitive.

AA: You said that you actually have this fear that you might wake up
and not be funny?
CJ: Yeah, or that you might make a picture and you've lost the whole
skill. Arthur Rubinstein said that when he walked out on a stage and saw
two thousand people who had paid money to see him perform, he said,
"I could not give them less than the best that I have."

You have no right to diminish an audience's expectations. You have
to give them everything that you have. And with children, with anything
that's supposedly being done for children, the requirement becomes
much more stringent. You've got to do the best you can. You have no
right to pull back. You have no right to "write for children." You do the
best thing that you can do. And the audiences—for children—all the
more so, because you're building a child's expectation of what is good
and what is bad. And all this stuff—the word "kidvid," which is used so
freely, is one of the ugliest words in the English language. It means
you're writing down to children. How are you going to build children up
by writing down to them?

There's only one test of a great children's book, or a great children's
film, and that is this: if it can be read or viewed with pleasure by adults,
then it has the chance to be a great children's film, or a great children's
book. If it doesn't, it has no chance. Every film should be pursued in
that way.

I've always felt that the very best I can is the very least I can do. I
don't think about the audience, I think about me. And I think about how

grateful I am that I blundered into that group of whimsical, wild, otterish-type people that are in there, all of them nutty and all of them intense. Because don't forget, we talked a lot about how free times were then, but every one of us had to turn out ten pictures a year, in order to get the thirty that Warner Bros. needed. And so, it was frivolous, to be sure, plenty of frivolity and plenty of laughter, but for every bit of laughter there has to be 90 percent of work.

I do three to four hundred drawings on every picture—the three to four hundred pictures that I used. But sometimes I might draw fifty drawings trying to get one expression, so that it will look right for Bugs, or Daffy. Or something like this. Sometimes it came quickly, like writing, sometimes you come to a dead stop. And I'd have to haul off. I'd have to go and do something, because I couldn't break through, couldn't find what the guy was supposed to be doing, and that's all. You don't have to worry about drawing. After a while it's as easy to draw Daffy, or Bugs, or anything as just movement. I know how to do that, but what's he thinking about? And I have to get that expression to indicate what he's thinking about.

AA: You've said of your work directing animation, that there's a sense in which you're almost married to the character. Could you talk about that?
CJ: Yes. You depend on them. You have to trust one another. In a lot of marriages, people don't, and that results in bad pictures and bad marriages.

Often, when I'm halfway through a picture, I don't know what the hell I'm going to do. How am I going to end it? And then have to think more carefully, "What would Bugs Bunny do in a situation like this?" In other words, I can't think of what I would do, or what I think Bugs Bunny should do. I have to think as Bugs Bunny, not of Bugs Bunny. And drawing them, as I say, is not difficult. Just like an actor dressed like Hamlet can walk across and look like Hamlet. But boy, when he gets into the action, he has to be thinking as Hamlet.

AA: Tell us that little anecdote about the writer who wrote to his grand-mother that he was writing scripts for Bugs Bunny.
CJ: Yeah. Bill Scott, he later did most of the work on Rocky and Bullwinkle. He was the voice of the moose and other voices. He was the lead writer. He was bright. After the war, he came to work for us as a writer. And he was very proud he was there, and he wrote a letter to his grandmother in Denver and told her he was writing scripts for Bugs

Bunny. And she wrote back a rather peckish letter that indicated she wasn't very happy about that. She said, "I don't see why you have to write scripts for Bugs Bunny. He's funny enough just the way he is." He was delighted with that. We were delighted with it, too.

If you want to know what a triumph is, it's the feeling that people really believe these characters live, just like we do. But if we don't, there's no chance anybody else is going to.

AA: Where do you see animation going now? How do you feel about the way it's going?

CJ: Animation is going very well right now. And to a great extent because of these young people at Disney that are doing the films. We must understand, this is a whole new generation that's starting with *The Great Mouse Detective*, and *Oliver*, and *The Little Mermaid*, and *Beauty and the Beast*, and *Aladdin*, and all done by people in their thirties and twenties. And that's where we started. We were all young like that.

When I went into animation, I was like seventeen, and the old man of the business was Walt Disney, who was twenty-nine. Walt Disney was not forty by the time he finished *Fantasia*, and *Snow White and the Seven Dwarves*, and *Pinocchio*. And the people that worked with him were younger than that. So it takes young people. And that's what I'm—I think I've just about gotten to where I've finished to work out a deal with Warner Bros. to do some more films. But I want to be the old man that pulls together the young guys today if I can. I want to be a magnet, pulling in creative young people from the art schools, and get them started again, doing some of the old characters, but in new stories, and so on. But new characters too, and hopefully a Warner Bros. feature. That's what I'd like to do. And I've written a couple of scripts that are not too bad, I think.

AA: What is directing animation?

CJ: Well, directing is doing the key drawings, not the key animation, mind you. If the coyote is falling, and he looks at the audience and holds up a sign saying, "Please end this picture before I hit." I have to make that particular drawing to show the attitude I want on the drawing. Plus the action of getting in there, the action of running, if he's going to fly like Batman, or falling over the cliff. Also, I have timed the entire scene.

It scares cameramen and anybody who works behind the camera to find out that in animation in Warner Bros. we weren't allowed to edit. You couldn't over-shoot—it was too expensive. So all of us as directors had to learn to time the entire picture on music, on bar sheets, just like you were writing a symphony. That's carrying it on a bit, but anyway— so by the time it came out to 540 feet, that's six minutes. Leon Schlesinger wouldn't let us make them any longer than six minutes, and the exhibitor wouldn't let us make them any shorter than six minutes, so they had to be six minutes. So we had to learn to do that, and it drives people like George Lucas or Spielberg crazy. "How can you make a picture without editing?"

Well, it is edited, but it's edited before it goes into work. There are a few live action directors, like Hitchcock, that shot a meager amount, but not the way we did it. At Disney's, they always have enough money so they could over-shoot. They could do entire sequences and take them out. It was heartbreaking, of course, for the animator. Because where an actor might have a fifteen-second, or twenty-second scene, even if they did it three or four times, it would take less than twenty minutes. But with the animator, if he's animated a scene that runs twenty seconds, it might be two weeks' work that's been thrown out.

AA: Music is such a key element in those Warner Bros. cartoons. You must have a musical bent.

CJ: I know something about it, but mainly through experience working with people like Carl Stalling and Milt Franklin. These were two incredible people with great memories. Stalling was particularly useful because he had been a silent-movie organist in Kansas City. In the Road Runner, for instance, people think of that as just helter-skelter, but it wasn't. A big percentage of the music was Smetana's *Bartered Bride* music. And whenever I had undersea stuff or so on, I always used Mendelssohn's Overture to *Fingal's Cave*. Later, when we did *How the Grinch Stole Christmas*, we used original music, but curiously enough, the Christmas music was done to a square dance call. We used it, because the rhythm sounded right, it was very cheery.

AA: Thanks for talking with us. And thanks for all the great cartoons.

Interview with Chuck Jones

MARK THOMPSON AND BRIAN PHELPS / 1996

From the "Mark & Brian" radio show,
KLOS-FM, April 1996. Interview
transcribed by Stormy Gunter, edited by
Maureen Furniss. Copyright © 1996 ABC
Radio Networks. Transcript printed with
permission.

M&B: That's perfect timing, because Chuck Jones just arrived, just came in the studio, sat down. Welcome back, Chuck.

Let us introduce Chuck, for anybody who's sitting there and doesn't quite know who we're talking about. This gentleman here created and brought to life Bugs Bunny, Daffy Duck, Elmer Fudd, Road Runner, Wile E. Coyote, Marvin Martian, Pepé Le Pew, and many, many others of the Warner Bros. classic cartoons. This year, we just saw him a month or so ago receive a Lifetime Achievement Award, an Academy Award, for his work over a lifetime of bringing the cartoons to the big screen.

Sixty years in animation. Now usually when he visits us, he brings a cel from one of his cartoons, and he gives it to us. This time he brought—and this is what, only a month old now?—the Oscar, the Academy Award he won . . .

M&B: . . . two weeks ago . . .

M&B: . . . it's sitting right here. And we'll go ahead and tell you what you've heard other people say: they're a lot heavier than you would think. Really heavy. A good workout actually . . .

M&B: . . . if you were just to curl it while you were in the car . . .

M&B: Now, welcome back Chuck. How are you?
CJ: [laughter] It's good to be back. I always enjoyed you birds. I just can't get up early enough to hear you.

M&B: [laughter] Now, this is your second Academy Award, but this particular one you were saying means so much more because it is an honorary award for the lifetime of work you've put forth.
CJ: Yes, you'd have to have lived a lifetime.

M&B: To get one of these.
CJ: That's right.

M&B: Which does help out.
CJ: It doesn't require any special [pause] talent. But you'd have to have lived a lifetime. I am entering my eighty-fourth year, and I just got back from Washington, where Herb Block, the great cartoonist of the *Washington Post*—they had had a party for him because he has been drawing cartoons for the *Washington Post* for fifty years.

M&B: And excellently done also.
CJ: Marvelous, one of the great cartoonists of all time. I think one of the greatest political forces of our life, or of my lifetime, which is a lot more extended than yours.

M&B: The last time you were here, you talked about a really interesting scenario. When you and the guys and gals you were working with when you first were starting out, you all kinda had gotten together. Was it Tex Avery that you were talking about, who all of you would work with— that he kind of passed down the way that he liked to draw cartoons and the creative force that goes behind them.

CJ: Well, Tex came over and was really the driving force for the kind of animation that he did. Nobody had ever done that kind of thing—the absolute nutty, wild timing and so on. People have tried to imitate it and have probably studied it a long time. It's flashing all over television today. But Tex was a very conservative man in many ways. In other words, he would start out any cartoon with a feeling that it was going to be a normal cartoon. And then suddenly it'd explode. These people think that you always explode—and of course you don't. And that is what made his pictures so remarkable. You knew that it was coming, but you didn't know when. But, yes, Bob Clampett and Tex and Bobe Cannon, who went on to do *Gerald McBoing Boing* and things, we all worked together there. We didn't know we were doing anything historic.

M&B: Just working.

CJ: Or hysteric for that matter. Um, as a matter of fact, we never, we . . . I don't know of anybody that's accomplished anything that really knew that they belonged in history. I'm part of history because I've been at it longer than anybody else. [laughter]

M&B: Very historical. Let me ask you about Wile E. Coyote. I heard somewhere, somebody told me that the inspirations for Wile E. Coyote were from your own experience, your own lack of skills with tools. Is that correct?

CJ: Although that would be Daffy, more than anything else. But it all comes back to the same old story, doesn't it? Where do you get your characters? And there's only one place that any actor, any director, or any cartoonist can find these characters, and that is inside himself, in you, because the core of every character is within you. We all are the ultimate failures, and we dream about being the heroes.

M&B: The Bugs Bunny.

CJ: Oh, I dream about being Bugs Bunny, but when I wake up, I'm Daffy Duck.

M&B: Right.

CJ: Or the Coyote. And before I proceed, I'd like to say that there were so many wonderful people that were contributors to these characters. Because as you get older, one of the values of getting older, if there are values, is that there are fewer people around that contradict you.

M&B: [laughter] Which is nice.

CJ: I can take credit for almost anything.

M&B: Well, sure, go ahead.

CJ: I tell my great grandchildren what a nice man Lincoln was, you know.

M&B: You know, it's kind of interesting with the cartoons and the characters involved—it's much like some of the characters on this program or some characters on *Saturday Night Live*, in that, when they first start out they are kind of what they are and as time goes along, the characters will change a little bit. They become more fully developed. Which is the case with Daffy Duck. If you look at a very early Daffy Duck cartoon, Daffy in the very first ones was a loon. Right. Right exactly. [Daffy's laugh]

CJ: He was crazy.

M&B: And Bugs.

CJ: Bugs—the same thing. But after Tex left and went to MGM and did some great films over there, Friz Freleng and I were pretty much in charge of the development of the characters. And we realized that pretending that you're crazy is much nicer than being crazy. The Spaniards used to chain up an idiot, and let him foam at the mouth. They thought that it was very funny, you know. Since that time, crazy is not enough. Pretending you're crazy—Groucho Marx pretends that he is crazy. But he isn't, and you know he isn't. You know he's playing at it. The Road Runner, however, was just a force. He's not a personality. He's more like electricity.

M&B: But he has a personality.

CJ: He has, yes.

M&B: A great personality.

CJ: But people say, why would anybody chase anything like that for food? Well, you have friends who would do almost anything for a one-ounce jar of caviar, rather than fifty hot dogs or money. I'd choose the hot dogs anytime. But there are some people that would die for that, you know. They die for little things like diamonds. You know, like Mark Twain said, "Diamonds are the hardest substance in the world, particularly to get back."

M&B: [laughter] Chuck, who wrote the majority of the dialog in the cartoons?

CJ: Well, in my case, the ultimate dialog I wrote, by translating into my own terms how I would think. Mike was brilliant at writing dialog. But he wrote in a broad sense, then I had to bring it down so that it fit the character. You must understand that we could never write a line for Daffy that Bugs could say, in the same sense that Groucho wouldn't say the same line that Chico would.

M&B: Sure. Daffy couldn't be too cool. Bugs got all the cool lines.

CJ: Well, a good way of stating it would be that Bugs talks and Daffy talks too much. [laughter] And that is the history of almost all of our problems isn't it?

M&B: Interestingly enough, I was watching a movie on Showtime or HBO the other day. I just kinda popped on it while I was clicking around, and it was a movie about a real live action kid who fell into his television and found himself in a cartoon. And in the cartoon he's in this house, and he was a cartoon figure, and the vacuum cleaner came alive and was coming after him. And the kid is sitting there thinking, "Okay, okay, okay, what do I do? What would I do if I were a cartoon? Well, I am a cartoon, so what am I gonna do? Here's what they always do in the cartoons." He wrote a letter very quickly and mailed it off to the ACME Company. And of course, seconds within mailing it he got whatever he needed to save his life.

CJ: It was an automatic dog.

M&B: Yes, it was as a matter of fact! It certainly was. You know the movie that we're talking about?

CJ: Sure. I directed it.

M&B: Oh. [laughter] Great. Good that you're in. OK. Good that you're here. [laughing] That's great. Well, you know what? The cartoon work on that was fabulous.

CJ: Yeah, it wasn't the greatest picture in the world, but—

M&B: But still, the cartoon stuff was great. And I remember thinking "Wow!" And you bring up a good point. You can always tell a Chuck Jones cartoon because it's more detailed than the rest. I mean the most detail always goes into yours. And I always wondered whose idea was it to put Bugs in drag the very first time? And did you have any negative connotations from whatever organization?

CJ: Well, at that time, which was before you guys were even born— it may be difficult for you to imagine a time when you weren't born. And I'm sure the public would agree that it's far better that you're here. But—

M&B: Depending on the day, Chuck.

CJ: The thing was at that time, if a man dressed up like a woman, there was no transvestite. Nobody even knew the term.

M&B: It was just funny.

CJ: It was just funny. The man would put on a woman's hat, and they would think that was funny. They wouldn't think that the man was turning into something "inappropriate."

M&B: Little did they know he really liked it.

CJ: Yeah, he did. We found that out as we went along.

M&B: *Wayne's World* even dealt with it in the first movie *Wayne's World*. Garth looked at Wayne and said, "When you see Bugs Bunny in drag, do you get sexually turned on?" [laughter] It's one of the most fabulous things that Bugs has ever done.

M&B: Chuck, you had told me the name of this last time, and I want to ask you again, so you can tell me. It was a Tex Avery cartoon, and it caught me by surprise. I was watching the Cartoon Network one day while having lunch, and this cartoon popped on about, I think it was a cow or something, and his uncle comes to his house in a big fancy car and takes him to town. And they're in a club, and they're watching the show, and the country hick is going to whistle and his uncle plugs up his whistling mouth with his finger and the whistle goes down his arm and out his own mouth.

CJ: That's right.

M&B: Do you remember the name of that cartoon, by chance?

CJ: No, it followed up from *Red Hot Riding Hood*. It may have been *Red Hot Riding Hood*. There had been two or three of them.

M&B: But it was a Tex Avery cartoon?

CJ: Oh, yes. All of those were Tex Avery's.

M&B: That's about as funny as it gets, those cartoons.

CJ: You bet. One of the strange things about that was that during the war, and it's hard I suppose for many people today—young people—to realize there was a war in which everybody was cool to the idea of winning a war. We had great villains, which you don't have in most wars, because you had Adolf Hitler, Hirohito, and Mussolini and all those lovely people to hate. Well, Tex made a picture called *The Blitz Wolf*, and there was the same wolf. Only this time it was Adolf Hitler and he took a terrible beating. Well, they had a producer there, and I won't use his name because he's the kind of man that's probably still alive and would be 105 and still irritating the world. He had one thing in common with George Washington in that his dentures didn't fit. So he'd talk through his teeth "like this." And Tex said, he'd come in and say, "Tex have you noticed"—they'd called him Fred, because his name was Fred—"Have you noticed how beautiful the eucalyptus trees are along the road?" [laughter] And he went on, he said, "I was just looking at the storyboard of the *Blitz Wolf*" and he said—you think, this is 1944, right in the middle of the war—and he said, "Do you think you're being a little rough on Mr. Hitler? 'Cause we don't know who's going to win the war."

M&B: My god. Oh, my god.

CJ: Can you imagine that?

M&B: No.

CJ: He was a brilliant man. He was in charge of animation at MGM.

M&B: Many people may not know this and would be very excited to know that Chuck Jones Film Productions is making new cartoons for theaters, including *Chariots of Fur*, that'd be a Road Runner and Wile E. Coyote, and *Another Froggy Evening* with Michigan J. Frog—that's not been released yet. What are the differences these days of making feature cartoons for theaters?

CJ: These are six-minute films.

M&B: Right.

CJ: Everybody's making features.

M&B: Right. But for the movie theaters back then.

CJ: Well, when Bob Daly and Terry Semel were the head of Warner Bros., through the advice of John Schulman, who's my friend over there,

they asked me to come over and make some cartoons. I said that I'd
come over and do so providing the end purpose was to get rid of me.
Because hiring an eighty-year-old man to do cartoons seems a little
chancy, you know. And I said the other reason I wanted them to get rid
of me was because I wanted to set up a situation where young people
could come in—young people under forty, hopefully thirty, would come
in with new ideas, give new adventures to the old characters and invent
new adventures for new characters. In other words, the purpose of this
was not for me to make cartoons, but for me to help young people get
started making cartoons.

M&B: Well, it must have been fabulous when the line was as long as,
you know, five city blocks to the door with young people wanting to
come and do this.
CJ: Yeah, yeah, well I'm glad they're willing to do what is necessary.
I don't know if I ever told you that when I went in to art school, and this
professor got up in front of us, he wasn't really a professor, he was a
maestro—a great artist—got up in front of us and said, looking down at
us, he said, "Everyone of you birds has a hundred thousand bad drawings in ya. The sooner you get rid of them, the better it'd be for everybody." [laughter] He said, "The better it'd be for everybody." That's
wonderful. And one of the things he wanted us to realize is that facing
the public is our duty. That's a thing that's hard for everybody to understand, that although you must make pictures for yourself, you have
to face the audience, no matter what it is. It may not even be in your
lifetime. Vincent Van Gogh never faced an audience. He only sold two
paintings in his lifetime, to his brother. But nevertheless, eventually his
paintings had to face the audience. And now they're worth millions and
millions and millions of dollars.

M&B: So do you enjoy playing the role as the mentor?
CJ: Well, I would if I thought of myself in that way. You don't change.
I mean you always have extraordinary doubts about your own ability.

M&B: Maybe you can help with this. Because this is just an observation
I've made and I can't quite put my finger on it, but it's a fact. When you
watch some of the Bugs Bunnys, the Daffy Ducks, the Coyotes, this is
also the case with Foghorn Leghorn, even Tom and Jerry for that
matter. The cartoons have such a—the ones I'm talking about, from the
sixties and fifties—they have such a robustness because the color is full

and the activity of the character is so almost human in a sense, as compared to the cartoons of now in most cases. Even with some of the Disney stuff now, it's not the same, it's not as active or full or animated or something. I don't quite understand what it is that grabs me and lets me know that it's different. Can you explain?

CJ: No, I can't explain how that works, but I do know the abiding factor in any creative work is that you must never talk down to your audience. You must be aware of them. One of the worst sins of all time is to write down to children. And to think your audience is a bunch of dumb people is the dumbest thing you can envisage. So you must, at least you owe the audience the best you can do. And that's not true today; so many of the people are writing down. An example of that would be when Mike Maltese and I worked together, we turned out an hour a year. That's ten six-minute cartoons. And we thought we were put upon because Disney only made six or seven cartoons a year and maybe five. And so we thought we were terribly put upon. But it turned out it was a very good thing for us, because you must work under a discipline. You guys, Mark and Brian, work under an extraordinary discipline. If you went out and were given all the time that you were allowed, you would be lost. Because once you're used to working, like Mondrian, the great painter who painted lines parallel to the sides said, "I cannot envisage not working under a discipline." A discipline is vital, and if you're open at both ends, goodbye. The creativity goes out.

M&B: Which is why I never studied for a test more than one day before the test. A discipline of cramming. I never. It's true. All right let's go to Dave on seven. Dave, you're on the air with Chuck Jones.

Dave: Hi, guys. Hi, Chuck. I just want to say that I'm a huge fan of Chuck's. Loved your work my whole life. I'm twenty-nine now and I have a son and I can't wait to turn him on to Bugs Bunny. My question is, do you have a favorite cartoon or a favorite character?

CJ: Well, how many children do you have?

Dave: I have just one son.

CJ: Ok, well, if you have more than one, you're going to have a favorite. But it would be very wise for you to keep that to yourself. [laughter] Otherwise you'd have a war on your hands.

Dave: I guess so.

CJ: The same thing holds true with us. If I said Daffy Duck is my favorite character, then I would be putting more effort into Daffy than I would into the other characters. Actually I'm more comfortable with Daffy because he's much more like I am. Like when I did *How the Grinch Stole Christmas*, I loved doing it because everybody hates Christmas a little bit, and here's a guy that hated it completely. For the first time in my life, I could haul off and hate Christmas the way it should be hated. [laughter]

M&B: Fully.

CJ: So, Daffy, I'm comfortable with him, but he certainly isn't my favorite because he's kind of anti-kindness.

M&B: You know, you bring up another point that was interesting in that this year for some reason, and I never really noticed this, I only knew I really loved *How the Grinch Stole Christmas*, but this past year as I'm sitting there watching it with my kid, I became aware of just how much of another color in the cartoon the voice of Boris Karloff was. How wonderful he is in that selection and what an odd selection to choose Boris Karloff's voice to narrate that cartoon. Did you know him before that cartoon?

CJ: No, I didn't. Ah, well, I did know him, but he didn't know me, because he had done a lot of recordings. Many people didn't know he was a wonderful narrator.

M&B: Nobody can say the two words "roast beast" quite like he could.

CJ: When he got up in front of a microphone there and started reading this thing, I realized what a wonderful dear man he was as a personality. He would praise the way it was written and the rhythm of it.

M&B: Ah, that ought to make you feel good. He looks down from the microphone and says, "This is great stuff."

CJ: Yeah, very dear.

M&B: He really should be appreciated for his work there because it was another labor of love that made a classic.

CJ: That's right.

M&B: Let's go to Kevin on line one. Kevin, you're on the air with Chuck Jones. Kevin are you there? All right, we lost Kevin. How about Jim on fourteen? Jimmy, how ya doin' there buddy?

Jim: Pretty good. How are you?

M&B: You're on the air.

Jim: Alright. Hi, Mr. Jones.

CJ: Hello Jim. How are you?

Jim: Good, good. It's an honor and a privilege to talk to you. I've been a fan of yours and Mr. Freleng for years and years.

CJ: Yeah, we just lost Fred. He was a great loss, a wonderful man. I learned so much of what I knew about animation from him. His timing is exquisite—

Jim: Yeah.

CJ: —with some of the greatest things ever done. He made a picture called *Birds Anonymous* which is magnificent, one of the greatest cartoons ever made. We miss him.

Jim: Yeah, me too. Um, I've got a couple of questions for you from a couple of people. Hold on a second here. [changes voice] Hi, uh, Mr. Jones. This is Tom. And I am really a great fan of yours and of course the late, great Mel Blanc. And um, I was wondering if you could tell me any stories about him. And um, hold on, Tex wants to talk to you too. [changes voice] Aye, Mr. Jones, aye this is Tex, yeah I'm an aspiring voice actor and, uh, just kinda wonderin' if you could give me any advice.

CJ: Is this a casting session?

M&B: Yeah, boy. Jim sounded great though. Thank you, Jim.

CJ: What am I supposed to do, answer this?

M&B: Yeah, he wants to know if you have any advice for him as an aspiring voice actor.

CJ: Find an agent. [laughter] I don't mean to brush you off, but it's a very, very highly selective thing. The way to do it is to make a recording of your voices, but to make a record of all of the voices that have been done won't help you any. What you have to do is prove your versatility. If I were doing a goat and here's this personality that knows what he'd sound like, then you're able to express something that will awaken in the agent some feeling of something that could be done. But there were a lot of people that said they could do Mel Blanc's voice after Mel died. The thing is that there are many, many people that could take a line that Mel Blanc had spoken, like "What's up, Doc?" or Daffy, but if you gave them a new line and asked them to do it the way Bugs would do it, that's where the artistry comes in.

M&B: Mel Blanc was—I never met him and don't know what it was like to work with him, but the work that he himself put forth, the versatility—to watch a cartoon and realize he was the only voice in it. He was the one man that threw out everything that we're listening to for the most part.

CJ: Well, the thing is that when we had finished the dialog, Mel never even saw the dialog till an hour before he recorded it.

M&B: Really?

CJ: And I'd go over the entire story with him, and Friz would do it the same way, and we would—actually the intonation and the way a line was spoken must be the director's. And Mel was brilliant. In an hour we'd have the whole thing in hand. Let's say I was doing Daffy and I would read the line to him the way I wanted it spoken, because I'd been living with it for ten weeks by that time, so each line was carefully fashioned in my own mind. "Oh, no you don't. Not again. This time I'll start it." [laughter] "Shoot him now! Shoot him now!"

M&B: What about the formation of a character when you have a new character and you're going to form the personality and the voice of that character to be recorded? Would Mel throw out a couple of three things, and you guys would say, "Yeah, I don't like this. I like that. Try some more of that."

CJ: Oh, for a new character, yeah, we would probably try different things. At the time of recording though, that wasn't true, because we'd know what the character was.

M&B: Right, but in the development, like with Daffy Duck, did he just come out with it and OK that's it, or did you guys tweak with it a lot?

CJ: Daffy Duck was, uh, Daffy Duck's voice came from our producer, who'd come by and say, "What cha workin' on fellas?" [laughter] And he'd put in lots of jokes. So Cal Howard suggested to Tex that that would make a funny voice for the duck. We didn't have that voice like Daffy—like Bugs's first voice wasn't like this voice—the way it is now. So we called Mel and said can you do the voice of Leon Schlesinger, our producer? I shouldn't say—no wait, it's all right, he's in heaven now.

M&B: Chuck, we have to take a break, but when we come back if you could stay one more, we have a surprise for you. One of your biggest fans is here. He wanted to shake your hand. He's across the hall doing a

news radio thing, interview or something, and he'd like to come shake your hand. So, if you could just sit here for two more minutes.
CJ: If he doesn't mind.

M&B: I think he'd be fine with that.

M&B: Before we bring this person in, here's what happened. You were into your last story, and we looked across the glass in the news room, and there this man stood. And come to find out he is a major fan of yours, and he was doing an interview on the AM side, and he just wanted to shake your hand. So we thought we'd bring him in. Dan Quayle is here.

CJ: Hi, Dan. How are ya?

Dan Quayle: Chuck, nice to see you.

CJ: You, too.

DQ: Congratulations on a marvelous career. Oh, I'm just traveling around and just stopped in to see Brian and Mark. They always tell me if I'm in the vicinity to drop by.

CJ: Pretty scenic room.

DQ: Yeah, I know. What's this Brooklyn business, uh?

M&B: You know it's just a shirt somebody gave me for free, and so I figured why not wear it?

DQ: Aren't they paying you here? [laughter]

M&B: Not a great deal.

DQ: Not a great deal?

M&B: Boss, if you're listening there, uh, Mark needs a little bit of a raise there. It's a shiny shirt. Dan, what is your favorite character that Chuck Jones has done?

DQ: Road Runner.

M&B: Road Runner is your favorite?

DQ: No doubt about it.

M&B: The one you relate to most. I can see it in politics I guess.

DQ: I grew up in Phoenix, Arizona, so the Road Runner was very popular over there, and I loved it as a cartoon.

CJ: My daughter went to school up at Black Canyon. So, we're familiar, and we're square dancers, too. Did you ever square dance?

DQ: I've tried it. Marilyn says I'm not very good at it, so I leave that to the younger generation.

M&B: Yeah, it takes his wife to tell him that he's not good at it. He didn't know it himself.

CJ: In my viewpoint, you're the younger generation.

M&B: That's why he came in here—to make him feel good like that.

DQ: Yeah, that's right.

M&B: There in front of you is an Oscar. That's the Academy Award there, Dan.

DQ: I've, uh, actually that's the first time I've seen one.

M&B: You ever held one?

CJ: Pick it up.

DQ: Never held one. It's uh . . . heavy.

M&B: Everybody, that's the first thing everybody says. How heavy it is.

DQ: That's something I don't think I'll ever get.

M&B: Well, you never know. You're very young. You've got a lot of time left, so who knows?

DQ: That's right. Maybe get into an acting career. How do you think I'd do out there?

M&B: Well, it was between you and Clooney for Batman, wasn't it? Dan, thanks for coming in. You should come in when we have more time, okay?

CJ: Good to see you.

DQ: Congratulations on a wonderful career.

CJ: Thank you.

DQ: Thank you very much.

M&B: Good to see you sir. All right, Chuck Jones—
CJ: I'm all for corporal punishment, if I'm not the recipient. [laughter]

M&B: Good point. Now, one thing, we did touch on the subject a second ago, there are two new cartoons we wanted to mention earlier. One is *Chariots of Fur*—that's a Road Runner, Wile E. Coyote cartoon—and the other is *Another Froggy Evening* with Michigan J. Frog. This has been finished, but it has not been released yet. And it will be released in conjunction with a full-length feature film.
CJ: That's right.

M&B: Alright, now the way the bum made Michigan J. Frog dance [singing] with his fingers, with just the limp frog—it has to be some of the best and funniest and most on the money animation ever. That was brilliant. And Chuck has just presented us with a cartoon cel of Michigan J. Frog. Man. And it's got the official Chuck Jones seal and the whole thing. You are always very giving and very kind when you drop by this program. We appreciate this so much.
CJ: Give a man a tool he can use. [laughter] You guys bring a lot of laughter and if it will help you continue.

M&B: Well, you are very kind. Now, let's talk for a moment about what they'll see on Friday night. Your showroom has original—in many cases—original cartoon cels, from many of your classic cartoons and these are available for purchase, are they not?
CJ: Yes, so I'm told.

M&B: Okay.
Guest: There's some limited editions that Chuck has. Most of those original production cels were destroyed back—I mean millions of them back from the thirties, forties, fifties.

M&B: Hanna Barbera broke in or uh? [laughter] Gimme that! That's mine! Let me have it.
Guest: So, Chuck has a lot of new stuff. New limited editions that he continues to create and those are on display as well.

M&B: Well, Chuck, let us say, we here on this program, we had a viewing party of the Academy Awards with listeners of ours over on Sunset Blvd, we mentioned this earlier. We were sitting there watching the Academy Awards with them, several hundred of them as a matter of fact, close to a thousand. When you were up on the big screen, the big monitor we had there for people to watch, when you were up there it was very much for us like there was a relative up there that was receiving a long overdue Academy Award for a lifetime of fabulous work that you've put in. And we felt proud—you had not only allowed us to benefit from your cartoons but allowed us to speak with you personally, and shake your hand, and that you continue to come back to the program. And that you are so great to our listeners, too.

CJ: Well, you don't have to deserve something in order to enjoy it. Coming here is very much a pleasure because I respect you people, and I respect and I love your laughter. That's all we tried to do, to never talk down to an audience. We were fully aware that we were to give them the best that we could do. When you people watch the Academy Awards and cheered, told me that you cheered, this is one of the most endearing things that ever happened to me. Because being up there you say, "I don't belong here. Everybody else belongs here—should be Friz and Tex and the rest of them." They're long gone and that's too bad, you know. So, here I am getting something I don't deserve but still enjoying it.

M&B: First of all, maybe you do actually believe that, but it isn't true. Your name is synonymous with quality cartoons. Well, wait, if he doesn't think he deserves it, we'll take it. He brought it with him. You can just leave it here. If you don't want it, we'll take care of it for ya. You do deserve it, fella.

CJ: Well, I'd have to split it down the middle.

M&B: Yes, you would. It'd be half an Oscar. Ah, okay. Please come back. You're welcome here anytime.

CJ: Thank you, I'd like to.

M&B: Well, A: because we really, really like you; B: because we really, really respect you; and C: because we've got quite the wall of your cels that you bring every time that you come.

CJ: I'm trying to fix it so that you won't have to buy wallpaper ever again. [laughter]

M&B: Keep it coming, Chuck.

CJ: Okay. Thank you.

The Inner Daffy: Chuck Jones and the Creative Process

JO JÜRGENS / 1996

Unpublished interview. Copyright © 2004
Jo Jürgens. Published with permission.

JJ: How important are the personalities of the characters in animation?
CJ: The personality is the essential thing. It started with the three little pigs. Most people don't realize that *Three Little Pigs* in 1933 was the first picture with three characters that looked alike and were differentiated by the way they moved and the way they spoke. From that point on, acting came to animation. Not everybody used it. I don't know how many ways there are to animate, but in our pictures, Bugs and Daffy and all our characters were defined by the movement. None of them are funny to look at if you've never seen them in movement. It's like good actors. Woody Allen or Charlie Chaplin aren't funny to look at, but they are funny by the way they move. That's the whole point about character animation. But that's one way of animating. There are many people who don't do it that way. I admire a great deal the Yugoslavian school.

I talked down there a couple of times and enjoyed it enormously, but what they were doing wasn't what I was doing. They had different ways of expressing themselves.

JJ: So do you think that personality is the most important thing in Hollywood animation?
CJ: It isn't Hollywood; it's acting. It's simply carrying on what is done in live action. Great acting in any mode of motion pictures must be done with the character and the personality. That goes for Laurence Olivier or Chaplin or Bugs Bunny. I don't wanna get into an argument about what is the best kind of animation. What we are talking about is personality animation. That's what Frank and Ollie practised and Joe and Bill did when they were doing the Tom & Jerry cartoons, but stopped doing after that. The characters they made for television were what they were basically for what they looked like. That's true of *The Simpsons*, and they're darn good because they have good scripts and so on, but if you turn the sound off, you can't tell what's happening. But in full animation, character animation, just as it is in live action, you can get a pretty good idea of what's going on by the way the characters move, without hearing them. It isn't only the Coyote and Road Runner. Whenever I finished a cartoon, I would run it in pencil test form, without colour and backgrounds, just the characters moving around without dialogue. If it worked then, it would certainly work with dialogue. The dialogue would probably enhance it.

JJ: Would you always take the personalities of the characters when doing the stories for your films into consideration, that this character wouldn't do this or that and so on?
CJ: Of course. That's what individuality is all about. If you're writing for the Marx Brothers, a line written for Chico would never work for Groucho or vice versa. Same thing would be true of Laurel and Hardy. The writers were careful to define the way the line was written in relationship to the character. Same thing with us. Bugs would never say a line the way Daffy would say it, and Daffy would not say it the way Elmer Fudd might say it. Of course you design the dialogue to fit the characters. If I'd known you for a while, I'd pretty much know what you're like. You speak English very beautifully, but you have what the psychologist call displacement activities. If you scratch your nose or pull your ear, you'll do it in a certain way. An animator, if he's working in full animation, must find out what those little idiosyncrasies are and include

them in the action. That's what gives the character and makes Bugs what he is. The way Bugs would look at a carrot for example.

When Sylvester was building something, like a ladder or some way to get up a tree or a swing or anything like that, Friz Freleng would always have him carry the materials across the scene and do some of the work off scene. But if he went across, he would drop a board or a bunch of nails or something. That's not necessary to the action itself, but it's very necessary to establish what kind of person he is. He's not a carpenter; he's Sylvester trying to build a ladder, so he would make mistakes.

JJ: Is it important for you to show the motivation of what each character does? You always show Bugs being provoked by somebody before he gets aggressive.

CJ: Well, we didn't have to really; that's something that's true of anybody. Only a scoundrel would go and pick on people just for the sake of doing it. I wanted Bugs to be believable, to be the way I and most other people would feel. So you'll put up with him no matter what he does, but you must believe that he has a reason for acting like he does. Bugs is minding his own business, he's sort of a Professor Higgins, down in his hole or somewhere you'd find a rabbit, and then someone comes along trying to kill him or disturb him, and he will fight back. The fact that he's fighting back is what makes him sympathetic. If he did it without a reason, he'd just be a bully.

I heard Laurence Olivier talking about acting once. They asked him where he got his ideas from. He said there's only one place any actor can get any ideas, and that's from himself. Lurking within all of us is King Lear and Macbeth and all other characters. What you have to do is realize that within yourself there is a Daffy Duck, but you're not normally that way. Everybody has that cunning little Daffy Duck personality, but very small; we keep it under control. Daffy doesn't. If you're acting the part, you bring Daffy to the surface and expand him, let him spread out. Then you don't have any trouble knowing what he'd do. The murderer is within us, the lover is within us, and many things we aren't proud of, because we don't wanna be a scoundrel, but it's there. We had Leon Schlesinger as our producer. He would say, "I'm not gonna be nice to people on the way up, because I'm not coming back down." Not many people would say that, but he didn't have much care about what happened to other people. Daffy would probably say the same thing. Daffy is not a particularly social-minded person. Very few of us are.

It's often been said that any woman in the world, including a nun, would rather loose her virtue than her good name. That suggests that all humans are human. We all have a Daffy Duck working within us. We'd like to be like Bugs Bunny. Bugs is an ideal. He's a person who's minding his own business. Someone comes along and tries to disturb, shoot him or eat him or do something with him, but then he fights back. But he's far too strong a character to just go out and bedevil people the way Woody Woodpecker might do, or Heckle and Jeckle, who seem to need no motivation. Bugs needs motivation. Daffy doesn't, because he's that kind of a personality; you kind of expect him to do anything that'll protect him, that will see to that he gets his share. Well, we all want our share, don't we?

I think everybody hates Christmas a little bit. That's why I did a picture called *How the Grinch Stole Christmas.* If your brother gets a bigger package than you do, your pleasure of Christmas becomes dimmed a little bit. You want more than he's got. As Mark Twain said, he wasn't speaking of Christmas, but he said, "Not only must I try, but my brother must fail." That felt pretty brutal, but when you examine it, you find out that when you're young, it holds true.

But these are profundities of an eighty-three-year-old man. Now I can look back and see it, but at the time we did those things because they seemed natural and because it brought the characters to life. We never would examine a character and try to find these philosophical attributes. But these things are certainly what made them work. They were done intuitively in the sense that all creativity is intuitive. You have to take what you know and let it spark into something new.

Mondrian said that he couldn't imagine not working within a discipline. I think that's one of the things that went wrong with animation to a great extent from 1963 to the present. It just went in all directions. People said they're drawing the way Tex Avery did. They aren't, and there's no way that anybody has quite mastered that. If you look at any of Tex's pictures, with the movement and the wild animation, he'd always start his pictures in a very quiet way. You knew these characters were going to do something wild, but you didn't know when, and that was the whole point. So much in today's television, people start out crazy and go crazy. Even Roger Rabbit, which was very well done, the guy never came to a rest. You never had a chance to know who he was. At the end of the picture I cared a lot more for Bob Hoskins than the rabbit, because he was so wild that he was not believable, at least not to me. People may say that the picture made a lot of money. Maybe so, but they haven't made another one.

JJ: Let's talk a little about how the shorts were made. What was your job as a director?
CJ: The director did everything. He worked with the writer all the way through the picture while the story was being developed. The picture wasn't complete when the storyboard was finished. It was my job or Friz's job or Bob McKimson's job, or whoever was doing the film, to then make three or four hundred character layout drawings to show what the expression might be, to imply the action, although we didn't expect the animators to follow them slavishly.

We never edited anything. We were told from the beginning that the pictures were to be 540 feet long. That's six minutes. We weren't to go over that because it would make them cost more money. So we learned something that people at Disney and people at perhaps any other studio never learned: to make a picture precisely 540 feet before it went to animation.

When I was doing the character layouts—the relationship between the characters, close up, medium shot, whatever they might be—my layout man, Maurice Noble, would be designing the picture and taking it from the angle of an art director. The design isn't my job. My job is to put all these elements together as a director. After about a week he would come in with little colour sketches and inspirational things, and I would take those little roughs and work them into the scenes I had already done. When those were all done, they ended up with the animator. The dialogue was all written by that time—I wrote all final dialogue in my pictures. Then you called in Mel Blanc, who had never seen the picture before, and let him have a go at it. He was a remarkably fast study, and he knew the characters pretty well. But he couldn't change his lines, because the dialogue was made to come out the right length. So no actor would be allowed to fool around with the dialogue, as they implied that he did. No actor can do that, because when you're working within a discipline, the discipline must be steadfast.

I would go over the storyboard, my drawings, my layouts, carefully with Mel, or whoever the other actors might be, and read the line the way I wanted it read. He was very quick on that. So we'd go through while he was getting to know the story. I would read Bugs's line, and he would record Daffy. Then I'd be Daffy, and we'd record him doing Bugs.

Whoever the character was, each director had to know every line exactly the way he wanted it.

Each of us three directors did ten pictures a year. You'd have, say, five thousand drawings per picture. With ten pictures that's fifteen thousand drawings in the studio at the same time. Anybody could come in with any single drawing and ask the director what he had in mind with this drawing, and he had to be able to answer. It's the same thing that Arturo Toscanini had to remember when he was going to conduct the orchestra, and the man who played the double bassoon came in and said that the valve was sticking on the double bassoon so he couldn't hit an E flat major. Toscanini said, "Don't worry. There's no need for the E flat major to be played by a double bassoon in this symphony." Think of all the notes there were and how many people playing them.

JJ: How carefully would the animators follow your poses?

CJ: Pretty exactly. That was the whole point. My job was to present what I wanted to see on the screen, and their job was to animate it. It was the same thing as conducting an orchestra, where the individual musician has no right to change a note. The director served as the composer and the conductor. But these were great animators. I couldn't animate the way they did. The pose drawings that I did simply indicated the general posture. If I had Wile E. Coyote falling off a cliff, I showed his attitude and look, but I sure as hell didn't animate him. But I would like the animator to give him a certain expression. Anybody falling off a cliff would look frightened. But I wanted him to be puzzled. He looks at the audience as though he's thinking he will have to wait to the next time. That's a very different expression. I don't expect the animators to have to know all those things. As far as the action itself is concerned, that's up to them.

In all the years I was making Bugs Bunny pictures—and I think I directed maybe fifty of them—I never had the character walk or run the same way. Never. Why? Because like the Hindus say: you can't step in the same river twice. There's different conditions; different water flowing down the river. The difference between Bugs Bunny chasing and being chased is as great as the difference between a walk and a run. One is a frantic run; the other is a determined run.

Somebody asked Grim Natwick what the basic tools of an animator are. He said, "Well a good example would be a horse trotting. That would be one of the things you'd have to know." And he said you would subdivide that by a fat horse trotting, a sick horse trotting, a young horse trotting, an old horse trotting. So you have to know first of all what a trot is, then you have to be the kind of a person who understands the difference between those different trots. You can have a determined horse, a scared horse, a frightened horse, an exhilarated horse. Then you apply that principle to Bugs Bunny. So you have Bugs walking, walk in a hurry, walk when he's afraid, you have him walking when he isn't afraid but pretending that he's afraid, and so on. All these are subdivisions. Anybody can animate a walk, but what good is that if you don't know who the person is who is doing that walk. Chaplin had a kind of a walk and a kind of a run that applied only to him. The Keystone Cops together had their own walk, a choppy thing where they went on one foot and hopped around the corner.

Many people don't even know the mechanics of a basic walk. A walk can be defined very simply as falling down and catching yourself. Otherwise you would always be pulling yourself along, and you get very tired. As you turn, you're talking to someone, you decide to leave, you'll turn on one foot and then you'll fall and catch yourself on the other foot. So you don't have to pull yourself into the walk. You fall into it. You always have gravity on your side. In running it's even more so. A runner's head and shoulders get so far ahead of his feet that he would fall down if he suddenly had to stop.

JJ: In all your films the characters have strong storytelling poses, unlike Bob Clampett's cartoons for example, where the characters are jumping all over the place all the time.
CJ: Oh sure. When I did studies of ballet, which I had to do when we did things like What's Opera, Doc?, I noticed that when a dancer is twirling, she doesn't just keep turning and turning. She makes a flip, comes to a front view and makes another flip to a front view. It's very fast so it looks like she's going around, but she isn't. It jerks around into a still position for maybe three frames, but it feels as if she's stalling every time. I noticed that in every action, you move when you have to move. There is no such thing as an even inbetween, even if it's something as simple as lifting your arm and reaching for something. In a walk you have the position with the legs spread, and then one with the leg crossing the knee. That's not a walk on its own; that's just a series of poses. That's what you call pose to pose, but it's not the way we worked.

Kandinsky or Klee or one of those guys said, "When drawing you make a single dot. That's your first tool. Then your little dot goes for a walk." He meant that that becomes a line that you move. Then every point of that line is of equal importance. So many people, as you said, what they're doing is going from dot to dot; they dart from one position to another. But the animator, or the artists, anybody, must be aware that the line in the drawing requires the greatest attention.

When I studied Degas, I noticed that he would draw a straight line coming down the inside of the girl's leg, then he would make an almost direct angle to the left, then he would tell the whole story of the leg on the other side. So that straight line gave you the feeling of the power and the weight coming down, and the other one would show you what you're talking about, which is the leg. It's very beautiful. So that's what I tried to do when I wanted to be certain that the characters are firmly set upon the ground.

When I was very young, about sixteen or seventeen years old, I worked in a puppet theatre for a while, actually marionettes on strings. Puppet manipulators, like animators, have the most extraordinary ability to control the motion. From way up above where they can't even see where the character is, they feel the weight of the character and can let the foot appear to drop solidly on the ground. That's why great puppet manipulators are artists, and the people who just dangle the puppets are not. The stuff isn't believable. There's no weight to our animation like there is to a marionette, but if we want the character to be believable, we'll animate him so that he appears to have weight. Of course you don't want weight if you're animating a butterfly, but a lot of guys who animate don't even know the difference between a butterfly and a moth. If you're animating a butterfly, its wings will be straight up when it lands. If you animate a moth, it will flap its wings when it lands.

JJ: Do you think that the other directors, like Freleng and Clampett, had a different approach to Bugs and Daffy than you did?
CJ: Sure. Friz would always think of the characters and get inside their heads, just like I did, but his way of solving that problem was different than mine. He's Friz Freleng and I'm Chuck Jones, whatever that may mean. That's why I don't think Bob McKimson ever got all of it right. He was more concerned with how they acted than who they were, and there's an enormous difference there. Bob could make certain kinds of pictures work, like the Tasmanian Devil or the rooster, because he didn't

need to get inside those characters, because they didn't require it. To a certain extent that goes for Tex, too. Tex never went very deeply for personality. He was probably the greatest master there ever was of physical comedy. But I don't know. Friz worked in his own way with his own animators. I didn't get inside of Friz's head. The only person in the world any of us can get inside of is ourself. Your observation of Friz is just as valid as mine. I had enormous respect for him. One thing I did try to learn from him was his exquisite sense of timing. I think he had one of the greatest senses of timing in animation. He'd know down to a twenty-fourth of a second how much difference that would make to something he was doing. He was brilliant at it.

JJ: How about Bob Clampett?
CJ: Well, I never quite understood . . . Clampett was a contemporary of mine; we went into direction within a year of each other. I think in certain cases he tried to imitate Tex. I don't think he ever succeeded in that. But he had his own style, and he had some interesting pictures, but I would have no way of knowing about him. His attitude toward everything was different than mine. That's alright, I never questioned that. Then UPA came along and all the critics jumped on that wagon. They felt that anything that looked different was different, and it had some effect on animation. The truth is they had no effect on animation at all. If you look at the UPA cartoons, you notice that nearly all of them have a narrator. The narrator tells you what to think rather than showing you. Our way has always been show them, don't tell. That's an old Americanism, but it's a basic truth of teaching, too.

All the pictures were made to be shown in theatres, so we didn't know who the audience was and had no way of knowing how we could control the people in a theatre. We knew that we weren't making pictures for children, so we felt that the only thing for us to do—it was obvious—was to make pictures that would make us laugh ourselves. So here we were, at that time Tex Avery, Friz Freleng, and I, the directors, and Tedd Pierce, Mike Maltese, and Warren Foster were the writers. Probably the finest group of short subject directors that have ever been and will ever be. By making each other laugh, we hoped that the audience would follow. And they have.

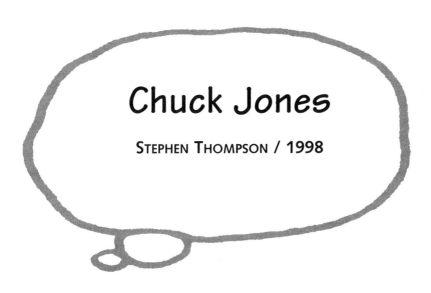

Chuck Jones

STEPHEN THOMPSON / 1998

From *The Onion* 33, no. 13.
Copyright © 1998 Onion, Inc.
www.theonionavclub.com. Reprinted
with permission of The Onion A.V. Club.

Chuck Jones is one of the greatest animation directors of all time, having worked on hundreds of classic Warner Bros. cartoons, from *What's Opera, Doc?* to *Duck Amuck* to *One Froggy Evening* (which Jones recently sequelized), as well as the Dr. Seuss masterpiece *How the Grinch Stole Christmas.* At eighty-five, Jones still keeps a busy professional schedule, but his cartoons from the '40s, '50s, and early '60s have taken on lives of their own: they've never stopped airing on Saturday mornings, and *The Bugs Bunny Film Festival*, a big-screen collection showcasing thirty favorites, makes its North American debut in Chicago on April 10. Jones—who personally created Road Runner, Wile E. Coyote, Marvin Martian, Pepé Le Pew, Gossamer, and more—recently spoke to *The Onion* about animation past and present, modern depictions of Michigan J. Frog, and the personalities of his characters.

The Onion: Have you been at this for sixty years now?
Chuck Jones: Well, yes. As far as drawing is concerned, I've been at it for longer than that. I've been directing for sixty years, but I started in animation in 1931. So we're getting close to seventy years. As far as drawing is concerned, I've been drawing since I was big enough to hold a pencil, or a burnt match; I didn't care.

O: Do you ever plan to retire?
CJ: I don't know what I'd retire from. I had a splendid uncle . . . If you've read my book [*Chuck Amuck*], you know who he is. I'm not suggesting you do so, because I'd hate to suggest things that might bring evil into your life. But anyway, he told me an old Spanish proverb: "The road is better than the inn," which simply means that when you receive an Academy Award [*Jones has three, plus an honorary award in 1996*], or anything, you're at the inn, but then you've got to go outside and start up the road again. So there's no end to it. And another one you might find useful: He said, "No artist ever completes a work. He only abandons it." It's true: Nobody ever completes anything. The great American novel can't be written, because somebody is going to write a better one. So my feeling is that the question of retirement is absurd; I hope that when I'm buried, they'll leave a place for my arm to come out so I can make a drawing. [*Laughs.*]

O: You mentioned that someone will always top the great American novel. Whom do you feel is carrying on your legacy?
CJ: Well, I don't really know. Animators today have technical and electronic tools that I wouldn't know how to use. We proceeded as all artists did before us: with pencil and paper. Nevertheless, if anybody wants to be an animator, they should learn to draw the human figure. That sounds strange, doesn't it? You don't want to copy Bugs Bunny or anything like that. If you learn how to draw the human figure, you will learn something that will stand you in good stead, because practically everything you will be doing throughout your life—whether you're an illustrator or an art director, or whoever you may be—will be based on the vertebrates, all the animals that have backbones. You see, anything from a shrew to a dinosaur has the same bones we do. So if you draw a dinosaur, or a shrew, all you have to do is look at it and compare it to

your own anatomy, and you'll soon learn that a shrew is simply a very much diminished vertebrate. The big difference—and I don't know if this is really what you want to talk about—is in the skull. And if you think about it, our bodies aren't that much different from those of alligators. But our heads are quite different. So, anyway, I'm sure you want to talk about other things.

O: Whom do you feel is carrying on your legacy? Besides yourself, of course.
CJ: Well, for one thing, a legacy is what somebody else says about your work; you can't say it about yourself. My wife objects to the term "legend" because she says, "Legend is what somebody has done." She wants to know what I'm going to do.

O: Well, that was my next question.
CJ: What am I going to do? Well, I just continue on. People come in and ask me to do things, and I do them. But mainly I've been painting, and drawing oil paintings of beautiful women and beautiful rabbits, and beautiful ducks, whatever. I'm not sure that I have time to direct a feature, and I'm not sure I want to. I did one once, called *The Phantom Tollbooth* (1971), when I was at MGM. I had that experience, but mainly I'm a cartoonist and an animator. And I'm an animator of short-subjects: I've done three or four hundred of them in my lifetime—I've never counted them carefully—and that's my field. You go back to the great essayists, like Samuel Johnson and people of that caliber, and they didn't make any excuse for being essayists. I make no excuse for being an animator. I came up that way, and all the great directors—and I don't mean to include myself, but those who surrounded me . . . every one of them had been an animator first, in order to learn how to time, because we had to time our pictures before they were animated. It's very different from live action. That's why Steven Spielberg and George Lucas and Martin Scorsese can't believe that you can make a picture by timing it out to 540 feet, or six minutes. They don't understand how you can do that, because their idea is to take 25,000 feet of film and then cut it down to feature length. Well, we had to figure all that out before we even started. It's a curious craft, but as in all work, the most important thing is to have a discipline and a deadline. A lot of people figure that when you start writing, you don't have to have discipline. Well, oh, yes, you do. And when Scorsese starts cutting down a picture, he's tearing bits of his heart out and throwing them on the floor. Because his first inclination is to

shoot the thing the way it should be shot, which is probably about six hours. And then he has to go chopping away at it, and that hurts. So at least we're not chopping beforehand.

O: As far as pacing goes, you must have to know what's happening in each individual second.
CJ: Yes, you do. You have to know what's going on in each twenty-fourth of a second. We had to time our pictures down to that. But if you look at any craft, you've got basic tools that you use. With writers, it's words and syntax; with us, it's timing and drawing. And unless you can do that, you'd better find another occupation, like grave-digging. [Laughs.] And that's rewarding work, because people are always dying. It's probably a good thing to learn.

O: What do you think of some of the other cartoons being produced today?
CJ: Well, I have a lot of respect for The Simpsons, but it's in the same tradition as Rocky & Bullwinkle: They're very clever scripts, and they had no intention of animating them. Animating goes back to that basic term that Noah Webster wrote in his dictionary—"Animation: to invoke life." Last night, when I was signing some cels, this deaf girl came up. She could read my lips, and she said that the thing she likes about the Warner cartoons and the Disney cartoons is that she could tell what was happening without hearing the dialogue. And that's what we tried to do: We always ran the pictures without dialogue, so we could see whether the action of the body would somehow convey what we were talking about. And she said that she'd watch Rocky & Bullwinkle or The Simpsons, and she couldn't tell what was happening, because so much of it is vocal. It's what I call "illustrated radio." The thing has to tell the whole story in words before you put drawings in front of it. But the basic tool, as I say . . . a great artist once said—in describing lines, which is really what we work with—that respect for the line is the most important thing. He described the line: "My little dot goes for a walk." You must have an equal amount of respect for any point on the line. You don't zip from one place to another like you're likely to do when you're young. When you watch your little dot go for a walk, it has to be carefully done, and thoughtfully done, and respectfully done.

O: How do you feel about Michigan J. Frog becoming a corporate logo for the WB network?

CJ: I had no control over it. They own all the characters, so there wasn't anything I could do about it. I could spend my life lamenting it, or I could continue to draw. I prefer to draw. See, the thing that makes all these characters is personality. *The Three Little Pigs* is one of the first pictures to use three characters that look alike and act differently; therefore, they had personality. A pretty woman isn't pretty because she's pretty; she's pretty because of the way she moves—her eyes, her mouth, and everything else. That's what makes beauty. Sure, it helps to have the proper features. But I remember someone asking Alfred Hitchcock what he required from actors, and he said, [*imitating Alfred Hitchcock*] "Well, I prefer them to have a mouth, and two eyes, hopefully on opposite sides of the nose . . ." He didn't care whether they were great actors or not; he could make them great actors by the way he directed them. So personality is what counts. The reason Bugs Bunny and the rest of them endure, I think, is that when you wrote lines for Bugs Bunny, they wouldn't ever work for Daffy or Yosemite Sam. Each one of them had a personal way, when you wrote dialogue for them, in the same sense that you'd never write dialogue for Chico Marx that you'd write for Groucho. So the whole point here is personality, individuality—the character of each one—and this goes for the Disney people who worked on the early pictures, too. The same thing is true of them. You knew how Donald would act, and you knew how Daffy would act, and they're very different. You move your hands a certain way and move a certain way, and if you sat down with an animation director for two hours, he would be able to move a character the way you move. We not only have to figure out what a character looks like, but we have to find out what those little differences are. Moving your hands a certain way, or chopping your hands like Harry Truman did . . . That made him Harry Truman. That's the way he moved.

O: And Michigan J. Frog didn't talk, or rap . . .

CJ: No, no. He only sang, and his personality was pretty flamboyant. But I didn't know who the hell he was; all I knew is, he could sing. I was as puzzled by him as anybody else is. [*Laughs.*] But I did know that he didn't talk, and shouldn't talk. And the only person who could ever hear him sing would be the man who uncovered him, and the audience. They shared that, but nobody else in the picture could hear him. Those are the disciplines. You know that in writing, you've got to have disciplines. And so, when you work with a character like Bugs Bunny, at first, he was crazy. And then we soon discovered that pretending like you're crazy is a much better way to develop personality. It's like Groucho Marx: He wasn't crazy; he was pretending to be. Daffy is a blatant loudmouth; that's his personality. With Yosemite Sam, for example, which [*animation director*] Friz Freleng did, he took a grown man and had him act like a baby. If anything displeased him, he'd bellow and scream. My father was kind of like that, so I pushed him into a few characters of mine. Fortunately, he only saw them after . . . [*Laughs.*] I was going to say, "He only saw them after he was dead." I guess that's true.

O: Your relationship with your bosses influenced some of your Warner work, right?
CJ: Well, I had a boss who came to Warner to run our operation when they bought us out in 1945, from Leon Schlesinger; this guy went through life like an untipped waiter.

O: He was the origin of the bullfighting cartoon [*Bully for Bugs*], wasn't he?
CJ: Yeah, yeah. Mike [*writer Michael Maltese*] and I were sitting there looking at each other across the table, and suddenly here's this furious little man standing in the doorway, yelling at us. He said, "I don't want any pictures about bullfighting! There's nothing funny about a bullfight." And he walked out, and Mike and I looked at each other in wonderment, and he said, "My God, there must be something funny about a bullfight." We'd never even thought about doing a picture about a bullfight, but since everything he ever said was absolutely wrong, we were certain that we had to pursue it. We worked our asses off making that picture; I even went to Mexico City to see a bullfight. I figured that if we were going to do it, I might as well have fun with it and do it the way it should be done. If you're doing a take-off on something, make sure you're doing it in an honest way.

O: What characters are most enduring for you?
CJ: All of them. It's like somebody saying, "What's your favorite child?" Are you married?

O: Yes.
CJ: Do you have children?

O: No, not yet.

CJ: You know how to get them, don't you? When you have them, if you have more than one, you will have a favorite. But if you value your sanity, you will never mention it to anyone. The same thing is true here: each character represents a part of me. You never find a character outside of yourself, because every human being has all the evil and all the good things, and it's how you use them, how you develop them. Those who enjoy Daffy obviously recognize Daffy in themselves. And with the heroes, like Bugs Bunny, what you have there is that that's the character you'd like to be like. You'll dream about being like Bugs Bunny, and then you wake up, and you're Daffy Duck.

Chuck Jones, in His Own Words

RON BARBAGALLO / 1999

Unpublished interview. Copyright © 2000
Ron Barbagallo. Reprinted with permission.
www.animationartconservation.com.
All rights reserved.

Someone once told me that art can be defined as "that which survives." Whether an artifact—like King Tut's death mask—or a draft of Jefferson's *Declaration of Independence*, or a painting by Leonardo Da Vinci, all crafts are reflective of the people and times when they were created. A mirror into the life the artist has traveled and, when hugely embraced, a testament to the people who enjoy them.

Over the last eighty-seven years, Chuck Jones has seen animation grow from its inception, on through its heyday in the 1930s, '40s and '50s, past the depths of the 1970s, onto the renaissance that has been the last twelve years. During that time, he has worked in nearly every capacity in the art form, leaving behind a body of work as a director of animation that boasts three of the four Warner Bros. shorts included in the National Film Registry.

I met Chuck Jones in 1996. Later that year and on November 8, 1999, I had the opportunity to interview him. Our conversations revolved around history and the art and philosophy of animation.

Condensed from these two interviews, in his own words, are the reflections and inspired insights of Chuck Jones, a true statesman of animation.

RB: What are you working on these days?
CJ: The older I get, the more I find myself sketching. I don't call it work. I do it because I want to. Right now, I happen to be sketching a drawing of Daffy Duck as Uriah Heep [a clerk who continually talks about his humbleness from Charles Dickens's novel *David Copperfield*], which is a pretty good role for him.

RB: Maybe it's the role he was born to play?
CJ: Well, perhaps, though it's kind of hard to think of Daffy ever calling himself humble.

RB: Chuck, I wanted to start off with some questions about your youth. You were born in 1912 in Spokane, Washington, and relocated to California. Where in California did your family relocate?
CJ: My father moved down here from Spokane when I was about six months old. So, I was only there a very short time. We moved here to southern California. My brother was born in Washington, my two sisters were born in the Panama Canal Zone.

There are many things about my childhood, I don't remember, of course. I have faint memories, like falling off things. I remember I was once attacked by a rooster when I didn't have my pants on. That sticks in my memory, but I don't know where it happened.

Memories of life were more vivid when I was about six. I can remember things happening then because that's when we moved to our home on Sunset Boulevard, right across from Hollywood High School. My father owned a very nice home there on the first block going west on Highland Avenue. We had an orange and lemon grove; we had that whole block.

RB: Was there was an orange and lemon grove on Highland Avenue and Sunset Boulevard?
CJ: Yes, there weren't any buildings on that whole block, as I remember it. But I remember that I could walk out and sit on my front porch and

watch Mary Pickford ride by on a white horse as the Honorary Colonel of the 360th Infantry of the Rainbow Division of the United States Army.

I remember going a few different places, including down to Newport Beach, in the summer time.

My brother is still alive and lives in Colorado. He is a very unusual creature; he was a combat photographer during World War II, but he worked in my unit before he went overseas. When he came back, he went into photography and teaching. He's retired now from a career with UNICEF and a person who can't get away from the mountains. And I'm a person who can't get away from the sea.

RB: I read when you were young you were constantly sketching and drawing. Who or what was your inspiration?

CJ: I just wanted to draw. The difference between our family and many others and—teachers, too—was that my mother didn't judge our work, good or bad. She didn't criticize what we did, nor did she overpraise it. And, that's the key isn't it?

Constant praise is as bad as constant criticism to anybody who wants to draw. If every time I had brought a picture to my mother and she said, "That's wonderful," and stuck it up on the refrigerator or wall, I'm sure I would have very soon lost respect, both for her and my drawings. After all, I knew, as all children know, that every drawing isn't wonderful. The result of overpraise, or over-criticism, seems to be that children fail to develop a sense of their own judgment.

People who continue to draw are those who either have the guts to ignore praise and criticism, or are guided by wise parents and teachers.

RB: When you were young, what type of images did you draw? In some way, I want to hear you felt compelled to draw coyotes and roadrunners. . . .

CJ: Well, no. I didn't draw coyotes and roadrunners. But, I discovered coyotes, in Mark Twain's book, *Roughing It*.

From the time I was very young, I have always read a lot. One of the great fortunes of my youth was that I always had books around me. My father always made it a criteria for every house we rented that it be furnished and have lots of books. One of the greatest houses was on Mount Washington Drive in Highland Park, California, where we rented a house owned by Harry Carr, the book editor for the *Los Angeles Times*.

The house was crammed with prepublication books Carr had accumulated and never thrown away. Books were behind the piano and in the basement. Every place in the house, it seemed, was filled with books. My father and mother were both avid readers, but my sisters, brother and I had never seen such a plethora of books, outside a public library. That's where I found Mark Twain.

RB: What do you like most about Mark Twain's work?
CJ: The way I found Mark Twain, well, I was just browsing around, I was probably about five or six years old, and I ran across this book, *Tom Sawyer*. I picked it up, flipped it open to the first page, and saw: "Tom. No answer. Tom. No answer." I knew right away what was happening.

I proceeded to read everything he had written, with the exception of the two volumes he did on Christian Science. I loved it all. Not many people know that he did that. People don't know that he wrote *A Trap Abroad*, one of the greatest books. They know *Innocence Abroad*, but they don't know *A Trap Abroad*, which is the difference between a young man and a more mature man—with a great love of his craft.   ·

I found the coyote in the fourth chapter of *Roughing It*, which is a journal he wrote about traveling by stagecoach to Carson City, Nevada. During that period, he kept hold of the things he'd seen and among them were things like tarantulas, and so on. Twain opens that chapter with a description of the coyote, which is about as accurate as anybody has ever described one. He also humanized him. And that was kinda news to me. I hadn't run into anything where I felt that a coyote was like a human being.

He described how the coyote dressed and so on. At the end of the paragraph, Twain wrote, "He may have to go ten miles for his breakfast and thirty miles for his lunch and fifty miles for his dinner, and we ought to pay attention to that and give him his credit, because he does that instead of laying around home, being a burden on his parents."

It was a new concept to my young mind, this way of humanizing the coyote's traits. It's a concept that stayed with me. Every year I re-read that book [*Roughing It*], including this year. Each time I re-read it, I find something I don't expect. Obviously, I wasn't looking for ideas when I was five or six years old, but I got them anyway. Mark Twain gave me the whole key to thinking that animated characters think the way we do.

Because you must understand, I was born in 1912, two years before Winsor McCay did *Gertie the Dinosaur*. There was a long dead period after that when animation was just moving comic strips, you might call them, until *Steamboat Willie*. And, then it came to life again.

By the way, I'd like to reiterate that the term "animate," as defined by Noah Webster, is "to evoke life." "Evoke life." And that's what animation is all about. To some extent, that's what's missing in what is currently called animation.

What I am afraid of is, I've seen the birth of animation, the growth of animation, and in some way, the decline of animation. I am glad to see films like *Toy Story 2*. That is wonderful animation, true animation.

We were fortunate in the early days [1930s–1950s] because nobody at Warner Bros. paid much attention to us. As long as we made cartoons that could be sold, no one bothered us much. No one ordered us to make anything better, and I don't think we were making much effort to make things better either. We were experimenting and looking for different ways to evoke like, if that's not too presumptuous. When Bugs became popular, why they asked us to make some Bugs Bunnys.

RB: Was there much instruction or involvement from Leon Schlesinger?
CJ: Nothing, zero. I'm certain that's why we were as successful as we were. Leon Schlesinger owned Pacific Art and Title and created the titles for most of the feature films all over the country. He had a lot of money from that.

He would come back where we worked at Warner Bros. and look around with disdain and say, "This is dirty back here, but on the other hand, many a masterpiece has been made in a garret." Schlesinger had a pretty pronounced lisp, by the way, and our director Tex Avery, came up with the idea of imitating his speech impediment for Daffy Duck.

Between 1938, when I started, to 1964 or '65, when Jack Warner shut the studio down, we made about thirty characters that are known internationally. In addition, we created forty-five or fifty other characters known well enough here in the United States to support an enormous licensed product industry. And why was it possible to create so many successful characters? I think it's because we didn't have to answer to anybody. It wasn't until some of the characters became especially popular that we were ordered, or encouraged, to make more pictures about them.

There were three units, each making ten pictures a year. If management wanted six more Bugs Bunnys, we would just split them up and do two each. That was our decision, not anybody else's.

You know, I believe the process of success involves stumbling. Winston Churchill once said: "Many people stumble over a good idea. But they get up and brush themselves off, and walk away as though nothing had happened." We were fortunate. We didn't do that. We stumbled over some good ideas and didn't walk away. We were able to continue drawing for its own sake.

You know, most people are most comfortable and like Daffy Duck. Why? I think it's because Daffy makes the same kind of mistakes we all make.

And, I think the Coyote is the same way. I think people will continue to enjoy the Coyote cartoons we made because he makes the same kind of errors we do. We tried to inject *character* in them, but we didn't do it consciously.

All of us knew we were drawing *character*, not drawings. Drawing is simply a way of getting it on the screen.

I think it's worth noting that the Seven Dwarfs [from Disney's 1937 feature film, *Snow White*] were really seven attributes of a human being. They didn't try to crowd them all into the same character. Yet, if you look carefully, you'll see the idea of one character who sneezes, one who was sleepy, one who was happy and so on. It is simply an examination of a single person, who is every one of those things. That's why we all recognize them.

RB: Recognizable, humanistic qualities inside the drawings?

CJ: Yes, it's *character* we can recognize.

RB: Another filmmaker who put humanistic qualities and mannerisms in his performances was Charlie Chaplin. When you were younger, you lived near where Chaplin worked?

CJ: His studio was two blocks from us at La Brea Avenue and Sunset Boulevard. Because there was no sound, they shot the films outside. As kids, we could go there and look through the fence and watch him work. He was kind of a hero to us, and we loved his films.

When we watched them in the theaters, it never occurred to us that anything was done over and over. When we watched them shoot, we discovered how difficult it was to get it just right.

My father saw Chaplin do one scene sixty-two times before he got it the way he wanted it. Well, I don't have to pretend to do anything like that. On many occasions, I have drawn over fifty drawings to get one right.

RB: Let's talk about some of your colleagues from the early days. A good place to start would be when you left high school at fifteen and went to the Chouinard Art Institute. You graduated during the depression. What type of work were you able to find?

CJ: I tried to get work at a commercial studio but couldn't letter professionally. Unless you could letter professionally, you might as well forget it. Fred Kopietz, who had been in art school with me, called and said he was working at Ub Iwerks's studio on Western Avenue and wondered if I wanted to come to work there.

I couldn't believe I might get paid to draw. I was right. They didn't want to pay me to draw. In 1931, they hired me as a cel washer and then as a cel painter, a cel inker, and eventually, an in-betweener. I wasn't a particularly good in-betweener.

That was the time when Shamus Culhane and Bernie Wolf and Grim Natwick were working there. They had all come out from New York, where they had been working.

When I was hired, it seemed to me that Ub was an old man. He was an old man in the animation business. I was about eighteen then, and he was thirty-eight. He was ten years older than Walt Disney and Carl Stalling. It's hard to imagine how young everybody was.

RB: At that early age, what films were you and Grim Natwick working on for Ub Iwerks? Flip the Frog?

CJ: Yes, and on Willie Whopper and a couple of other horrible things. Ub was a brilliant animator but didn't seem to have much of a sense of humor. Walt Disney, on the other hand, probably had the most acute knowledge of humor around in animation. He knew when it was good and when it wasn't. He was the one who made the whole thing work. Ub was a technician in terms of being a great animator. So, Ub's studio didn't go very far.

RB: How did you go from working for Ub Iwerks to working at Warner Bros., where you helped redefine the way characters behaved and the way comedy was portrayed in cartoons?

CJ: I don't know if I can take credit for that, but I can say I needed a job. I had tried working at Charles Mintz's studio, where they were doing Oswald, the Lucky Rabbit, then went back to Iwerks.

About that time, Leon decided to start his own studio, and he hired a couple of directors from Disney.

RB: Was Bobe Cannon [the future director of UPA's Academy Award winning short *Gerald McBoing Boing*] directing when you started?

CJ: Oh, heavens, no. Bobe, Bob Clampett, and I were just in-betweeners. The term animation assistant wasn't used then. There were animators and in-betweeners, and that was it. They may have been called assistants at Disney, but not at Schlesinger's studio. There were also no clean-up artists. Each animator did his own clean up. In fact, there were several animators who didn't have to clean up their drawings at all because they animated clean. Bill Nolan, Ub Iwerks, and Benny Washam were like that. Their finished extremes were always finished.

RB: One of the most interesting things about Warner Bros. in the late thirties through the fifties is that whether through lack of corporate planning, or the benevolence of being left alone to experiment—the directors at Warner Bros. each imbued the evolving cast of Looney Tunes' characters with their own individual personality and unique vision.

In a lot of respects, the approach taken by the Looney Tunes directors more closely parallels that taken by live action directors like Kubrick or Scorsese when they are redefining an accepted film genre, like science fiction or the gangster picture. The manner of storytelling is reflective of the personality of the director.

How did this step forward take place at Warner Bros.? Was it when Tex Avery arrived?

CJ: The man who was really the leader was Friz Freleng, I think. He was an extremely competent, talented, and able director. When Friz came over, he really saved the studio.

Tex had been an animator at Universal and when he came over to Schlesinger's, he had it in his mind to be a director. Tex told Leon Schlesinger that he had been directing pictures at Universal. Leon never checked, so he hired him as a director. Tex may have helped direct at Universal, but Walt Lantz [creator of Woody Woodpecker and Chilly Willy] didn't credit anyone but himself.

Tex was in charge of one unit. Friz Freleng was in charge of another unit and Frank Tashlin had the third unit. Each unit turned out ten cartoons a year, each almost five hundred and forty feet, give or take ten feet.

Originally, there were four animators, a director, a layout man, and a background man in each unit. Each unit would work on a picture for five weeks and then start another one. At the end of five weeks, the picture would go to ink and paint, and then to camera.

No one was criticizing or lashing out at anyone. No one set themselves up as better judges of our work than we were.

For me, the most important person at Schlesinger's studio was Friz Freleng. Tex Avery was great, but he wasn't there very long when we were making Bugs Bunny cartoons. He only made about three, maybe four, and then Bob Clampett took over when Tex went to MGM. Personally, I think Tex's best pictures were made at MGM.

He didn't have the time to develop the Looney Tunes characters. I am not downgrading him, because he was one of the great innovators—he stretched a gag to its limits. He'd play with film within film. He had guys running right through the screen. I think he was one of the geniuses of animation. He was a vital and necessary force in animation.

People try to imitate that absolute nuttiness that Tex had, and most of them miss the boat completely. You see his influence all over. Did you see *The Mask* with Jim Carrey? That was practically pure Tex Avery; very funny.

Tex never knew how good he was. He was a very sad and hurting person when he died. When Tex was dying, I remember, he was in the hospital watching the baseball game with another animator. He said to his friend, "I don't know where animators go when they die, but I guess there must be a lot of them." Then, he thought for a moment, and said, "They could probably use a good director though." Those are pretty much his last words.

RB: Background art is a subtle and, at times, undervalued element in animation. If background artists, such as your colleague Maurice Noble, do their job correctly, you are not supposed to notice them. They set a stage and a mood for animation to fall upon. At times, they can transcend and lift the animation to another place. I think Maurice Noble's backgrounds are a good example of this.
CJ: Absolutely. Maurice is brilliant. In most of our films, Maurice would do all the scene layouts and art direction, while I was doing the direction, layout drawings and writing the dialogue. We didn't interrupt each other. The understanding we had was that we were both enhancing the storyline. He was and is wonderful. The best I have ever worked with.

RB: And you worked with him for a long time?
CJ: I think it was shortly after World War II that Maurice joined my unit. Mike Maltese, the great writer and gagman, came to me about that time, too.

RB: Could you talk a little about Michael Maltese?

CJ: He was a brilliant writer. He and I worked extremely well together. Mike was a great storyman, and we came up with some great stories together. He didn't write the dialogue; I did that as I did the layout drawings. We didn't have a script until after I had done all the layout drawings. Mike was a vital factor. Mel Blanc was, too, but Mel didn't originate characters or write dialogue. He was a great, great actor. We would tell him what we wanted to hear and he took direction brilliantly. The dialogue was written before we recorded it, though. It wasn't open for change at the recording session.

RB: You also worked with Shamus Culhane, the legendary animator who imbued so much individual personality into each dwarf marching along the mountain crests in the "Heigh Ho" sequence from Disney's *Snow White and the Seven Dwarfs*. What was it like working with him?

CJ: Shamus Culhane didn't work with me very long. He had a work habit that drove everybody crazy. He'd come get a sequence from me that would run maybe seventy-five or a hundred feet, take it back to his desk and just stare at it for three or four days, not drawing anything. Then, he would come up with an idea about how it worked. When he started animating, and he could animate fifty feet a week, he worked it all out in his head before he began, carefully thinking and analyzing the whole sequence before he ever started to draw.

RB: Did you or your colleagues have any idea that your films would have the long range popularity or influence that they've had?

CJ: God, no. We never were conscious that we were doing anything that had any lasting quality. It's a great surprise, as I am sure it was to Mark Twain, William Shakespeare, and so many others. You know, the Globe theater owned Shakespeare's plays. Talk about history repeating itself. Warner Bros. owns all the characters we developed, and we don't get any residuals. Not that I'm a Shakespeare, but just to make the point, he didn't get any residuals either. Shakespeare continued to do what he did because it was his life—he had to do it. I feel that way, too. It never stopped me from continuing to draw. The saddest thing in the world is to find some artist who just stops drawing.

RB: Will you direct again?

CJ: I doubt it. After all, I'm eighty-seven, I'll continue to draw and write. If something comes along I just can't refuse, I'll do it if I have time.

RB: Recently, there has been an explosion in animation. Inspired by the success of Disney's *The Little Mermaid, Beauty and the Beast,* and *The Lion King,* studios have jumped on the feature animation bandwagon.

With raised expectations, the animation industry has entered a new phase where the studios focus less on storytelling and more on merchandising films into video games, happy meals, and licensed toys. Direct to video sequels and television series are planned before a feature film has even been released.

In the midst of all this commercialism, a lot of films have come out. What over the past decade have you liked and what have you disliked and why?

CJ: Well, I don't know where it's going. As I mentioned I recently saw *Toy Story 2,* and I wrote John Lasseter [the director of the Pixar/Disney film] to tell him how much I loved it. There is hope when films like that are being made.

I surely hope the art form persists. A lot of what is happening now reminds me a great deal of what happened in New York stage in the late 1930s. Many people in the legitimate theater were so intrigued with stage craft that they believed it was more important than the play itself. The result was that set designers, like Norman Bel Geddes, were given more credit than they deserved. They started doing enormous sets and overwhelming everything. It got to a point where Bel Geddes built a set for *The Miracle,* or one of those plays, that extended the stage out over the first twenty rows of the orchestra, and the people in the balcony couldn't see what was happening. It was ridiculous. They forgot what they were doing.

Along about that time, *Our Town* was staged. No stage craft at all. It was such a relief. It allowed the audience to imagine everything, which was great. And, that's true for great cartoons as well. Backgrounds aren't the dominant factor; they are there solely to support the characters and the story. Like I said about Maurice, we were doing the same job—enhancing the storyline.

Most of the people who are doing computer animation today have gone overboard. The backgrounds are so enormous and wonderful and beautiful that you thought you were seeing something better than you were. They've gotten so enthralled with the technology and what it can do that they've forgotten, or never knew, what they're supposed to be doing—telling a story and introducing audiences to real characters. The characters have no warmth, no humanity. As Dorothy Parker once said, "There's less here than meets the eye."

Why do they want to make it more realistic? I mean, Bugs Bunny doesn't look anything like a rabbit and Daffy doesn't look anything like a duck. They're not realistic, they're believable. That's the key.

In some of the new huge films, it seems to me that they are showing off instead of entertaining. It's using a tool just because it's there.

When Walt Disney needed an opening for *Pinocchio*, they invented the multi-plane camera, and it worked. But they didn't invent the multi-plane camera and then use it for everything.

The question becomes, is animation an art form or isn't it? If it is, I would like to see more people respecting it as an art form. I believe that the artist, and the art still exists—that you can take a sheet of paper, and a bunch of drawings, and bring something to life. Too many people are overlooking the essence of animation. It is bringing something to life, with the simplest tools. They show off with tools they don't know how to use and miss the point completely.

When Alexander Woolcott first saw *Snow White and the Seven Dwarfs*, it was in pencil test. And he didn't know anything about animation, but he looked at this thing and he said, "It'll never be any better than it is now." And it's true. In the final analysis, all of us are in business because the thing that you're going to see is always the animator's work.

The essence of any great animation is the animator's work. A director can guide and inspire the animator, but you can't substitute for what the animator must do. It's the same principle that exists in acting—a moving picture of a photograph is not the same as an actor acting.

RB: Yes, that is what's lacking, but even more than that, the incentive behind making animation today is not as it was when Walt Disney was making the original *Fantasia* and *Pinocchio*.

Artists working at Disney in the post-thirties Depression were classically trained fine artists—who in a stronger economy would have been pursuing their own careers. They came to animation with life experience and an appreciation of art, literature, and music. They were not trade-schooled cartoonists or animators retreading old territory.

They also had the benefit of a genuine storyteller in Walt Disney.

Today, studio executives make animation for entirely different reasons.

Their impulse to put commerce before craft has removed the art and the essential need for artistic forward vision from the process and replaced it with meddling executives trying to be artists, hired technicians—albeit talented—and a line of licensed products.

The motive behind making the animation in the thirties and forties had more to do with inspiration and passionate storytelling in a medium that was steadily redefining itself.

CJ: Yes, you are right. Animation seems to be downgraded these days. When *Fantasia* was made in 1940, they were artists. Creativity is the key.

RB: Of all your projects, what are you the most proud of?

CJ: Well, I'm not proud of any of them. The main thing about any creative work, including animation, is you can't do it the best. You can't become the president of animation. There's no such thing as the best piece of animation because someone will come along and do it better.

I'm surprised that the cartoons we made have been around so long and continue to make people laugh. I'm not being excessively modest, it just continues to surprise and delight me.

These days, I'm drawing and painting in oils and watercolors. I'm doing the characters, life drawings, and other things too. I've never stopped drawing. I doubt if a day goes by that I don't do a drawing of some kind. Drawing is something that is catching. It's a wonderful and terrible disease.

I never try to compete with anyone. I don't even try to compete with myself.

There are two essentials for me.

I have to imbue personality into each character with a simple line.

The other thing is I have to read everything that I come across. It really doesn't matter what it is. When I got in the habit of reading at such a young age, I started to develop taste. I didn't have to be told what was good or bad by others.

The same thing is true in animation and in any other career or interest. The more you know about it, and the more you study it, the more you build your own attitude towards it. Those things are the most vital.

When my daughter, Linda, was in junior high school, she was a fan of the book based on Ben Franklin, *Ben and Me*. When she saw the Disney film *Ben and Me* [1953] she was incredibly disappointed at the fact that it didn't have much relation to the book at all.

Later, she discovered that the director of the film [Hamilton Luske] had not read the book. I feel that way, too. It's hard to understand how someone can use the title without respecting the author enough to use the story.

The Sword in the Stone [1963] was another example. The book is a great example of our literary heritage, but the film minimized it, bringing it down to a light tale about a witch and a wizard. There was some funny stuff in there, but it had nothing to do with the book.

Because of my strong feelings about this, when we [Chuck Jones Enterprises] set out to do *Mowgli's Brothers* from Rudyard Kipling's *The Jungle Book*, I read it over and over again. We had signs up all over the studio saying, "Rudyard Kipling is the screenwriter of this film." We did everything we could to stick strictly to the story as Kipling told it. It's still used extensively in schools all over.

After Disney made *The Jungle Book* [1967] I was unsure about the pronunciation of the lead character's name, Mowgli. I had always heard it pronounced as if the first syllable rhymed with "cow," rather than "crow."

Before we started our film, I discovered that Kipling's daughter was still alive and called her. In an elegant, British dowager-like voice, she confirmed my pronunciation and added, "and, I hate Walter Disney." It was the only time I ever heard anybody call him Walter. In her lifetime, she said nobody ever pronounced anything but Mauwgli.

RB: You were at Disney for a brief time—between July 13 and November 13, 1953—to work on the early stages of *Sleeping Beauty* [1959]. What brought you there and what did you do there?
CJ: I went to Disney because Jack Warner decided to close our studio. He had brought out a film called *House of Wax*, one of the first three-dimensional films. It was a novelty, but he seemed to think the future of films was in 3-D, so he closed the studio.

I worked on *Sleeping Beauty* for a short time, but the conditions were so completely different that I went to Walt and told him there was only one job worth having at Disney, and he had it.

RB: Any closing thoughts?
CJ: I was very fortunate. I have done almost three hundred cartoons in my lifetime. I think a lot of them were insufficient. Some of them are really bad, I guess. But I was continually diverted and urged by myself

and by the conditions that existed, not by the people that I worked for. I had the opportunity to express myself in so many ways.

Nobody could ever convince me that there is anything more wonderful than being paid for doing what you love to do. I couldn't have been more fortunate because that is what happened to me.

The author would like to thank Chuck Jones, Linda Jones Clough, Craig Kausen, Dean Diaz, Dave Smith, Dina Andre, and Amy Genovese for their time, assistance and encouragement in assembling this work.

Index

Conversations with Comic Artists Series
M. Thomas Inge, General Editor
The collected interviews with notable comic artists, including

CARL BARKS ~ MILTON CANIFF ~ R. CRUMB
CHARLES M. SCHULZ ~ MORT WALKER

CENTER MORICHES PUBLIC LIBRARY

3 0817 00   771 7

741.5809 Jones, Chuck,
JON   1912-

        Chuck Jones.

$20.00

DATE			

CENTER MORICHES FREE PUB LIB
235 MAIN ST
CENTER MORICHES NY 119345024

05/05/2005

BAKER & TAYLOR